D1583191

WAITING FOR
THE END

Leslie A. Fiedler

WAITING FOR THE END

The American Literary Scene

from Hemingway to Baldwin

Jonathan Cape
Thirty Bedford Square
London

First published in Great Britain 1965
© 1964 by Leslie A. Fiedler

Published in the United States of America by
Stein and Day

Printed in Great Britain by
Lowe and Brydone (Printer) Limited, London
On paper made by John Dickinson & Co.
Bound by A. W. Bain & Co. Ltd., London

CONTENTS

TO MY SONS:
Kurt,
Eric, and
Michael

Shall we go all wild, boys, waste and make them lend,
Playing at the child, boys, waiting for the end? ·
It has all been filed, boys, history has a trend,
Each of us enisled, boys, waiting for the end.

WILLIAM EMPSON

1

THE DEATH OF THE OLD MEN

It is with a sense of terror that the practicing novelist in the United States confronts his situation today; for the Old Men are gone, the two great presences who made possible both homage and blasphemy, both imitation and resistance. It is a little like the death of a pair of fathers or a pair of gods; like, perhaps, the removal of the sky, an atmosphere we were no longer aware we breathed, a firmament we had forgotten sheltered us. The sky we can pretend, at least, is Heaven; the space behind the sky we cannot help suspecting is a vacuum.

At any rate, both Faulkner and Hemingway are dead, a slow suicide by the bottle in one case, and a quick one by the gun in the other, as seems appropriate to our tradition; and we must come to terms with our surviving selves; yet first, of course, with them. Their deaths have made eminently clear what the passage of time had already begun to establish (and our sense of outrage over the awarding of the Nobel Prize to John Steinbeck merely emphasizes the fact): that these two writers represent to us and to the world the real meaning and the true success of the novel in America during the first half of the twentieth century.

Nevertheless, it must be added immediately that the moment of their world fame has not coincided with the period in which they produced their greatest work. In a sense, each received the Nobel Prize posthumously, though both lived long enough to accept it with thanks; and Faulkner, at least—perhaps Hemingway, too, though we still await evidence of this—continued to write to within months of his actual death. Yet each, in the last decade or so of his life, had published either second-rate imitations of his own best work (Faulkner's *The Town* and *The Mansion*, Hemingway's *The Old Man and the Sea*) or atrocious parodies of that work (Faulkner's *The Fable*, Hemingway's *Across the River and into the Trees*). Naturally, there are in all their books, even the worst, small local triumphs, flashes of something we wonder whether we perceive or remember; but we should not, in any case, deceive ourselves about either how bad their late books are or the way in which they are bad.

If Hemingway and Faulkner ended by parodying themselves, it is because their method was from the beginning actual parody or something (for which we have, alas, no name in the critical lexicon) which attained its effects by skirting the edge of parody. We should not forget what we are now in a position to see clearly, when polemics and envy no longer matter: that our two greatest recent novelists were essentially comic writers. We realize now that *The Torrents of Spring*, the Hemingway travesty of Sherwood Anderson, is not a trivial *jeu d'esprit* but one of his central achievements; and we have long been approaching the realization that the most abiding creation of Faulkner is the Snopes family, especially Flem Snopes, that modern, American, bourgeois, ridiculous version of Faust. We should not, then, be surprised that, having exhausted the worlds they began by caricaturing (and having succeeded in those very worlds at the same time), the two comic geniuses of our century ended by caricaturing themselves.

Despite their self-travesty, however, both Hemingway and Faulkner still continue to influence the fiction of younger men, and, even more deeply, the image of themselves as writers with which such younger men begin—the possibilities of success and failure they are able to imagine as they start their careers. The legend of Faulkner is a parable of success snatched from failure: the artist abiding, in loneliness and behind a smoke screen of lies, the day when the neglect of the great audience and the critics (everyone is aware that at the end of World War II no novel of Faulkner's was in print) will turn to adulation. There is something profoundly comic and satisfying in the notion of the great talent lying hidden, like Poe's purloined letter, in that obvious place which guarantees its invisibility, the place of its belonging and origin; of Faulkner safely concealed until the destined moment of revelation—in his home town, in the very Oxford, Mississippi, where, just after his death, Federal troops were deployed to insure the registration of a single, indifferent Negro student in a less-than-mediocre university. It is as if history itself were subscribing to Faulkner's view of the South—his notion of a baffled aspiration to the tragic, nurtured by dreams and memories, falling away always, in fact, into melodrama or farce. Surely Faulkner is involved as deeply in the legend of the South (which, indeed, he has helped create) as in the all-American morality play of success and failure. In a sense, he can be seen as the last of the old Southern writers, the final descendant of Edgar Allan Poe, the ultimate seedy Dandy, haunted by the blackness of darkness embodied in the Negro, and seeking in alcohol an even blacker darkness, in which the first may be, for a little while at least, lost. Unlike Hemingway's death, the death of Faulkner escaped both mythicizing and exploitation in the press, perhaps because the pressures which drove him to his last spree had already become a legend and certainly because they drive us all, so that no one need feel guilty of his death.

Faulkner died as the culture which sustained him was also dying, died in history, that is to say, rather than against it. For surely the Old South—as he foresaw and desired—cannot long survive him; and though we can applaud no more wholeheartedly than he the emergence of the New South, whose coming Faulkner projected in terms of the rise of the Snopeses, we can find in him a model for how best to hate it, along with the New North and the New West—how to hate any world to which we are bound by the accident of birth and a heritage of love. How to deal with Faulkner himself is another matter. We have already

[11]

begun to teach him in the universities; and when, inevitably, Negroes come in large numbers to the classrooms of colleges even in the deepest South, he will be waiting for them there to show them how they, too, must learn to excoriate not the Other but themselves. Meanwhile, the tourist booths in his native Oxford are already displaying picture postcards of Faulkner's house; and when the plaque or monument to his memory is dedicated, as it must be soon, when speeches by fellow-citizens he despised are duly delivered, the joke he all along foresaw will be manifest. It is, of course, a joke we have heard before, yet a healthy one for young writers of fiction to be told over and over.

The legend of Hemingway is more commonplace: like the legend of Scott Fitzgerald, for instance, a mythic retelling of the failure of success; but, in Hemingway's case, the old story has somehow taken us by surprise. Only now has it become clear to all of us, for instance, what some of us have long suspected—that his truest strengths presented themselves all along in the guise of weaknesses, his most disabling weaknesses in the guise of strengths. Only the ultimate disaster was able to strip Hemingway of bravado and swagger and reveal behind the mask of the self-loved bully, which it pleased him to put on, the figure of the scared poet, which he hated to confess himself. He, who had lived for so long elsewhere, had come again to America, to the American West, to be stripped naked and to die, following, in a fated way, the path of Gary Cooper, with whose legendary image he had hopelessly confused himself by then. When Cooper died, Hemingway sent a strange telegram of condolence to the survivors, saying that he had never expected the actor to "beat him to the barn."

It was for the "barn," then, that Hemingway felt himself to be "headed" even before he pulled the trigger, a place of warmth and darkness where he could rest from the long day's posturing in the pasture. Enough of being the prize Bull, watched warily over the fence by idle onlookers! In the barn, perhaps, and just before sleep, Hemingway could become again the Steer he had originally imagined himself —not the doomed, splendid victim in the bull ring (this is

[12]

the role of the celebrity rather than the writer), only the patient nudger of bulls on the way to the ring. In *The Sun Also Rises*, which seems now the greatest of his novels, it is the image of the Steer which possesses Hemingway, and this is appropriate enough in a book whose protagonist is impotent. Moreover, the castrated anti-hero of Hemingway's first novel is succeeded by the deserted anti-hero of his next, *A Farewell to Arms*; while beside these two stand the comic alter egos of Jake Barnes, Yogi Johnson of *The Torrents of Spring*, and, especially, Nick Adams, nearest thing to a frank self-portrait in Hemingway's work. Nick, who continues to reappear in the later fiction, is already set in those early stories which Hemingway gathered together in *In Our Time* —a harried, frightened boy, who can witness but not act, register but not influence events.

In the mouths of his early non-heroes, in flight from war, incapable of love, victims of history and helpless beholders of infamy, the famous Hemingway style seems suitable, really functional. Such anti-heroes demand anti-rhetoric, since for them there are no viable, new, noble phrases to replace the outworn old ones—only the simplest epithets, and certain short-breathed phrases, not related or subordinated to each other, but loosely linked by the most non-committal of conjunctions: *and . . . and . . . and . . .* In a world of non-relation, only non-syntax tells the truth as in a world of non-communication, only a minimal speech, the next best thing to silence, the equivalent of silence, gives a sense of reality. In the Hemingway style, so simple at first glance, a score of influences are fused: the sophisticated baby talk of Gertrude Stein; the passionate provincial stutter of Sherwood Anderson; the blending of poetry and dialect invented by Mark Twain; the laconic idiocy of upper-class British speech; the muttering of drunks at bars, and, most notably perhaps, the reticent speech of the American Indian and of the white frontiersman who imitated him.

Beyond a few deep, childhood memories of actual Indians, it is apparently through books that Hemingway learned to write Hemingway-ese—through the eye rather than the ear. If his language is colloquial, it is *written* colloquial; for he

[13]

was constitutionally incapable of hearing English as it was spoken around him. To a critic who once asked him why his characters all spoke alike, Hemingway answered, "Because I never listen to anybody." Except, one imagines, to himself, to his own monologues, held, drunk, or sober, over a book or before a mirror, in the loneliness of his own head. He was, of all eminent writers, the most nearly inarticulate—garrulous, when garrulous at all, like the friendly drunk who claims your ear and at great length manages to say nothing. To the end of his life, "articulate" was to Hemingway a curse word, an epithet applied with mingled admiration and contempt to certain rival writers. And yet he, who spoke with difficulty, and surely wrote with more, managed to invent, without betraying his inarticulateness, one of the most imitated prose styles of all time.

What terror drove him to make speech of near-silence we can only guess; but whatever the spur, he made, with the smallest verbal means any major novelist ever had at his disposal, a dazzling success. What was in him he exploited fully, though too fully, too early in the game, perhaps. For the kind of perfection he attained was drastically limited, could only be reached once and for all, without the possibility of further development. Certainly, after the first two novels and the early stories, he was able only to echo, in the end parody, himself. But he was not, of course, his only parodist. In the conversation of the young, life frequently imitates art; and by a fitting irony, Hemingway, who listened to no one, was, after a while, listened to and emulated by all. He invented, scarcely knowing it, a kind of speech adequate to an age: the age of between-the-wars—when the young delighted in being told over and over (since they prized their disillusion as their sole claim to superiority over the past) that all was nothing, that nothing was all.

Hemingway's initial appeal, then, was as the exploiter of the self-pity of the first in a long series of American Lost Generations. But the feeling he evoked went deeper than mere self-pity, touched the depths of a genuine nihilism which may not have told the whole truth about existence, but which told a truth for which that generation hungered.

[14]

That he loved nothingness more than being, death more than his own life, and failure more than success, is the glory of the early Hemingway, which is to say, of the best Hemingway. His authentic work has a single subject: the flirtation with death, the approach to the void. And this subject he managed to treat in a kind of language which betrays neither the bitterness of death nor the terror of the void.

There is, however, a price to be paid for living always with the savor of one's own death on the tongue. One can sustain the mood of Ecclesiastes only in brief, ecstatic moments. The living experience of the void around us, like the living experience of God, is inevitably followed by what the Saints have called a dark night of the soul, doubly dark when the initial vision is itself of nothingness. And in the darkness, one is tempted to leave off one's death, to escape into suicide. To exorcise this temptation, to immunize himself against the urge toward self-destruction, Hemingway evolved a career of vicarious dying, beginning at the bull ring, and (so easily does the coin flip over) of vicarious killing in which lion and rhinoceros served as substitutes for the hunted self. In 1936, he wrote, speaking of himself— the only beast in view—in the third person: "If he had not spent so much time at shooting and the bull ring . . . he might have written much more. On the other hand, he might have shot himself."

But he did shoot himself in the end, losing finally the life for which he had paid so terrible a price. He became, in the course of time, the *persona* he had invented to preserve himself, became the hunter, the *aficionado*, the gusty, super-masculine, swaggering hero—in short, the Bull. Abandoning, first in life and then in art, the role of the anti-hero, the despised Steer, in whose weakness lay his true strength, Hemingway became first a fiction of his own contriving, then the creature of articles in newspapers and magazines, as unreal as a movie star or a fashion model. And it was the unreal Hemingway who wrote the later books, creating a series of heroes no more real than himself: men who sought rather than fled unreal wars, and who, in the arms of unreal women, achieved unreal delights. The boy, Nick Adams, who dreamed the first stories, the son of a failed father, proud only of his impotence, became himself a successful imaginary father, the legendary "Papa" of the newspaper columnists.

Beginning with the confusion of *To Have and Have Not,* rising to a climax in the fake nobility and sentimental politics of *For Whom the Bell Tolls,* and culminating in the sloppy self-adulation of *Across the River and into the Trees,* Hemingway betrayed again and again the bleak truth it had been given him to know, betrayed death and the void. Naturally enough, his anti-style went to pieces as his anti-vision of the world was falsified, becoming a manner, a tic, a bore. In *The Old Man and the Sea,* trying to recapture the spare horror of his early work, he produced only an echo, a not-quite-convincing counterfeit of his best. All this he must have known. Certainly, after *The Old Man and the Sea,* self-doubt overwhelmed him as the felt failure of his later work undermined his confidence even in the early, and the confusion about his identity (was he Papa? Gary Cooper? Nick? Jake Barnes?) mounted toward the pitch of madness. In his distress, he scurried back into his earlier life, seeking some self that might have written books worthy of survival. The articles on bullfighting in Spain which appeared in *Life* shortly before his death, the book on the 1920's in Paris on which he was working at the very end, are evidence of this search: a man without a future ransacking the past for the meaning of his career.

But the meaning of his career was there all the time in the authentic work of his youth, as the critics might have told him had Hemingway been able to read them less defensively. When he turned to the critics, however (and for all his pretended contempt, he was driven to them), he could find there, in his torment and self-doubt, only the reservations, the cruel judgments, the unkind remarks. And to whom could he have appealed for reassurance anyhow, having made himself the sole Papa of his world? At last, even the flesh betrayed him, the great, muscular body he had willed for himself shrinking beneath his handsome, old-man's head and his small-boy's beautiful smile. On the night

[16]

before his death, we are told, he could not find a pair of pants he would wear, for even retailored to appease his vanity, they sagged around his skinny shanks. How to exorcise the demons, then, when not only art had failed him, but his body, too, and with it the possibilities of ritual killing, those vicarious deaths with which he had bought, for years, his own life?

He had long been unable to hunt big game, and after a while could no longer even shoot birds from cover, since he could not manage to crouch down. Now, perhaps, the moment had arrived when he would no longer be able even to fire walking. One quarry was left him only, the single beast he had always had it in his power to destroy, the single beast worthy of him: himself. And he took his shotgun in hand, improbably reasserting his old faith at the last possible instant, renewing his lapsed allegiance to death and silence. With a single shot he redeemed his best work from his worst, his art from himself, his vision of truth from the lies of his adulators.

In any case, both early and late, at his best and at his worst, Hemingway, like Faulkner, continued to influence the actual practice of the younger writers of fiction. Yet his influence has worked quite differently from Faulkner's. Hemingway, that is to say, has invented a style to which it is impossible for more recent American novelists not to respond, in one way or another; but he has not, in the United States at least, founded a school. Faulkner, on the other hand, whose style is impossible to imitate fruitfully, is the founder of an important school of fiction, which, in its several subdivisions, fills the pages of our magazines and books to this very moment.

There are, it is true, a few self-declared disciples of Hemingway: writers of "hard-boiled" fiction, who exploit a certain tough masculinity and a certain boyish ideal of heroism, neither of which quite successfully conceals a typical brand of sentimentality, an overriding self-pity. John O'Hara, for instance, or even Norman Mailer and Vance Bourjaily, make such claims; but, in the end, they are less like Hemingway than they think—or, perhaps, only assert. The one line

[17]

of fiction which demonstrably descends from Hemingway is not quite literature: a special sort of vulgar, pseudo-realistic detective story, that grows progressively more debased as it passes from Dashiell Hammett to Raymond Chandler to Mickey Spillane to Richard S. Prather (the last sold exclusively in paperbacks and to the young, to the tune of some fifteen or twenty million copies).

On the level of art, Hemingway is a diffuse influence, found everywhere and nowhere, more often in nuance and inflection than in overt imitation, and especially in a language not merely written but spoken by two generations of young people, who may, indeed, claim to find him unsympathetic. No one these days, however, claims to find Faulkner unsympathetic. Such an assertion would be considered blasphemous by most literate Americans under, say, forty, especially by those with any pretensions to being writers themselves. Among them, he is a universal favorite; and everywhere his popularity increases, even among the aging, who despised him in the Thirties (for his presumed reactionary social content) only to make amends in the Sixties.

Moreover, there descends from him what has already become a tradition, a familiar kind of fiction which takes the South as its background, terror as its subject, the grotesque as its mode, and which treats the relations of black men and white as the chief symbol of the problem of evil in our time. Actually, three separate groups of writers have derived from Faulkner: the Southern Lady Writers, of whom Katherine Anne Porter is the most distinguished representative, and which includes Carson McCullers, Eudora Welty, Flannery O'Connor; the Effete Dandies or Homosexual Decadents, from Truman Capote to Tennessee Williams; and a one-man line of development, stemming from the popular and anti-feminine elements in Faulkner (so oddly transmuted in the first two groups), in the novels of Robert Penn Warren.

It is, perhaps, because the Negro question continues to be a pressing concern of contemporary America and threatens to become that of the whole western world that Faulkner has seemed a living influence in the sense that Hemingway has not. The mythology of bullfights and safaris and aggressive innocence seems to us, these days, less viable than that of slavery and war and the compounded guilts of segregation. Nonetheless, behind what is parochial and peculiar to him, Faulkner shares with Hemingway certain key experiences—experiences important not only in biographical terms but imaginatively as well—which make it meaningful to speak of both as members of a single generation, that of the Twenties, to which, of course, Scott Fitzgerald and Glenway Wescott also importantly belong, and against which the generation of the Thirties, as well as that of the Forties-Fifties, and that of the Sixties, have had to define themselves.

2

WAR, EXILE, AND THE DEATH OF HONOR

What, then, were for our eminent Old Men, and remain still for the few survivors of the Twenties, the critical life experiences out of which they were able to make their most authentic art? First, of course, was World War I, for them eternally the Great War, to which they compulsively returned during the whole of their lives, Faulkner writing his account of that conflict in *The Fable,* published in the Fifties, and Hemingway leaving behind, according to reports, a long narrative poem on the bravery of the foot soldier in that first of our international wars. But the War was followed by the return, at once to peace and to America, which ended in the great disillusion (how could the home dreamed of in trenches be realized in fact?), which, in turn, culminated in the great expatriation—the flight, chiefly to Paris, of a whole generation of artists and intellectuals. And the experience of Paris, in personal terms of a flirtation with irresponsibility, alcohol, and sex, in literary terms meant the exposure to European avant-garde literature, toward which the generation of Hemingway and Faulkner were attracted, but which ultimately they chose to reject. It was an affair, not a marriage, this temporary cohabitation of the American artist and the European avant-garde, but like many short-term affairs, it continued to influence the lives of those who moved back (with the coming of the depression) to more sober and permanent unions.

It is tempting to think of the practice of our writers of

the Twenties as representing a decisive disavowal of the temptations of avant-gardism, and, in a sense, this is true; but it is not true enough. Hemingway and Gertrude Stein may have become at last, symbolically as well as personally, enemies; yet the example of her war on syntax and coherence made him to the end a more insidious subverter of common speech than the readers of *Life* magazine could ever permit themselves to recognize even if they were capable of doing so. And however stubbornly Faulkner insisted on reinventing stream-of-consciousness in his own home-made terms, the experiments of Joyce surely inspired the effort. The ostensible rejection and the abiding nostalgia, the pride and shame of the generation of the Twenties in its encounter with Europe, is, in fact, the reaction of the tourist, the provincial tourist. It matters little whether the writers played abroad for a long time like Fitzgerald, or retreated immediately to their home towns like Faulkner, or kept seeking on foreign continents images of Montana and Upper Michigan like Hemingway—the writers who came of age in World War I remained what they were to begin with: country boys perpetually astonished at meeting the Big City and the Great World, provincials forever surprised to discover themselves in London or Paris or Antibes, and afterward dazzled to remember that they had ever been in such improbable places.

It is this "provinciality" which has distinguished their exile and return from that of both the writers who preceded them and those who followed them. We think of the generation of the Twenties, perhaps because they were so self-conscious about their exodus—composing manifestoes before and apologies afterward—as holding the patent on flight from home, but scarcely a major American writer has not been drawn (along with a host of minor ones) to Europe. Not only have some, like Pound and Eliot and James, lived most of their adult lives as declared expatriates, but others, who would have hooted in derision at the title, have spent long periods abroad. Benjamin Franklin, for instance, wrote most of his *Autobiography* in England and France; and, indeed, that first of American books which we can still read with delight appeared in French before there was any edition at all in Franklin's native tongue.

From Washington Irving (who spent seventeen years in Europe), through Hawthorne (who did seven at one stretch), to Melville (whose first voyage took him in that direction, and who, at his life's critical moments, always headed across the Atlantic)—through the generation of the 1920's and that lone exile of the Thirties, Henry Miller, to the present moment, American authors have sought in Europe a refuge from our weather and their friends, as well as a place for indolence and work. Only a short while ago, James Baldwin, who had lived many years in Paris, finished a novel in Istanbul; while William Burroughs, the Black Saint of the American very young, refuses still to return to his homeland; and Allen Ginsberg, who has made of Burroughs' exile a standing charge against America, recently walked in the mountains above Delphi, in search of whatever it is that for more than a century and a half our writers have sought in the Old World and not found—found perhaps by not finding.

Not only certain great European cities like London and Paris and Rome have provided our writers with a literary climate more favorable than their own, but the single, small hill of Bellosguardo in Florence lists on a memorial tablet the names of more American novelists of first rank who worked there on major books than any single spot in America could boast. It is, indeed, astonishing how many *especially* American fictions were conceived or actually executed abroad, from "Rip Van Winkle" through the Leather Stocking Tales, the *Marble Faun* of Hawthorne, and Twain's *Pudd'nhead Wilson*, to Fitzgerald's *Tender Is the Night* and *The Sun Also Rises* of Hemingway.

Some of these books are, of course, precisely studies of the American abroad; and since Henry James brought the theme to full consciousness, it has been an almost standard subject of our literature. I have before me, as I write, a list of "Outstanding Books for Summer Reading," chiefly by Americans, and my eye following the plot summaries sees at a glance, "on a Greek island," "self-discovery on the

[22]

French Riviera," "a busy Left Bank street in Paris," "a voyage from Mexico to pre-Nazi Germany." Remembering such books as these, we remember, too, that most of them end with their protagonists *going home*.

Such novels of exile and return reflect the deepest truth, the *mythical* truth of the experience of Americans abroad, a truth of art which life does not always succeed in imitating, though it is one to which it aspires. T. S. Eliot may never go back to St. Louis to live out his declining years, while Pound, released from captivity in the States, seems set on dying in Rapallo. And if Rapallo looks, as Karl Shapiro has somewhere observed, just like Santa Barbara, California, that is just one of those irrelevant jokes which history plays on us all. Nonetheless, Hemingway, after long wandering, did come home to the American West to die; and Henry Miller, who threatened for a while to freeze into the image of the Last Exile in Paris, has managed to thaw out in California. As for the generation of the Twenties, its backward trek has been memorialized in that Bible of repatriation, Malcolm Cowley's *Exile's Return*.

In literature, the pattern of exile and return works with more consistency; indeed, in some cases going home seems to be lived out vicariously in books, to spare the writer the indignity of living it out in fact. In the key books of Henry James, for instance, from *The American* to *The Ambassadors*, the protagonists go back to the place from which they started, whether it be San Francisco or Boston. And though, in *The Ambassadors*, the departing Lambert Strether tells his young friend Chad to stay in the France he is leaving, we cannot help suspecting that Chad will, for ignoble reasons, take the path back to America already followed, for quite noble ones, by his senior. Whether in self-sacrifice or cowardice, the displaced American returns. At least in literature.

The Dick Diver of Fitzgerald's *Tender Is the Night* is living in Geneva, N. Y., as his book closes; while Kenyon and Hilda of Hawthorne's *Marble Faun* are headed for marriage and America at their story's end; and Twain's Connecticut Yankee, who has traveled in time as well as space, returns to Connecticut to mark the close of his strange fable. Even Eliot, Anglo-Catholic and Royalist, returns home in his imagination, making a pilgrimage in the *Four Quartets* not only to New England, but even, less foreseeably, to Huck Finn's Mississippi, beside which he was born.

In the deepest American imagination, Europe represents a retreating horizon, opposite to but quite as elusive as the retreating horizon of the West. And like the West, it is thought of as a place in which we find it difficult to remain, like the place of a dream from which we wake in pleasure or fear. Or alternatively, we view it as the object of a romantic flirtation from which we return to the realities of marriage or loneliness. Most typically, we represent Europe to ourselves as a woman we cannot hold: a saint to be worshiped from afar, or a whore to be longed for and left—from Henry Adams' Virgin, through Twain's falsely accused St. Joan, to the "clouded" Mme. de Vionnet of James, and Pound's symbolic "old bitch gone in the teeth . . ." Only homosexuals, and the women who these days let homosexuals prefabricate their fantasies, imagine Europe as the bronze-and-black Mediterranean boy appropriate to a Roman spring.

Longfellow, for many years the chosen intermediary between the American middle classes and Europe, found once in a Roman *stornello* what struck him as the perfect expression of the feeling with which the American artist goes home. *"Se il Papa me donasse Campidoglio,"* the song runs, *"E mi dicesse, 'lascia andar sta figlia.' Quella che amavo prima, quella voglio"*; which means in English, "If the Pope would offer me the Capitoline Hill and say to me, 'let your girl go,' the one whom I loved first, her would I choose." And after "the one whom I loved first," Longfellow wrote, transcribing the lines in his notebook, "(America)." America! The image is customary enough: the presentation of the longing for Europe as an unworthy impulse to adultery, and of the return as a righteous reassertion of loyalty. And with it as a clue, we can begin to resolve the contradiction between the fact that our writers have constantly warned us off Europe and constantly sought it out.

The American, let us say, goes to Europe to see if he can triumph over temptation, and he learns that even if he cannot always leave what allures him, at least he can write accounts of leaving it. Discovering in Europe that his own country is myth as well as fact, and Europe fact as well as myth, he comes to see that one myth is as good as another, and he might as well stick to the one to which he was born. Meanwhile, he learns that in *fact*, in terms of plumbing and class relations and politics, America is clearly preferable; for even the superior comforts of Europe, cheap services and greater leisure, for example, are for him guilt-ridden advantages. In Paris, obviously different from the dream of Paris, the American discovers he can bear Kansas City, which he began knowing was different from all dreams of it; and this is worth his fare plus whatever heartache he pays as surtax.

Yet the American is typically not sure that the choice he has made in leaving is what in his deepest of deep hearts he desired. On the streets of Athens, his inner picketers chant, "Go home!"; as he boards ship or plane, they cry, "You fool!" Which is to say, he has fallen in love. In the erotic dream, he has committed his waking self. And he is dogged thereafter by the sense that if he had not got out in time he might have been captured forever, might have been held by precisely what, in his right mind, his stateside mind, he believes to be worst in Europe: its venality, its indolence, its institutionalized cynicism, its idle sensuality, its class distinctions, its shoddiness and dirt, its oppressive concern with the past. There is no reason, of course, that he should love only what is worthy of him; but as an American he is possessed by the mad notion that he *must*.

In any case, in our most serious books, representative Americans do not give up Europe gladly. Fitzgerald's Dick Diver blesses the Riviera beach from which he turns; and James's Lambert Strether departs from France as close to tears as his dry eye will come. But the regret itself is ambivalently regarded, Diver's blessing felt as blasphemous, Strether's regret as a betrayal of all New England taught him to honor. When the tone of rejection is not nostalgic, it is likely to be—as in the case of Mark Twain, for instance—shrill and unconvincing, the tone of one who has awakened from a dream left only reluctantly but remembered with pain. It is not, in any case, the ambivalence of the Twenties writer to Europe, or the tone with which he renders one aspect or another of that ambivalence, which distinguishes his kind of European novel (*The Sun Also Rises, A Farewell to Arms, Tender Is the Night, Three Soldiers, The Enormous Room*) from such earlier works as James's *Ambassadors* or *The American*.

And even the naïveté, the small-town point of view with which he starts, is not sufficiently distinctive, since, though it separates him from James, it joins him to Mark Twain. It is rather his motive for going that makes the novelist of the Twenties unique: the fact that not personal curiosity but world-wide catastrophe takes him across the Atlantic, not the ordinary impulse of commercial tourism but the exigencies of war.

Twain's defensive witticisms and cracker-barrel cynicism had as little appeal as James's involutions of syntax and deep exploration of sensibility to the generation of the Twenties, for their European experience was not a pilgrimage or a revelation but a binge, and they saw the Old World from the vantage point not of *salons* or museums, but of bars or trenches. Their books, that is to say, are not merely accounts of Americans in Europe but of Americans in war, or just out of it, as well. And though there is a sense in which the anti-war novel is merely a late sub-variety of the international theme (and another in which it is a sub-genre of the class-struggle book), we are compelled now to recognize it as the greatest and most characteristic literary invention of the Twenties.

Perhaps the kind of pacifism such books embody is the sole product of World War I to have lasted into our era. Certainly the official aims in whose name that war was fought, and which were theoretically assured by the Treaty of Versailles, have not come to very much. The dissolution of the League of Nations, the successes of Stalin and Hitler, and the outbreak of World War II made clear that the outward forms of democracy, national self-determination,

[26]

and international cooperation, imposed by fiat or invoked in pity, had little to do with the inward meaning of the world after 1919. Not peace and order but terror and instability were the heritage of the postwar years: an institutionalized terror and a stabilized instability, in whose honor two minutes of silence were observed for the score of November elevenths between the first great Armistice and the second great eruption of violence.

But pacifism, too, was a victim of World War II, which saw thousands of young men, who earlier had risen in schools and colleges to swear that they would never bear arms, march off to battle—as often as not with copies of anti-war books in their packs. Those books were real enough, like the passion that prompted them, and the zeal with which they were read; only the promises were illusory. The unofficial war-resisters, who for twenty years had pored over evocations of battlefield atrocities to immunize themselves against the appeals of patriotism, found their own slogans finally as irrelevant as the catch phrases they pretended to despise. To be sure, the end of still another war has seen the upsurge of still another pacifism; but this seems by now part of a familiar pattern, the zig which implies a zag before and after.

Perhaps then, we must settle for saying, more modestly, that the chief lasting accomplishment of World War I was the invention of the anti-war novel: a fictional record of the mood out of which the pacifism of between-the-wars was born and of the hopes and fears which sustained it through all the horrors of peace. It is certainly true that before the 1920's that genre did not exist, though it had been prophesied in the first two-thirds of Stephen Crane's *The Red Badge of Courage*, and that since the 1920's it has become a standard form: both a standard way of responding to combat experience and a standard way of starting a literary career. In the United States, it has been especially the examples of Hemingway and Faulkner which have encouraged young authors to pursue the genre, though we have always translated, and often exaggeratedly admired, similar books from abroad: Henri Barbusse's *Le Feu*, for

[27]

instance, or Hasek's *The Good Soldier Schweik*. At any rate, the generation of Americans who broke their pacifist oaths in World War II have sought to make amends by keeping faith with the kind of novel that had made war real to them before life itself had gotten around to doing it.

Certainly the flood of anti-war novels produced since the Forties owes more to certain books their authors grew up reading than to the actual fighting many of them did. A typical case in point is Norman Mailer's *The Naked and the Dead*, begun at Harvard before Mailer had lived through any battles but fictional ones; and quite properly so, since, for those of his age, the meanings of their wars had already been established by men twenty and thirty years their senior. As a matter of fact, for the generations from Pericles to Pershing the meaning of their wars was established before the fact—in Western culture, largely by works of art. The writers of Europe and America who were young enough to fight in World War I were, in this light, unique, endowed with a peculiar freedom their successors have vainly tried to emulate by imitating the forms in which it was expressed. Only the former, however, actually lived in the interval between two conventional ways of understanding war, serving as gravediggers to the one and midwives to the other.

For a thousand years or so, roughly from the time of Charlemagne to 1914, the wars of Christendom, whether fought against external enemies or strictly within the family, had been felt and celebrated in terms of a single, continuous tradition. And those who lived within that tradition assumed without question that some battles, at least, were not only justifiable but holy, just as they assumed that to die in such battles was not merely a tolerable fate but a glorious event. Doubts they may have had, but these could scarcely be confessed to themselves, much less publicly flaunted. Full of internal contradictions (what, after all, had any military code to do with the teaching of Christ?) and pieced together out of the ragbag of history, nonetheless the Christian heroic tradition proved viable for ten centuries. Yet all the while it lived, it was, of course, dying, too—so slowly, however, that only under the impact of total war were those who fought shocked into admitting that perhaps they no longer believed in what they fought for.

Last to learn that the old tradition had in fact died were the heads of state, kings and emperors, prime ministers and presidents. In their mouths, the shabby slogans, "For God and Country," "For Christ and King," "*Dulce et decorum est* . . ." rang ever less convincingly. But they were not the simple hypocrites their earliest critics took them for; they were merely dupes of history, in whom self-interest conveniently cooperated with confusion. Even more absurd than they, however, seemed the prelates of churches, on whose lips the more bloody battle cries, always a little ironical, appeared suddenly nothing but ironical. Yet it was not the believers who felt the absurdity, only those to whom God was presumably dead—only the Lost Generations.

Small wonder, then, that priest and potentate alike remained unaware that history had rendered them comic; no one told them so except those whose opinions they discounted in advance. Indeed, some to this very day have not realized that the words they speak in all solemnity have been to others, for over forty years, household jokes. One function of totalitarianism in its manifold forms is precisely to forestall the moment of awakening, imposing by decree the heroic concepts which once flourished by consent. Not only in totalitarian societies, however, is the anti-heroic spirit assailed by the guardians of the pseudo-heroic. In democratic nations, mass culture is entrusted with the job assigned elsewhere to the secret police; and if those who snicker at pretension are not hauled off to prison, they merely find it difficult to make themselves heard over the immensely serious clatter of the press. Yet recent writers, from Norman Mailer to Joseph Heller, continue to feel obliged to carry to the world the comic-pathetic news it is still reluctant to hear: the Hero is dead.

In the battle front against war, however, there is these days no more possibility of a final victory or defeat than on the battle fronts of war itself. In each, the end is stalemate; for the anti-heroic satirists who have carried the day in the libraries and the literary magazines elsewhere seem to have made little impression. The notion of the Christian Hero is no longer viable for the creative imagination, having been destroyed once and for all by the literature of disenchantment that followed World War I. Yet we fight wars still, ever vaster and more elaborately organized wars, while senators and commissars alike speak and are applauded for speaking, in all seriousness, the very lines given caricatured senators and commissars in satirical anti-war novels. Worse still, the anti-heroic revolt has itself become a new convention, the source of a new set of ridiculous clichés. Shameless politicians are, in fact, as likely to use the slogans of between-the-wars pacifism to launch new wars as they are to refurbish more ancient platitudes. The wild freedom with which the authors of A Farewell to Arms and The Enormous Room once challenged millennial orthodoxies has been sadly tamed; its fate is symbolized by Picasso's domesticated dove hovering obediently over the rattling spears of the Soviet war camp. Nevertheless, such books still tell us certain truths about the way in which men's consciousness of themselves in peace and war was radically altered some four decades ago.

The anti-war novel did not end war, but it memorialized the end of something almost as deeply rooted in the culture of the West: the concept of honor. The *locus classicus* is to be found in A Farewell to Arms, of course: "Abstract words such as glory, honor, courage, or hallow were obscene beside the concrete names of villages, the numbers of roads, the names of rivers . . ." But it was not merely a matter of level of abstraction as Hemingway rather disingenuously suggests. The notions of glory, honor, and courage lose all meaning when in the West men, still nominally Christian, come to believe that the worst thing of all is to die—when, for the first time in a thousand years, it is possible to admit that no cause is worth dying for. There are various mitigated forms of this new article of faith—that no cause is worth the death of all humanity, or a whole nation, or simply many lives; but inevitably it approaches the formulation: no cause is worth the death of a man, no cause is worth the death of *me!*

[30]

There are, in the traditional literatures of Europe, to be sure, characters who have believed that their own death was the worst event and honor a figment; but such characters have always belonged to "low comedy," i.e., have been comic butts set against representatives of quite other ideals: Sancho Panza serving Don Quixote, Falstaff trembling before Prince Hal, Leporello cowering as Don Giovanni tempts fate. And they have represented not a satirical challenge to, but precisely a "comic relief" from, the strain of upholding, against the prompting of our animal nature, the demands of indolence and greed and fear, those high values once thought to make men fully human. What happens, however, when the Leporellos, the Falstaffs, and the Sancho Panzas begin to inherit the earth? When the remaining masters are in fact more egregious Falstaffs and Leporellos and Sancho Panzas, and all that Don Quixote and Prince Hal and Don Giovanni once stood for is discredited and dead? What happens is what has been happening to us all ever since 1914, what our novelists beginning with the great Old Men have continued to record: what happens is *us*.

We inhabit for the first time a world in which men begin wars knowing that their avowed ends will not be accomplished, a world in which it is more and more difficult to believe that the conflicts we cannot avert are in any sense justified. And in such a world, the draft dodger, the malingerer, the goldbrick, the crap-out, all who make what Hemingway was the first to call "a separate peace," all who somehow survive the bombardment of shells and cant, become a new kind of anti-heroic hero. And it is precisely such sad sacks, such refugees from honor and glory, who returned to America to beget or become the generation of the Thirties. In Faulkner's *Sartoris* and *Soldier's Pay* we can read the record of their coming home from the wars, just as in Fitzgerald's "Babylon Revisited" we can read the record of their turning back from exile. But other writers must take up the burden at this point—writers who dream Armageddon but live Hollywood, who foresee Apocalypse and inherit prosperity.

3

THE BEGINNING OF THE THIRTIES:
DEPRESSION, RETURN,
AND REBIRTH

It is with the backlash of the Twenties, the return from
Europe to America, that the literary Thirties begin. More
customarily, and indeed properly, critics describe the period
as having been born out of the Depression; for chronologi-
cally the Depression preceded the Return. The writers of
the Twenties, who, the first time around, had been drafted
into Europe, *bought* their way back the second time; and
the decline in value of the American dollar after 1929 sent
them scurrying home to a new politics and a new kind of
art. Yet, in their deepest consciousness, they were returned
Americans even before they became Marxist Americans—
the first generation of returned Americans in our history.
Understanding this, it is easier to understand how many of
them brought back with them, or were at least conditioned
to accept after coming back, a brand of European politics,
a theory of society and of social action that remained, and
remains, meaningless to the vast majority of other Americans—how they became, in effect, the first truly European
Americans, as opposed to certain pseudo-Europeanized
Americans of the decades before them, or to the Melting-
Pot Americans who had been their grandparents.

The classic account of the rebirth in America of certain
American writers who had gone to Europe (which then
meant Paris, of course) to be born as artists is to be found
in Malcolm Cowley's *Exile's Return*; and the classic case of
the twice-born European American writer is the career of

John Dos Passos, whose *U.S.A.*, so avant-garde European in its superficial aspects at least (as compared, say, with Hemingway's *The Sun Also Rises*, which had actually been written in Europe), seemed for a while the great book of the age. Dos Passos had written before the Thirties and has continued to write ever since; but only in that period did he manage to seem central and important, so that he provides a more dramatic instance of the odd upheaval of critical values which accompanied the political hysteria of those times, than, say, Edmund Wilson or William Carlos Williams, who, like him, were rediscovering in the Thirties an America which, like his, was astonishingly theoretical. Considered together, however, Dos Passos and Wilson and Williams represent fairly enough a group of contemporaries and near-contemporaries of Faulkner and Hemingway, who were influenced as deeply as they by World War I and the impulse toward expatriation but were unable somehow to make it at the height of the Twenties and came into their own as elder statesmen in the era of the great Depression.

For the true Twenties writers, however, the Depression decade tended to be disastrous, forcing them to distort their values and to betray the myths which informed their authentic work in pursuit of shifting critical acclaim and an audience that had radically changed its allegiances. Faulkner's *Pylon* is a case in point—a shrill and opaque novel, dealing with the class struggle among stunt pilots, it turns away from Yoknapatawpha Country, where Faulkner is most at ease, to seek, in New Orleans (a scene the author had avoided since his early, unsuccessful *Mosquitoes*), a setting urban enough to suit the city mode of the Thirties. Similarly, Hemingway had abandoned his more customary foreign settings and had sought, in *To Have and Have Not*, to project a conflict between sturdy, proletarian values and effete, bourgeois tastes against a background for once wholly American. But though Hemingway had lived and fished in the Florida Keys, as Faulkner had lived and drunk in the French Quarter of New Orleans, the soil of the United States proved as alien to his imagination as the city to Faulkner's. Even the propinquity of Spanish-speaking terri-

B

tories (by then Hemingway was talking to himself in pidgin Spanish) to the scene of his action was of no help, and the book was a shambles—bad enough to have inspired not one, but two execrable movies.

At its worst when most serious, *To Have and Have Not* comes to life only when Hemingway forgets the class struggle long enough to parody his favorite butt, Sherwood Anderson, who had attempted in *Beyond Desire* an unconvincing proletarian novel of his own. The heroine of Anderson's book, a Jewish Communist organizer with an unfortunate resemblance to that brief movie favorite of the Thirties, Sylvia Sidney, stirred for a moment the vein of parody which Anderson's early heroes had awakened long before to produce *The Torrents of Spring*. But this was not all; for once Spain, the homeland of Hemingway's imagination, had become to American Communists and their fellow travelers a symbol of the ultimate, doomed struggle for which they longed, he was bound to try again. *For Whom the Bell Tolls* marks Hemingway's abandonment, under the pressures of Popular-Front, anti-Fascist slogans, of the anti-war novel for the pro-war novel; the anti-hero for the hero; himself for Gary Cooper; failure for success. It is not a good book, though on the level of action an exciting one, for it is not a true book, finally as false to history as to language; but in it Hemingway, the laureate of a "separate peace" to the generation of his own youth, tries to be born again as the laureate of a common war to the youth of the Thirties.

Equally unsuccessful, and equally admired for reasons equally untenable, is F. Scott Fitzgerald's *The Last Tycoon*. There is a kind of sentimental taste for unfinished works, especially those left in the wake of disastrous careers. And Edmund Wilson, in particular, has touted his former classmate's final attempt at a novel, persuaded, perhaps, by his own success in making out of his obscure Twenties beginnings a Thirties career, into believing that his friend, too, might have salvaged from the failure that followed his first triumphs an ultimate, more lasting (because more socially oriented) victory. I, however, have always found *The Last Tycoon*, despite occasional convincing scenes, singularly incoherent and scandalously fashionable, a bow to the times rather than a return to Fitzgerald's deep self, and have wished that he might have resisted the temptation to do an *à la mode* study of class struggle among the script-writers, as he had earlier resisted the temptation to tack a "proletarian" ending onto *Tender Is the Night*. He apparently contemplated for a while converting its protagonist, Dick Diver, to Communism, in one of those rebirth endings so prized by writers who, all the same, never quite believe in the New World into which their heroes are presumably being reborn.

From the vantage point of today, the Thirties books of Faulkner and Hemingway and Fitzgerald seem curious aberrations, examples of the extraordinary power of a mode which was a kind of madness; and when we read them, if at all, we are likely to approach them less as art than evidence, incidents in case histories which concern us for other reasons. A novel like Dos Passos' *U.S.A.* tends to be less and less read as the importance of its author is revealed to be only, in the most chilling sense of the word, "historical." The fat copies of the once well-thumbed Modern Library Giant edition sit untouched on the book shelves of certain survivors of the Thirties or are taken down in idle curiosity by their children, whom they do not move. Not only does the one-time audience of such books find itself embarrassed remembering its former allegiances; some of the writers of such books themselves apparently find their early works now disturbingly hysterical or false. At any rate, they insist on rewriting them, in an attempt, perhaps, to make them readable not only to those now young, but also to their present selves. Typically, the two sources alluded to by Granville Hicks in 1933 (in his *The Great Tradition*) as casting most light on "the young generation" have been presently revised. Malcolm Cowley's *Exile's Return*, which was first published in book form in 1934, was drastically redone for the new edition in 1951; while Edmund Wilson recast his *American Jitters* of 1932 by lopping away "shallow or nagging . . . Marxist morals," and republished it in a more inclusive volume called *The American Earthquake*, which

[35]

appeared in 1958. Moreover, Wilson stubbornly refuses permission to anyone in search of the Thirties as it looked to itself to reproduce any portion of the earlier text. If the Thirties begins with authors being reborn, it ends with those same authors rewriting their lives, much as in the Soviet Union, which some of them temporarily admired, history is rewritten with every change of generation and regime.

How hard it is, therefore, for us to close with those times, from which, despite a rash of new studies of their politics and art, we seem now at precisely the wrong distance. We can no longer read at all the "proletarian novels" of which the age once pretended to be proud—those fictional accounts of inevitably defeated strikes, which we are not surprised to discover were read by hardly anyone then, too, though they pre-empted so much space in the critical columns of newspapers and periodicals. And even some of the novelists who were then considered major figures, and whose works still bulk large on library shelves (James T. Farrell and John Steinbeck, for instance) seem at the moment, here in the United States at least, oddly irrelevant, whatever their merits. There is something almost tragic in their plight, whether they be, like Farrell, currently indigent and ignored, or, like Steinbeck, currently prosperous and— ironically—accorded the Nobel Prize; and their situation is not less tragic for being involved in a comedy: the comedy of the relationship to their past of middle-aged men who today delight in remembering, and falsify as they remember, their youth, which was contemporaneous with the Depression.

Certain underground figures of the Thirties, however, writers who in their own period were labeled reactionary or eccentric, who were despised or condemned or simply overlooked, have come to seem to us to represent the abiding achievement of that period, an achievement which necessarily had to be accomplished in secret and to await in secret the collapse of the Cult of Social Consciousness (with its concomitant hostility to all art not *both* ideologically o.k. and properly middlebrow) and the emergence of a new taste. We have been busy rediscovering these novelists over the

[36]

past decade or so, with the special glow of satisfaction that comes with learning to relish "one of us" born out of our time. Certain Jewish writers, pioneer exploiters of the ghetto milieu and the rhythms of Jewish-American speech (Abraham Cahan's *Rise of David Levinsky* provided an example of the genre as early as 1917 but remained for nearly twenty years an isolated sport among vulgar or ineffectual novels of Jewish "local color"), have seemed to us, in light of the practice of the Forties and Fifties, especially significant: Henry Roth, Daniel Fuchs, and Nathanael West.

Other kinds of underground writers, however, were, in the Depression decade, preparing for quite other lines of fiction: John Peale Bishop, for instance, creating, in *Act of Darkness*, a model for Robert Penn Warren, on the one hand, and, on the other, an inspiration for the semi-proletarian novel with which Carson McCullers began her career as the Thirties died, *The Heart Is a Lonely Hunter*. Out of that oddly hybrid first work of McCullers, there has emerged the whole school of Distaff and Epicene Faulknerians, so that, from the point of view of the present moment, Bishop's scarcely recognized book seems the essential link between the Twenties novel of the South and more recent examples of Southern Gothic; a work which kept alive, at a point when Marxian critics were sure they had destroyed the standing of the master himself, the Faulknerian line.

The Thirties, too, was the period in which Henry Miller produced his most valuable work, though the Thirties themselves did not know what to do with his untidy dithyrambics or how to judge his half-comic, half-earnest prophetic stance. The critics of the era, as a matter of fact, left him to be explicated by a frenetic knot of his friends (Lawrence Durrell, Alfred Perlès, Michael Frankel), through whose adulatory obfuscations we have been forced ever since to beat our way in search of Miller's real import. It is hard to remember that *Tropic of Cancer* (1934) and *Tropic of Capricorn* (1939) are genuine Depression novels, for they have long seemed to us forbidden books in the sense in which *Fanny Hill* was until only yesterday forbidden, rather than subversive books in the sense in which some readers once fondly believed *Grapes of Wrath* to be subversive, dirty rather than revolutionary. Moreover, they are the novels of an expatriate, celebrations of the illusion of freedom from puritanism possible only to Americans abroad; yet they were produced at a moment when theoretically all American writers had turned their backs on such illusions in favor of home, responsibility and social progress.

To make matters even more difficult, the sentimentality of the two *Tropics* (and, in so far as they are not farcical, they are sentimental) was attached to certain quasi-mystical doctrines out of Krishnamurti, Nostradamus, Mme. Blavatsky and John Cowper Powys, rather than to the teachings of Marxism-Leninism, which lent to the more fashionable sentimentalities of the age an air of *Realpolitik*. And the style of Miller's books—his particular ideal of bad writing as an earnest of sincerity—was, in its pursuit of the garrulous and the centrifugal, quite different from the dogmatic and straightforward meagerness to which bad proletarian novels aspired. The anti-structure of his books, too, seemed unsympathetic to readers accustomed to the highly structured class-struggle novel, rigid, almost, as the Western story, because, like that popular genre, it denied personal expression in favor of ritual and cliché. In place of the mythos of the proletarian romance (the conflict of forces, the eruption of violence, the inevitable defeat of the preferred cause, and the conversion in the midst of defeat), Miller provided only erotic daydreams, broken by shrill exhortations to freedom, freedom not from economic exploitation but from conventional morality and from politics itself. Finally, however, it was his euphoria, his unrelenting hilarity, which baffled an era that could never manage to embody in its literature the optimism appropriate to its hope of social revolution. Over and over, but always in vain, the Marxist critics scolded the self-declared Marxist novelists for being unable to imagine in their fiction even minimal happy endings.

More to the black taste of the times were Ferdinand Céline and Thomas Wolfe, two other Thirties exponents of

[38]

anti-form and the exploration of the author's sub-mind as the only knowable world; for at least they were not happy! The compulsively rewritten autobiography which Thomas Wolfe presented as a series of novels, and which declined from the limited success of *Look Homeward, Angel* through failed book after failed book until death mercifully intervened, pleased many readers of his age. However they may have deplored Wolfe's politics, they applauded his *Weltschmerz* at least, that half-comic sadness of a country Gulliver fallen among big-city pigmies; and wherever the taste for *Weltschmerz* persists—in Germany, for instance, and among the young, who are Germans one and all, from fifteen to twenty-one—a taste for Wolfe endures. During the Thirties, Céline was the favorite of a smaller but more discriminating audience, to whom his assault on rationality, his nausea and total rejection, justified, in terms of a meta-politics appropriate to that apocalyptic era, his making of the dirty word the Word. This justification readers did not find in Miller.

In a late book, full of tenderness toward himself and his own youth, Miller has listed Céline's *Journey to the End of the Night* among "The Hundred Books Which Have Influenced Me the Most"; but it seems difficult to believe that Miller ever really understood the rage and terror of Céline as well, say, as he understood the blander vision of the writers he lists just before and after the French novelist: Lewis Carroll and Benvenuto Cellini. Clown and cocksman, finally cocksman-clown, Miller is too *funny*, both intentionally and by mistake, to be ranked with a true descendant of the Marquis de Sade. To Miller, sex is not an instrument of power and degradation but a howling joke, and the most comic of all created things is the female sex organ as observed by his own oddly objective, though properly concupiscent, eye. Even now, however, in the moment of recognition and triumph, when Miller has come to play the Old Man to many in the generation of the Sixties, and his best books are printed for the first time in his own country, the real meaning of his work is scanted by the enlightened prigs, to whom his present vogue is largely an occasion for self-congratulation and is overlooked by the religioid Beats, to whom his muddled "serious" pronouncements seem to qualify him as prophet-in-chief to the modern world.

In any event, Henry Miller is just now coming into his own, making the difficult transition from a cult favorite, smuggled past customs into the land of his birth, to a popular author, displayed on newsstands in airports and supermarkets. Miller, however, has not merely survived long enough to be admired for certain older books which seemed in their own time offensively irrelevant, but to feel obliged to write new ones, in particular the trilogy *The Rosy Crucifixion*, which he speaks of as the last, the ultimate as well as the final, work of his life. He has felt obliged, that is to say, to be reborn as most Thirties writers have not—the luckiest among them managing to die, in one sense or another, the unluckier continuing to repeat themselves with diminishing vigor and conviction (like James T. Farrell). And in this sense, he is a fascinating case.

A comparison of *Plexus*, his last published major work, and *Tropic of Cancer*, the first of his books to appear, is especially illuminating in this regard. *Plexus*, which came out in 1953, is the second volume of *The Rosy Crucifixion*, of which the first, *Sexus*, was published in 1949, and the third, *Nexus*, is presumably still in progress. Like his first book, however, which was printed in France in 1934, the last deals with the only subject that has ever interested Miller, i.e., himself, retelling, with only the merest pretense at order, a series of events from his life already twice told or a score of time foreshadowed elsewhere, and rehashing notions, picked up in his early reading, about the lost continent of Mu, metempsychosis, and other vaguely mystical matters for which he has always had an unfortunate affinity. The mask of the narrator remains still the same, despite the passage of twenty years (but Miller as a writer was never young, being nearly forty-five when *Cancer* appeared): the mask of a half-American, a Noble Savage who is not also a Puritan, a citizen of the United States without guilt, or any commitment, however diminished, to diligence, industry, frugality, or duty.

Even more astonishingly, readers of *Plexus* will discover once more an American novelist who despises whisky (peace to Fitzgerald, Hemingway, and Faulkner) though he affects a taste for wine and adores good food despite the notorious fact that good meals are as rare in American books as satisfactory love affairs. And they will find, too, one who lived through the Thirties without acquiring the slightest interest in politics or social justice or, indeed, in people in groups larger than two or three. Others have meaning for Miller only as they impinge directly on him, hurting or sustaining him; he finds it difficult to imagine them as real to each other, even in pairs, much less in communities or nations, except in the moment of copulation. Miller has, it is true, an extraordinary ability to re-create, in fiction, his friends and enemies joyous in bed, but he is an idiot when he tries to imagine them miserable in society. "For the world in general," Miller has written in a memoir of his friend Alfred Perlès, "the ten years preceding the war [World War II] were not particularly joyful times. The continuous succession of economic and political crises which characterized the decade proved nerve-racking to most people. But, as we often used to say: 'Bad times are good times for us.'"

The indifference of Miller to any *angst* except his personal one, his actual relish of the world's misery, seems the more incredible when we realize that the time on which he is commenting, the time, indeed, during which he found his authentic voice and style, was the period of the great Depression and of the terror of Between-the-Wars. It is an era which produced many brands of apocalyptic hysteria, but none so eccentric or so heartless as Miller's. That hysteria he is in the habit of presenting to us in the guise of joy; but it seems rather to be a symptom of the strange failure of the tragic sense, a way of apprehending experience as rich as it was black, which characterizes American literature from the time of Melville and Hawthorne to that of Hemingway and Faulkner, however desperately and vestigially in the latter. In this regard, perhaps, the work of Miller must be considered prophetic—a preparation for an age of maximum consumption and relative plenty, in which the tragic sense would become as obsolete as the maxims of *Poor Richard's Almanac*.

Miller represents, then, the moment at which a specially American way of coming to terms with human misery and evil, a way rooted in dying Puritanism and accompanied by obsessive guilt, particularly in regard to indolence and copulation, was being destroyed forever. In a sense, the concern with social justice, which so possessed those writers who were looking out at America at the moment Miller, in Paris, had turned his back on his country, seems a last effort to maintain and justify the long concern of our literature with "the blackness of darkness." But that concern, however little we knew it, was already doomed even in the Thirties, on the one hand by the attenuation of traditional guilts, and on the other by the replacement of a metaphysical or ethical view of man, a cosmic or social approach, by a personal one, self-congratulation or self-pity.

Miller is the laureate or, better, the prophet of the new personalism, and hence the first important self-consciously anti-tragic writer in America. It is a little misleading, all the same, to speak of him as a comic writer without further qualification, though he is howlingly funny, both intentionally (in the perhaps one-quarter of his books where he is at his best) and unintentionally (in the three-quarters where his self-awareness breaks down or his naïve susceptibility to pseudo-philosophy and mantic posturing takes over). What is funny in him, however, is rooted neither in social satire, whether directed against the deviant individual, like, say, Pope's, or a whole society, like G. B. Shaw's, nor in a vision of the total absurdity of mankind, like Chaucer's or, more recently, Samuel Beckett's. Miller's is the humor of mocking gossip, rooted in the kind of betrayal of friends (as his life-long friend, Alfred Perlès, somewhere suggested) in which many men and most women delight to indulge in private, but which committed to cold, public print scandalizes and disturbs us, as all revelations of the self we fear others see and hope they do not scandalize and disturb us.

In this sense we can identify Miller's humor as a function of the *persona*, the mask of the "Happy Rock" called Henry Miller, created by the form he loves best: transmogrified autobiography—not autobiography objectified by form and distance into proper fiction, but autobiography made truer to itself than mere fact by the skill of an inspired and malicious liar. The essential aim of that liar, as well as of the humor he makes his chief weapon, is to put down all the rest of the world and to glorify himself, without, however, denying that that self is a feckless, conscienceless sponger and deadbeat. In the very moment that Miller tells us how he rewarded by sleeping with their wives those who sponsored, clothed, fed, and subsidized him, he is further rewarding them by making a comic tale of that betrayal or by drawing comic portraits of the sex organs of those wives, thus compounding the initial treachery.

The man who disavows duty, work, and conscience—those moral burdens which our earlier writers chafed against without daring to slough—who really acts as if the world owes him a living, is likely to be loaded down with a new burden in place of the old, the burden of obligation and gratitude, unless he can laugh his benefactors to scorn. It is this desperate laughter, the last weapon against the last temptation to duty, the temptation to say thanks to those who sponsor a dutiless life, which rings through Miller's work. But even the desperation behind the laughter does not finally succeed in depressing him (though he confesses it overtly from time to time and betrays it unawares even more often) because he is convinced he is immortal, does not believe he will ever die, even now when he has passed his seventieth year.

How strange, for a grown man, this illusion which ordinarily sustains only the young! But it is characteristic of Miller to have begun to be young at forty-five, to have made the young man's move into exile precisely when writers like Fitzgerald (actually five years his junior) had begun the retreat toward maturity and despair, and it is typical of him, too, to be working at it still, or again, beyond the full span of three score years and ten. But it is this which makes him characteristically American as well as characteristically himself, for all of his rejection of Calvinism, guilt, and tragedy, and despite his preference for sex over whisky. He is not, however, an American in the line of Hawthorne, Melville, and Faulkner in this regard, but rather a late link in the chain that begins with Benjamin Franklin and passes through Emerson to Mary Baker Eddy: the line of self-congratulatory post-Christians who manufactured homegrown religions (often with hints of the mysterious East) to express their assurance that tragedy was an illusion and death was not real.

If, in his latest book, Miller sounds more like Franklin than Rousseau or even Whitman, this is not only because his personal success, his recent happy marriage (on the fourth try), and his first real relationship with children of his own have overtaken him late in life, at the moment he has returned to America, but also because America has at this moment returned to prosperity. From post-World-War-II America, Miller has returned, in *Plexus*, to the America of Post World War I, from one era of plenty to another, as well as from his old age to his youth. What has been dropped out is the middle of his life, the misery of his middle age memorialized in *Tropic of Cancer*, and the unnoticed years of the Depression, which coincided with that middle age. It is with nostalgia that he turns back to that earlier time, a nostalgia for old books, old buddies, and old loves. And though at the center of *Plexus* is the love affair with, and the marriage to, "Mona," Miller's second wife, it is only the best years of their relationship which he records.

He cannot stay away from the memory of her, even from the anticipation of her betrayal of him, any more than he can stay away from the Jews, to whom he has always been bound by a ferocious ambivalence; but this time everything is mitigated and blurred, rendered as a series of crucifixions not so much rosy in themselves as seen through rose-colored glasses. Even the pseudo-avant-garde style of

Cancer has peeled away, that violence of image and language bred of an anguish near madness, as well as of Miller's attempts to please his improbable Muse, the much-over-rated Anais Nin. This very joyousness of Miller, once frantic and subversive, his contemptuous negation of a prevailing melancholy ("No, this is a prolonged insult, a gob of spit in the face of Art, a kick in the pants to God, Man, Destiny, Love, Beauty . . . what you will. I am going to sing for you, a little off key perhaps, but I will sing. I will sing while you croak, I will dance over your dirty corpse . . ."), has become now mere smugness and cliché ("The first few months . . . it was just ducky. No other word for it. . . . We lived exclusively for each other—in a warm, downy nest . . ."), the banal nostalgia of an old man proud that he has lived so long, pleased with his still youthful vigor, and astonished that his published visions of failure and apocalypse have brought his success and peace.

Yet it has been only in the Sixties, at the point where his powers have flagged, that Miller has won the admiration of a practicing generation of writers; for those who came of age in the Forties and Fifties, he seemed, and seems still (except in the case of recusant members of the group like Karl Shapiro), less important both as a model and in his own right than certain unappreciated novelists of that era who died with that era, either actually, like Nathanael West, or metaphorically, into Hollywood like Daniel Fuchs, or into madness and consequent silence like Henry Roth. To that generation, West and Fuchs and Roth have seemed more a part of what has appeared, until recently, to be the mainstream of the modern novel; though, as compared with Miller, their achievement in terms of bulk is slight.

Roth is the author of a single novel, *Call It Sleep*; and Fuchs managed to write only three—one of them, *Homage to Blenholt*, of considerable merit—before his retreat to Hollywood and ladies' magazine fiction. There remains, then, Nathan Wallenstein Weinstein, who preferred to call himself Nathanael West, and whose long neglect by the official critics of the period is now being overbalanced by his enthusiastic discoverers, chiefly University Press authors and writers of Ph.D. theses. At the moment, all of his works are again in print, and *Miss Lonelyhearts* has been translated into a play and a movie; but there is no use in concealing from ourselves the fact that what has been restored to us is only another tragically incomplete figure, whose slow approach to maturity ended in death.

Like Wolfe, Céline, and John Peale Bishop (but also like Roth and Fuchs), Nathanael West is another of the exploiters of violence in whose work even sex tends to be treated as one more example of horror and aggression. Unlike their Gentile opposite numbers, however, the Jewish subscribers to the Thirties' Cult of Violence, Roth and Fuchs as well as West, declare their allegiance with a special pathos; for to espouse violence is, for them, to deny their fathers. Yet what could they do? In those shabby, gray years, the dream of violence possessed the American imagination like a promise of deliverance. Politics was violent, and apolitics equally so; whatever else a man accepted or denied, he did not deny terror. Obviously, the Thirties did not invent terror and violence in our fiction, for as far back as American books go, they are obsessed with images of horror; but there are, in the Thirties, two transformations of the traditional uses of violence.

The first is the urbanization of violence, its transposition from the world of nature to the world of society, from what man must endure to what man has made; and the second is the ennobling of violence, its justification as "the midwife of history." Under the aegis of "the Revolution," violence came to be thought of not as an evil to be avoided, but as the climax of social progress, the crown of social life. In light of this, it is easy to understand that, matters of ideology aside, it is the pure love-fear of violence which distinguishes the authentic novel of the Thirties—a kind of passion not unlike that which moved the Nazis before their final defeat, a desire for some utter cataclysm to end the dull dragging-out of important suffering. In official Communist terms, the vision of apocalypse is translated into that of the final conflict between worker and boss, proletarian Good and capitalist Evil.

[46]

This pat formula, the underground Jewish-American novelists of the Thirties could not quite stomach; and they fought it in a kind of camouflaged resistance movement which they were unwilling to confess even to themselves. Instead they subverted the glorification of violence they dared not openly reject with the ambiguities of humor. Toward the close of Daniel Fuchs's *Homage to Blenholt*, the *shlemiels* who are his anti-heroes have reached the end of their illusions and are confronting each other in comic despair. One has come to realize that he will run a delicatessen for the rest of his life; another to see that the greatest event in his career will be his having won three hundred dollars on a long shot.

"Well," said Coblenz, "don't take it so hard. Cheer up. Why don't you turn to Communism?" . . .
"What has Communism got to do with it?" Munves sincerely wanted to know.
"It's the new happy ending. You feel lousy? Fine! Have a revelation, and onward to the Revolution!"

Fuchs's characters are not merely anti-heroes but fools, incapable of any catastrophe more nearly tragic than a pratfall; for his means are comic, and his mode parody. Just as he caricatures briefly, here, the ending of the Proletarian Novel, he travesties, throughout the main body of his work, the Gangster Novel—that Thirties' urban equivalent of the Western in which the middlebrow author believes himself to be creating a modern version of the tragic hero. There are no Little Caesars, however, among Fuchs's Williamsburg and Coney Island hoods; only small businessmen, acquisitive slobs trying to make a living in tough times and succeeding, by and large, as ill as anyone else .That Fuchs ever quite knew what he was doing beyond this is doubtful; certainly he has subsided into a modest Hollywood success without a sigh or twinge of guilt, admonishing his old readers that "it would be foolish to expect writers not to want to be paid a livelihood for what they do," and assuring them that "we are engaged here on the same problems that perplex writers everywhere."

Henry Roth and Nathanael West, however, possessed more complex minds and more lofty ambitions, and were therefore able to achieve effects at once consciously anti-heroic and intendedly quasi-tragic; but, by the same token, they were subject to anguish and a prevision of defeat to which Fuchs remained immune, and were driven to devices more desperate than any of his. Roth's *Call It Sleep* appeared in 1935, yet the events which it describes occur in the years from 1911 to 1913; and they are funneled through the mind of a boy who is six as the book opens. Through the imagined sensibility of this dream-ridden, mama-haunted, papa-hating Jewish child, Roth manages to redeem to poetry the formlessness and the banality into which the ghetto novel had fallen since the time of Abraham Cahan. But the predating of the action serves another purpose, too, helping the author evade an ideology which might have hampered his artistic freedom, an ideology which in 1911 had not yet been frozen by the Russian Revolution. For the Marxian version of the class struggle, to which Roth was theoretically committed, *Call It Sleep* substitutes a Dickensian one: a view of the "Final Conflict" as taking place between a corrupt adult society and the pure child.

That conflict is resolved when David, Roth's young protagonist, thrusts the handle of a milk ladle down into the crack between two electrified streetcar rails and is shocked into insensibility. He has learned earlier of the power lurking in the rails and has come to identify it with the coal of fire by which the mouth of the Prophet Isaiah was cleansed; he considers himself cleansed when, in the moment before total unconsciousness, he sees a vision in which all that has vexed him, all the fear and rage and filth he has felt in himself, his family, and the world they inhabit, is dissolved in a glow of peace. But for this vision neither the eight-year-old neurotic nor the author has a name; and as the boy falls from awareness, he thinks: "One might as well call it sleep." It is an astonishingly beautiful and convincing book; but Roth was never able to write another. Bogged down in the midst of a second try, he seems to have undergone a breakdown from which he emerged only to disappear from public view. He has published two or three stories since, of little consequence, and has contributed an occasional statement to a symposium; and there have been, through the years, accounts of his working at some improbable job: attendant in an insane asylum, teacher of mathematics in a high school, most recently poultry farmer outside some small New England town. But what anguish works behind his near-silence we can only—remembering the terror of the novel with which he began and ended—surmise.

West, unlike the other two, survived the darkness of his inner world and the menace of the even darker world outside, survived both his own first novel and Hollywood. Yet his career, too, seems abortive, for he died in an automobile accident at the moment when he was approaching artistic maturity; and greatness lies like a promise just beyond his last novel. Nonetheless, he is the inventor for America of a peculiarly modern kind of book, whose claims on our credence are perfectly ambiguous. Reading his fiction, we do not know whether we are being presented with a nightmare endowed with the lineaments of reality, or with reality blurred to the uncertainty of a nightmare. In either case, he must be read as a comic novelist, and his anti-heroes understood as comic characters, still as much *shlemiels* as any imagined by Fuchs, though they are presented as sacrificial victims, the only Christs possible in our skeptical world. In West, however, humor is expressed almost entirely in terms of the grotesque, which is to say, on the borderline between jest and horror; for violence is to him technique as well as subject matter, tone as well as theme.

Much of this West learned, like many of his generation, in Europe. Especially in *The Dream Life of Balso Snell*, the influence of the French Surrealists is patent everywhere: in the brutal conjunctions, the discords at sensitive places, the tendency to move from belly-laugh to hysteria. Yet, like others of that generation, he brought what he learned home,

[49]

Americanized it. It is even possible to see him finally as just another of the "boys in the backroom," one more all-American tough guy; but he remains, for all his disclaimers, also a Jew, that is, a special brand of European-American eternally shocked to discover what any streetcorner loafer knows: "In America violence is idiomatic, in America violence is daily." And in *Miss Lonelyhearts* he created a portrait of a man whom the quite ordinary horrors of ordinary American life lacerate to the point of madness, but who is given, half as a joke, the job of answering "letters from the lovelorn" in a daily newspaper.

This is West's metaphor not just for his own plight but for that of the writer in general, whom he considers obliged to regard unremittingly a suffering he is too sensitive to abide. West is child enough of his age to envision an apocalypse at the end of this long torture; but his apocalypse is a defeat for everyone. The protagonist of *Miss Lonelyhearts* is shot reaching out in love toward a man he has unwillingly offended, while the hero-*shlemiel* of *A Cool Million* goes from one absurd anti-Horatio Alger disaster to another, and after his death becomes the hero of an American Fascist movement. But the real horror-climax of his life and the book comes when, utterly maimed, he stands on a stage between two comedians, who wallop him with rolled-up newspapers to punctuate their jokes—until his wig comes off, his glass eye pops out, and his wooden legs falls away, after which they provide him with a fresh set of artificial appurtenances and begin again.

4

THE END OF THE THIRTIES:
ARTIFICIAL PARADISES AND
REAL HELLS

Not until *The Day of the Locust*, however, West's last book and the most terrifying treatment in fiction of Hollywood, does one get his final version of the Apocalypse. At the end of the novel, a painter, caught in a rioting mob of fans at a Hollywood première, dreams, as he is being crushed by the rioters, his masterpiece, "The Burning of Los Angeles":

> Across the top he had drawn the burning city, a great bonfire of architectural styles. . . . Through the center . . . spilling into the middle foreground, came the mob carrying baseball bats and torches—all those poor devils who can only be stirred by the promise of miracles and then only to violence, a great United Front of screwballs and screwboxes to purify the land. No longer bored, they sang and danced joyously in the red light of the flames.

It is a dream prophetic as well as historical, predicting the disappearance of Hollywood which we are just now witnessing in fact, and reminding us that the great literary invention of the Thirties was not the "Proletarian Novel," so worried over by its theorizers, but the Hollywood, or more properly, anti-Hollywood book, which no one then took the trouble to identify. Just as in the Twenties a generation of writers went to war and produced the anti-war novel (and as in the Forties-Fifties a generation of writers were to go to the university and produce the anti-university novel, in

[51]

the Sixties to the madhouse and produce the anti-madhouse novel), so in the Thirties a generation of writers went to Hollywood and produced the anti-Hollywood novel, a form that has been a staple of our fiction ever since.

Everyone must be aware of the fact, and perhaps for this reason it is rarely recorded, that beginning in the Thirties a large number of quite serious American writers, some of the highest rank, went off to become script-writers for the American movies. Of the three novelists (Faulkner, Hemingway and Fitzgerald), generally considered the most notable in the generation of the Twenties, for instance, two spent a considerable period writing for the films: Fitzgerald, who died in terror and defeat in Hollywood, and Faulkner, who managed to come and go without suffering any irreparable wound. But they did not make the move, of course, until the era of the Depression; and their belated commitment to so alien a place seems a mistake, an aberration from their true careers, like the anti-Fascist fictions to which their contemporaries felt impelled to turn a hand at the same time. Sinclair Lewis, in fact, did his best to commit both errors, not only writing an anti-Fascist novel, *It Can't Happen Here*, but also preparing with Dore Schary an anti-Fascist film-play called *Storm in the West*. The movie, however, never appeared, and the script was not published until 1963.

The move to Hollywood which the generation of the Twenties attempted often out of desperation and always against the grain, certain writers of the Thirties managed to make typically, as it were, and without strain, being the first group of Americans to have been born into the world of modern mass culture, which had waited on certain technological breakthroughs for its full development. A notable example, as we have seen, is West, who died in California a script-writer to the end; and another is Daniel Fuchs, who, having abandoned his career as a serious novelist, has managed to work in Hollywood with some success and, if he himself can be believed, considerable happiness. To them should be added Christopher Isherwood, noted British novelist of the Depression era, who, when the Revolution failed him, chose immigration to an America which for him meant Southern California. He lives even now in Los Angeles, writing distinguished scripts that do not ordinarily get made into films at all—but which are paid for at a respectable enough rate to enable him to go on writing less profitable fiction.

Later writers have, of course, gone to Hollywood with the experience of their predecessors already known to them, and therefore without any of the original hopes and fears of the first generation to come of age under the regime of popular culture. They went to write movies at second-hand, wise with someone else's wisdom; but even so, of those who worked in the movie industry for a longer or shorter time (Norman Mailer, Budd Schulberg, Truman Capote, James Agee, Calder Willingham), the most persistent and success-ful have been those who are in some sense belated Thirties figures: like Mailer, who discovers everything twenty years late, and Willingham, who thinks he lives in the heyday of James T. Farrell. Perhaps this is why a gifted young Canadian like Mordecai Richler, whose country's culture limps a couple of decades behind ours, goes as inevitably into film writing as his contemporaries this side of the border find jobs in colleges.

Perhaps nothing less catastrophic than a total depression and the consequent questioning on all sides of basic values could have brought about the improbable and foredoomed marriage of the serious American novelist and the American movie industry. The America which our films have, from their beginnings until now, postulated is a country without books or audiences for books. Certainly, anyone who had learned about our country just from watching our films would be convinced that no Americans ever read anything, and that presumably there is nothing produced in our land worth reading—that, in short, America is the first post-literate culture. Who, for instance, can imagine the great figures created by the American films, those larger-than-life mythical characters who survive from movie to movie, read-ing a book? Think of Marilyn Monroe, Jean Harlow, or Gary Cooper; Charlie Chaplin, Clark Gable, Jerry Lewis,

[53]

or Kirk Douglas; John Wayne, Steve McQueen, or Mickey Mouse, entering a library or standing before a bookshelf with any serious intent in mind.

How many scenes involving books remain in the memory, out of the films of the last thirty years, excepting always those shelves of meaningless books in libraries, obviously bought by the gross like furniture? A volume of Proust, perhaps, discussed in *The Scoundrel* of Ben Hecht and Charles MacArthur, and Irwin Shaw's *The Young Lions'* being read by the gigolo script-writer in *Sunset Boulevard*. But there is no way to be sure that the Proust volume has been actually read in *The Scoundrel*, and anyhow the putative reader is an international type, played by Noel Coward, while the reading of Shaw's semi-serious book is symbolic: an act of revolt, a gesture almost un-American in its implications. Portraits of literary people in American movies, moreover, the bohemians who gather in *Auntie Mame*, for example, are travesties embarrassing to all but the most ignorant. It can be argued, of course, that movies as such are essentially anti-literary, concerned with a world of outwardness and action that has nothing to do with the readers and writers of books, and that intellectuals should be happy to be well out of so uncongenial a world. But there is always the example of certain European directors, Antonioni, for instance, in whose *La Notte* Broch's *Sleepwalkers* plays an essential role, and in whose *l'Avventura* Scott Fitzgerald's *Tender Is the Night* sets the tone of a crucial scene.

The fact is that the producers of American movies until only yesterday have been chiefly men who do not read but have others read for them and who, therefore, despite occasional pretenses to the contrary, are not the victims of commercialization and genteel taboos, but the beneficiaries of the only world in which they could possibly thrive, one of profit-taking and timidity. They do not merely suffer, but believe in, the taste of an audience which they share more than they like to admit, an audience in which they can be reasonably sure there are few, if any, readers of genuine books. And yet, for reasons difficult at first glance

[54]

to understand, the makers of big movies have been unable to keep their hands off serious literature while at the same time, for reasons even more obscure, many serious writers, especially, as we have seen, since the Thirties, have been unable to stay away from the big movies.

Perhaps the yearning for culture, prevalent among successful makers of commercial movies, can be thought of as the tribute which middlebrow vice pays to highbrow virtue; but it is more complicated than that easy formulation suggests. The motives which impel a certain kind of producer or director to meddle with the great American books, both schoolroom classics and more recent works, could be summarized as follows, in descending order of consciousness: first, a sense of duty; second, sheer condescension; and third, a secret hostility to art.

Certain kinds of rich men have always endowed libraries and museums with profits made from selling gunpowder while others have set up philanthropic foundations with fortunes made by peddling oil. The movie mogul, similarly moved, has an advantage over these since he can pay off in kind: losing on what he takes to be "good" movies, the money he has made on "bad" ones. And while he is salving his conscience, he may be convinced that he is also doing a favor for the largest public, and for the serious author as well; for he is likely to feel that the ignorant public which has made him rich cannot understand as well as he the great works of our literature, in *words* at least. He believes, therefore, that by translating them into the language of images, he has benefited not only that audience but also the writers, living and dead, who do not—for the best of reasons—know how to communicate as well as he. Behind all this array of self-justification, however, there lurks an unconfessed desire to desecrate that which he pretends to honor, to revenge himself for the insult which he feels the very existence of high art offers to all that he ordinarily does.

Obviously, the first of these motives leads to an insufferable piety and stuffiness in those films which Hollywood producers think of as attempts at art; the second to oversimplification and sentimentalization; and the third to downright parody and falsification. It is instructive, though disheartening, to recall what has become on the screen of the three books universally recognized as the greatest works of fiction produced in our country: *The Scarlet Letter*, *Moby Dick*, and *Huckleberry Finn*. The first has, in recent decades, not been attempted at all, perhaps because, being the most subtle, the most adult, it is the least amenable to travesty. And yet it begs to be filmed, since it, more even than the others, is scenically conceived, a study in scarlet and black and white, which already exists in the mind imagistically, its passages of action freezing into a series of stills.

Moby Dick, on the other hand, has been more often attempted, though chiefly as a vehicle for certain actors, John Barrymore, for example, and Gregory Peck, who have lusted to portray Ahab. Having no concept of the intellectual motives of Ahab's quest, and being aided not at all by their directors, they have ended by playing him as a lunatic—in the case of Gregory Peck (who would have been better cast as the whale) as a mad Abraham Lincoln, in the case of Barrymore as a mad Barrymore. And *Huckleberry Finn*, of course, has seemed fair game to everyone, striking producers as a natural family movie (i.e., no sex but lots of action), a real box-office draw for the kiddies, like *The Swiss Family Robinson* or *Journey to the Center of the Earth*. They have been only slightly disturbed, if at all, by the critical estimate of *Huck* as a great work of art, considering this a bonus to be accepted in cynical bewilderment. Samuel Goldwyn himself is the most recent violator of *Huckleberry Finn*; and the clue to his approach is to be found in the fact that he shot the Mississippi scenes on the Sacramento River, presumably on the theory that any touch of truth would be out of place. For a while, a rumor circulated that Tom Sawyer would be made a girl, since romance is a help, though sex an embarrassment; and there was no female available to Huck. Unfortunately, the rumor proved to be false, for the picture might have been a lot funnier that way.

[56]

More recent works have fared little better, though the worse they were to begin with the better their chance of being made into satisfactory films. Hemingway and Faulkner have been consistently bowdlerized and misrepresented, though never as flagrantly in Hemingway's case as in Faulkner's, who has had to see his prize villains parodied and redeemed to suit the talents (and accents) of current favorite leading men—Yves Montand, for example. A few books of second or third rank, respectable if not great, have, on the other hand, become movies of the same order, e.g., Steinbeck's heavily sentimental *Grapes of Wrath* and Robert Penn Warren's satisfactorily melodramatic *All the King's Men*. Sometimes good books by bad stylists are even improved, on the level of style at least, by splendid movie technicians, as George Stevens substituted for the clumsy, inaccurate plodding prose of Dreiser's *American Tragedy* his own dreamy, sunlight-through-water effects in the movie version called *A Place in the Sun*.

John Huston, least anti-intellectual of living directors but a child of the commercial movies all the same, is a fascinating case in point; for his great movies, his real contributions to American cinema, are not his abortive filmings of *Moby Dick* and *The Red Badge of Courage*, but movies he has made from bad or indifferent books: *The African Queen*, *The Treasure of the Sierra Madre*, and *The Maltese Falcon*. And behind him looms the figure of D. W. Griffith, whose *Birth of a Nation*, perhaps the best film ever made by an American, was inspired by what may well be the worst book ever written in our country, an inept and hysterical piece of anti-Negro propaganda called *The Clansman* (though in all fairness, it must be admitted that General Lew Wallace's *Ben Hur*, filmed at considerable expense at least twice, gives it a close race). Nor is the situation markedly improved when writers of the first rank attempt to adapt works of the first rank, even their own, to the screen, as West's own reworking of his *Miss Lonelyhearts* sufficiently attests.

None of this is a secret from anyone, yet in the face of it writer after writer, as we have seen, set out for Hollywood and a frustration which even then they must have known was inevitable. What drove them from the actual hells they inhabited to the most artificial of paradises? The tribute highbrow virtue pays to middlebrow vice, it is tempting to say—the shame of the lonely intellectual which answers the shame of the successful producer of mass entertainment. Of course, there were less complex and more immediate inducements: the simple need for money, in the first instance, at a moment when the general economic collapse made Hollywood salaries look especially tempting. And then there was the promise of a major change in the films, brought about by the introduction of sound. Fitzgerald, for instance, tells us in an observation worked into *The Last Tycoon* how films began to be *written* with the advent of the "talkies," and how the script-writer came to replace the mere "gag-man" who stood, in the old days, behind the director's shoulder, his only manuscript page the director's cuff.

Moreover, the Thirties had brought with them a sense, which was to grow deeper and acuter in the next three decades, that the novel might be approaching its end; that the first form of bourgeois commodity-art was about to be replaced by another, and that the fiction of the future might well have to be written on the screen, if it was to survive at all. And how much larger the audience which serious writers could reach if they could indeed adapt their ideas to the new medium, escape the restrictions imposed on them by the limits of literacy! It was a dazzling prospect, this notion of reaching the great audience of millions, especially to novelists whose published books had sold a thousand or fifteen hundred copies; and their illusions were fed by the half-literate producers and directors, who, for reasons we have already examined, needed artists by their side, as anti-Semites need Jews, and philistines, bohemians. What could lie ahead for such writers but grief?

At best they came and went, unsuccessful but unharmed; at worst they stayed and suffered and perished, Fitzgerald providing the classic instance. Indeed, so pat and moving is his case, that the movies themselves have tried to tell the story of his defeat in the very medium that destroyed him, thus heaping, with *Beloved Infidel*, a final indignity on his fallen head. But West's was, potentially, at least an equally disastrous career; and more recently James Agee lived out the pathetic pattern again, dying of a heart attack after a struggle to make of *The African Queen* the movie which he, as a poet and critic of films, had imagined. Yet he, in this single instance, was successful at least, unlike most of the other writers who had attempted similar tasks; and of them it must be said that, whether or not Hollywood liked their work well enough to keep them on, they have not succeeded in producing movies of real merit. By and large, their films have been worse than those turned out by certain Hollywood hacks with no pretensions at all. Here, for instance, is a typical list, a few of the movies written by Nathanael West, surely among the most talented of the lot: *I Stole a Million, Spirit of Culver, Men Against the Sky, Advice to the Lovelorn* (a miserable travesty of his own *Miss Lonelyhearts*)—not one worthy of note in a history of the cinema.

Yet in the end it cannot be said that the sole outcome of the romance between the serious writer and the big movies has been private grief; for a series of books have been written out of that experience which continue to provide readers with insight and pleasure. And in these books there is documented a case not only against the industry which some have hoped to make an art and others pretend is a public service, but also against the whole culture which sustains both the industry and the artist as long as he stays within it. The list of such books is impressive: Fitzgerald's *The Last Tycoon*, Christopher Isherwood's *Prater Violet*, Budd Schulberg's *What Makes Sammy Run*, Peter Viertel's *Black Land, White Hunter*, Norman Mailer's *Deer Park*, Mordecai Richler's *A Choice of Enemies*, and, pre-eminently, *The Day of the Locust* by Nathanael West.

All but the last treat of the conflict between producer and director on the one hand, and the writer on the other: a kind of version of the class struggle, after all, in which the writer, conditioned by the clichés of the Thirties, sees him-

[59]

self as worker, the producer as boss, but one passionate and personal rather than theoretical and abstract, and, therefore, quite ambivalent. Few accomplished writers of fiction in the Thirties knew deeply and from within the factories of Gastonia and Paterson in which they were urged to set their tales of exploitation and protest; but many knew Hollywood, and in Hollywood lived at first hand the relationship of artist and businessman—more unhappy marriage or ill-fated love affair than simple conflict on the barricades. It is with this strange passion, at any rate, that most anti-Hollywood novels deal, setting it against a background of sex, character assassination, and low-grade, Machiavellian struggles for power in the large studios.

The Day of the Locust, however, is about actors rather than directors, and about third-rate actors at that. West evokes no tycoon-hero-villains reminiscent of Irving Thalberg or John Huston, but only a handful of seedy extras— failed versions of figures who, successful and made into public myths, possess our waking dreams: a decayed and malicious pseudo-Gary Cooper; a mindless, provocative yet unattainable proto-Marilyn Monroe. But for West it is the audience, the great public itself, which proves in the end the ultimate villain and true enemy of the artist; the bored and rootless petty-bourgeois professional spectators, who, at the close of his book, are making the super-spectacle to end at once all mere Hollywood spectacles and their own boredom, are making, that is to say, Armageddon, which, just before his death, the artist manages to sketch in his head.

How hard it is, all the same, to think of Hollywood among the archetypal experiences of the writer of the Thirties. Surely his actual hells count more than this artificial paradise: the return to America, the great Depression, the radical movement, the Civil War in Spain—these seem more central, as they are, in fact, more real; but they are the occasions for literature of lesser merit. Out of the Depression, came the dull, pseudo-experimental novels of Dos Passos; out of the conflict of classes, such an inept performance as Clara Weatherwax's *Marching! Marching!*— which won the first *New Masses* prize for proletarian fiction

[60]

and ended the genre; out of the migrations of homeless farmers, a sentimental entertainment (hoked up with heavy-handed symbolism) such as Steinbeck's *Grapes of Wrath*; out of the Spanish Civil War, Hemingway's betrayal of his own deepest commitments in *For Whom the Bell Tolls*. Considered together, such books are revealed as representing the preparation for a new middlebrow literature, no longer sentimentally Christian and pro-feminist like the best sellers of pre-World War I days, but sentimentally liberal and pro-"little people"—the maudlin tradition carried on by such Forties-Fifties writers of the second rank as James Michener, John Hersey and Irwin Shaw.

Yet even the more serious novelists of the Forties and Fifties (Wright Morris, Saul Bellow, Bernard Malamud and Norman Mailer, for instance) are influenced by the Thirties, though in terms of theme rather than of technique. Their key experiences remain still Hollywood, as well as the return to America, the Depression, the left-wing movement, and Spain—even, at third hand, memories of the Great War and the exile from America which followed it; and they write the books appropriate to those experiences, express themselves in forms they never made: the anti-producer novel, the anti-war novel, the novel of social protest. In this sense, they must be considered not a generation proper, but a group without a center, moving uncertainly in their quest for identity between the writers of the Twenties and those of the Sixties. Like many writers of the first inter-generation group which flourished in the Thirties, many of them have had to be culturally twice-born. Conditioned to the values of the Thirties, schooled by its journals, brought up on its books, committed in earliest youth to its politics —with, perhaps, a first novel in the Depression mode already in manuscript—they have been forced to postpone their debut by the loss of faith in Communism, the revulsion from the Soviet Union and the dream of Revolution, which was the last critical experience of the Thirties and the first of their independent cultural lives

Being, then, typically twice-born, they are likely to be fully mature before they are willing to abandon all claims to their interrupted and extended youth. Certainly they are assured with the assurance of those granted *two* adolescences and *two* educations, sophisticated beyond anything imagined by their immediate predecessors of the Thirties (some of them twice-born, too), much less those genuinely callow youths of the Twenties. And they have, therefore, been able to propose, shocking those younger and older than they, an ideal of good writing rather than bad as an earnest of truth—a notion, we are presently being told, blatantly un-American. In any case, the writers of the Forties-Fifties brought to our literature, for a little while, an uncustomary aplomb in the face of the richness of experience as well as of the complexity of forms.

How different they are in these respects from the novelists of the Twenties! Though they may have lived through World War II, quite as their elders through World War I, though it may, indeed, have brought them to the same places, they know them in advance, if only through the books of those elders. France, so long the great, good place to the American highbrow and tourist alike, is likely to seem to them a bore, and if they go abroad they are likely to go elsewhere, most often not as tourists at all, but on official missions, with government portfolios, or fellowships or grants.

War as such astonishes them no more than Europe or Hollywood, it, too, being for them a second-hand experience; and the only conflict which has meaning for them at all is not World War II, in which most of them participated, but the Civil War in Spain, to which most of them never went, but in which many of them as children and adolescents invested their best hopes and deepest fears. Similarly, they have grown up with avant-garde literature (punished, perhaps, in their high schools for having passed from hand to hand beneath their desks in algebra class a copy of Louis Aragon's *Red Front* as translated by E. E. Cummings), and European culture is more likely to seem to them old hat than to dazzle them. No more are they overwhelmed by the Big City, being, by and large, city boys to begin with, children of immigrants who settled in New York and Chicago, to whom the American small town is the ultimately foreign place.

Only their own success surprised them, conditioned as they are by the literature of failure and defeat written by the two generations of writers before their own. But it is not merely their personal triumphs which bewilder them, the recognition and the rewards which set them to worrying about their income tax. Even more surprising has been the victory of what they had thought of as an advanced morality and the consequent disavowal of that morality by the very young. All literary generations from the Twenties through the Fifties have shared certain attitudes and allegiances which now oddly link them to the middlebrow establishment and separate them from the dissident youth. Most important of these are the ritual flouting (in the name of Freud) of traditional sexual morality, and the ritual dedication (in the name of Edgar Poe) to drunkenness. These are not merely matters of personal weaknesses or tastes, but a species of anti-religion based on contempt for the bourgeois family and the desire for a sort of release not always easy to distinguish from death. Faulkner and Hemingway and Fitzgerald were all three anti-Saints of this anti-Church, but they were perhaps its *last* anti-Saints. For the Dionysiac cult and the sexual revolt alike have been assimilated to bourgeois culture, becoming the cocktail party and campus —or country-club licensed carnival—with the psychiatrist-in-attendance waiting to pick up the pieces. As Puritanism dies, anti-Puritanism becomes middlebrow affectation; and it may, indeed, turn out to have been the function of the writers of the Forties and Fifties to have described this particular Thermidor.

In any case, at the center of the literary generation of the last few decades are a group of novelists who, following the example of Daniel Fuchs and Nathanael West, write as city-dwellers about the experiences of cities, and in whom the themes of isolation and terror in the wilderness and in Europe (as old as Fenimore Cooper and Edgar Allan Poe) are transformed into the themes of urban American loneliness and urban American terror. It is understandable and

[63]

proper that a sizable proportion of these writers be like Fuchs and West, American Jews. America's recent entry into world culture is, of course, by no means the accomplishment of Jewish-American writers alone; but surely they have played a key role in presenting to non-Americans living images of our contemporary life, while naturalizing for Americans certain ideas originally European—the doctrines, for instance, of Freud and Marx, Sartre and Camus and Martin Buber, Jung and Fraser and Wilhelm Reich. Think of Saul Bellow, surely the most talented and successful of the group, in whom most of these ideologies appear played out in a drama, by turns comic and pathetic, whose actors respond to the exchange of thought as to a blow or a kiss.

But how have we ever come from the Old Men with whom we began to so strange a situation? What has Saul Bellow—or Bernard Malamud or Philip Roth—to do with Hemingway or with Faulkner, with the defender of anti-intellectualism and polite anti-semitism, on the one hand, or the laureate of the Negro and Southern aristocrat, on the other? We can trace the roots of these novelists of the Fifties back to their fellow Jews of the Thirties, but beyond the underground novels of West and Fuchs, they seem to have no connection with the American past. Must we, then, consider them European novelists, grafted onto the American mainstream by the returners from expatriation, and writing in English, as it were, by historical accident? Surely, they cannot be considered descendants, or even collateral connections, of Hemingway, but are rather anti-Hemingways, avengers of the despised Robert Cohen, Jewish butt of *The Sun Also Rises*.

5

ZION AS MAIN STREET

Certainly, we live at a moment when, everywhere in the realm of prose, Jewish writers have discovered their Jewishness to be an eminently marketable commodity, their much vaunted alienation to be their passport into the heart of Gentile American culture. It is, indeed, their quite justified claim to have been *first* to occupy the Lost Desert at the center of the Great American Oasis (toward which every one now races, Coca-Cola in one hand, Martin Buber in the other), which has made certain Jewish authors into representative Americans, even in the eyes of State Department officials planning cultural interchanges. The auto-biography of the urban Jew whose adolescence coincided with the Depression, and who walked the banks of some contaminated city river with tags of Lenin ringing in his head, who went forth (or managed not to) to a World War in which he could not quite believe, has come to seem part of the mystical life history of a nation.

Even in the realm of poetry, writers of Jewish origin are beginning, for the first time, not only to project the most viable images of what it means to be an American, but to determine the cadences with which we glorify or deplore that condition. The very lines inscribed on the base of the Statue of Liberty are, to be sure, by Emma Lazarus, who called one collection of her poems *Songs of a Semite;* but it was not until the appearance of Delmore Schwartz and

c

Karl Shapiro, in the years just before and after World War II, that Jewish-American poets succeeded in producing verse capable of living in libraries and the hearts of other poets, rather than on monuments and in the mouths of politicians. And only within the last decade has a poet as Jewish in his deepest memories (whatever his current allegiances) as Allen Ginsberg been able to stand at the head of a new poetic movement.

Yet the moment of triumph for the Jewish writer in the United States has come just when his awareness of himself as a Jew is reaching a vanishing point, when the gesture of rejection seems his last possible connection with his historical past; and the popular acceptance of his alienation as a satisfactory symbol for the human condition threatens to turn it into an affectation, a fashionable cliché. Indeed, the recent recognition of even the most serious Jewish-American writers seems somehow less an event in literary history than an incident in the development of middlebrow taste, part of the minor revolution which has made Harry Golden into a modern prophet and has enabled newspapers to build circulation by running serializations of the latest pseudo-books of Leon Uris. Surely, a kind of vicarious shame at the monstrosities practiced against the Jews of Germany by the Nazis has something to do with this revolution; and the establishment of the State of Israel has tended to give even the Jews in exile a less ambiguous status, while the struggle against Great Britain leading to that establishment has lent them a certain sentimental cachet, ranking them, in the minds of American Anglophobes, with the Irish and the mythical revolutionary ancestors of us all.

But it is chiefly the resurgence of "intergroup understanding," the tidal wave of toleration that has flowed into the vacuum left by the disappearance of zeal and the attenuation of faith among churchgoers, which has carried the Jews along with it. And they have benefited, too, by the canonization of support for "little people" among the pieties of yesterday's liberalism which have become the orthodoxy of today's New Deal-New Frontier conservatism. Armenians, Greeks, Chinese, Cubans, low-caste Indians, Mexican wetbacks, women without suffrage, paraplegics, teen-agers—one group after another has been dubbed with that condescending tag. But, maybe, from this point of view the ordeal of the Jew is almost over, for he no longer occupies the number-one slot among the insulted and injured. Even the *New Yorker* has recognized that the Negro is, at the moment, *up*; and it is the Baldwins rather than the Bellows who have to wrestle now with the mystery of the failure of success in America. The general *détente* in the cold war between Gentile and Jew in the United States persists, and though other sentimental fashions challenge it, it remains chic in certain middlebrow, middle-class, middle-liberal quarters to be pro-Jewish. Philo-Semitism is required—or perhaps, by now, only assumed—in the reigning literary and intellectual circles of America, just as anti-Semitism used to be required—and after a while only assumed—in the Twenties.

But the Judaization of American culture goes on at levels far beneath the literary and the intellectual. The favorite wine in Missoula, Montana, which does not have a dozen Jewish families, is Mogen David; and for years now, "Nebbishes" have stared out of the windows of the local gift shop from greeting cards, ash trays, beer mugs, and pen stands. And why not? Everyone everywhere digs Jules Feiffer and Mort Sahl, just as everyone tells "sick" jokes and sends "hate" cards to celebrate birthdays and weddings and national holidays. The "sick" joke and the "hate" card, however, represent the entry into our popular culture not only of certain formerly exclusive properties of the avant-garde (the mockery of bourgeois pieties, a touch of psychoanalysis) but also of Jewish humor at its most desperate. There is nothing entirely unprecedented here, of course; Potash and Perlmutter were best-sellers in the opening years of this century, and Charlie Chaplin's debut was almost contemporaneous with theirs. As a matter of fact, the Jew enters American culture "on the stage, laughing."

It might be possible, indeed, to make a graph showing, decade by decade, the point at which it became possible for Jews:

1) to act out travesties of themselves on the stage;

2) to act out travesties of other "comical" ethnic groups (Chico Marx as an Italian, Al Jolson in blackface);

3) to write popular songs and patriotic sub-poetry and begin the wholesale entry into universities as students;

4) to produce comic strips and popular novels;

5) to argue cases in court and judge them from the bench, to prescribe for the common cold and analyze the neurotic;

6) to write prose fiction and anti-academic criticism;

7) to teach in the universities and help determine official taste in the arts;

8) to write serious poetry, refuse to go to college, and write on the walls, "Down with the Jews!"

Presently all of these things are possible at once, for no new gain has canceled out another, our successes expand at dazzling speed. Huckleberry Finn becomes Augie March; Daisy Miller turns, via Natalie Wood, into Marjorie Morningstar; Eddie Fisher is drafted as the symbol of clean young American love, while Danny Kaye continues to play the blue-eyed jester; and finally we enter an age of strange conversions to Judaism (Marilyn Monroe, Elizabeth Taylor, Sammy Davis, Jr.), and symbolic marriages. Eros himself turns, or seems to for a little while, Jewish, as the mythical erotic dream-girls of us all yearn for Jewish intellectuals and learn to make matzo-balls.

Even more startlingly, the literature of busy males, of politicians and executives seeking at once relaxation and the reinforcement of their fantasies, is Judaized, too. The long dominance of the Western and the detective story is challenged by that largely Jewish product, science fiction. There are a score of Jewish authors among the most widely read writers in that popular genre as compared with practically none in the two older types of institutionalized fantasy. The basic myths of science fiction reflect the urban outlook, the social consciousness, the utopian concern of the modern, secularized Jew. The traditional Jewish waiting-for-the--Messiah becomes, in lay terms, the commitment-to-the-future, which is the motive force of current science fiction. The notion of a Jewish cowboy is utterly ridiculous, of a Jewish detective, Scotland-Yard variety or tough private eye, nearly as anomalous—but to think of the scientist as a Jew is almost tautological.

Much science fiction, set just before or after the Great Atomic War, embodies the kind of guilty conscience peculiar to such scientist-intellectuals (typically Jewish) as Robert Oppenheimer, while the figure of Einstein presides over the New Heaven and New Earth which such literature postulates, replacing an earlier Hebrew god who is dead. Even in its particulars, the universe of science fiction is Jewish; the wise old tailor, the absurd but sympathetic *yiddishe momme*, plus a dozen other Jewish stereotypes, whiz unchanged across its space and time. Even secret Jewish jokes are made for the cognoscenti: the police on a corrupt, trans-galactic planet are called, in the exotic tongue of that only half-imaginary world, *Ganavim* (thieves). And in the Superman comic books (the lowbrow equivalent of science fiction), the same aspirations and anxieties are projected in the improbable disguise of the Secret Savior, who may look like a *goy*, but who is invented by Jews. The biceps are the biceps of Esau, but the dialogue is the dialogue of Jacob.

Even for those who read neither books nor comics, Jewish culture lies in wait—not only in the gift shop and the saloon, but in what is our only truly living museum, the real cultural storehouse of the average man: the supermarket. There—even in the remotest hamlets—beside the head-cheese, the sliced ham, the pseudo-hot-dogs composed of flour and sawdust, one finds kosher salami; beside the hard-tack, Rye Krisp, and löfsa—matzos; beside the chocolate-covered ants, fried grasshoppers, and anchovy hearts—Mother's Gefilte Fish. But whatever is in the supermarket, like whatever is in *Life* (both organized on the same pseudo-catholic principle: everything glossily packaged and presented without emphasis and distinction) is in the great democratic heart of America. In that heart, at least, Jewish culture, as defined by gefilte fish and Natalie Wood, the Jewish scientist and the Nebbish, has established itself as if it meant to stay. And it is in light of this cultural fact that Jewish-American writers must assess the mounting sales of their books and the warm reviews which greet them; but the confrontation leaves the best of them amused, the second best embarrassed, and the worst atrociously pleased.

Yet this kind of success is, in a way, what the Jewish-American writer has all along desired—though for a long time he was able to depend on the realities of his situation, the exclusion from which he began, to protect him against his own lust for belonging. From the start, the Jewish-American writer has desired not only to create living images of his people in the imagination of all Americans, and to redeem them from psychic exploitation at the hands of anti-Semitic Gentile authors; but also, by creating such images and achieving such a redemption, to become himself part of the American scene, a citizen among citizens, one more author on a list which begins with Benjamin Franklin and Washington Irving. The very notion of a Jewish-American literature represents a dream of assimilation, and the process it envisages is bound to move toward a triumph (in terms of personal success) which is also a defeat (in terms of meaningful Jewish survival). If today Jewish-American writers seem engaged in writing not the high tragedy of Jewish persistence in the midst of persecution, but the comedy of Jewish dissolution in the midst of prosperity, this is because they tell the truth about a world which neither they nor their forerunners can consider themselves guiltless of desiring.

Yet at first the striving of the American-Jewish community, through its artists, to become a fact of the imagination as well as of the census seemed merely gallant and happily foredoomed. In the beginning, the Jewish author and the Jewish character, whether invented by Gentile or Jew, played only a slight and peripheral role in the literature of the United States and in the deep mind of the American people which that literature at once reflects and makes. This is in part the result of the simple sociological fact that Jews were, in the earliest years of our nation, few and insignificant and that, therefore, the mythology of the Jew, which we inherited along with the English language and the corpus of English literature, moved the popular American mind scarcely at all. What could the figures of the Wandering Jew, of Shylock and Jessica, Isaac of York and Rebecca, Riah and Fagin mean to a people whose own guilts and fears and baffled aspirations were projected onto quite different ethnic groups? Associated with the names of Shakespeare, Sir Walter Scott and Dickens, authors sometimes revered, even loved, but chiefly, alas, resented as required reading in the classroom, such figures assume the vicarious reality of classroom facts, of something learned for the first time out of books, rather than *recognized* in books as the truths of nightmare and dream.

It is those whom the white Anglo-Saxon Americans persecuted in the act of becoming Americans, even as the Europeans persecuted the Jews in the act of becoming Christians, who live in the American psyche as Shylock and the Wandering Jew live in the European one: the Indian and the Negro, who are facts of the American imagination from the moment that imagination is formed. The Anglo-Saxon immigrant could maintain only a theoretical anti-Semitism in the New World, just as he could maintain only a theoretical opposition to the aristocracy; his real struggles were elsewere, and his attempts to project his own psychological difficulties onto the enemies of his ancestors never took root in literature. So, also, with later generations of immigrants, from other parts of Europe. The Germans, the Poles, the Czechs may have brought with them certain traditional anti-Semitic fantasies of their native lands; but at the moment that their assimilation to America moved from the social to the psychic level (and in the country of the melting pot this moment comes quite soon), they began to find their old nightmares driven out by new.

James Fenimore Cooper, greatest of American mythographers, tried to identify the evil Indian of the *Last of the Mohicans* with Shylock, and, in one of the last of his novels, portrayed the Indians as New World Jews re-enacting the crucifixion in the midst of the wilderness; but this major attempt to make transatlantic and cisatlantic attitudes of hatred and guilt reinforce each other failed. The Jew could not figure as the archetypal Other, the psychic whipping boy, in a society which was not bound to him by ancient and terrible guilts: guilts lived, as well as read about in schoolrooms or even sacred books. Exclusions from jobs and country clubs is no substitute for pogroms and massacres, and even the anti-Semitism implicit in Christianity has remained, in America, largely theoretical; an occasional schoolchild has been sent running home in tears with the cry of his classmates, "You killed our Christ!" ringing in his bewildered head; but practically nobody in the United States *has ever died from it!* And this is perhaps why in our classic literature, much concerned with precisely those conflicts from which men had indeed died, Jewish characters play such unimportant roles.

It is worth remembering that the poet who wrote and rewrote, from just past the middle of the last century to almost the beginning of ours, the four-hundred-page poem which declares itself the most broadly inclusive of all all-American poems, included no Jewish character or scene in his mythic world. There are no Jews in *Leaves of Grass*; and the single appearance of the adjective "semitic" recorded in the concordances to that work turns out to be an error. Whitman, meaning to describe the ideal American poet as "plunging his seminal muscle" into the "merits and demerits" of his country, miswrote "semitic muscle" the first time around, but changed it when some amused reader called it to his attention. White, red, and black make up his America, and even the yellow oriental makes an occasional appearance; but the Jew was represented by no color on his palette and constitutes no part of the myth he has left us. No more are there Jews included in that otherwise universally representative crew: the Manx, African, Irish, Spanish, Italian, Polynesian, and Middle-Eastern human flotsam of the world who, under a mad Yankee skipper, sail a ship called after a defunct Indian tribe in the pages of Melville's *Moby Dick*. Nor does Huck Finn meet a single Jew, either ashore or afloat on the great river whose course he follows down the center of civilized America.

[72]

There are, to be sure, occasional Jewish characters else-where in Melville, and in Hawthorne, Henry James, even Longfellow; but, by and large, these are either borrowed bugaboos, male and female, or inventions of a sentimental-ity which kept itself pure by keeping its Jews imaginary. In Melville's long narrative poem *Clarel*, for instance, one finds the major attempt to adapt for American uses the archetypal pattern story which has most appealed to the American imagination when it has sought at all to deal with things Jewish: the myth of Shylock and Jessica, the sinister Jew deprived of his lovely daughter. But the Ameri-can imagination does not permit the Gentile hero to get the Jewish girl in a blithe Shakespearean ending; on this side of the ocean, a tragic blight falls over the European myth of assimilation: the dream of rescuing the desirable elements in the Judaic tradition (maternal tenderness and exotic charm: the figure of Mary) from the unsympathetic ele-ments (patriarchal rigor and harsh legalism: the figure of the High Priest and Father Abraham with a knife).

The trouble is that the Jewish girl is thought of not in terms of Mary, but of Lilith, and becomes one with all those dark ladies (otherwise Latin) who are paired off against the fair, Anglo-Saxon girl: the former representing all the Puritan mind most longs for, and fears, in passion; the latter standing for a passionless, sexless love. At the very beginnings of our literature, Charles Brockden Brown could permit his hero to marry a Jewish woman, but neither Mel-ville nor Hawthorne could forget his own pale, Anglo-Saxon bride long enough to follow Brown's example. Even in our presumably post-Puritan times, the protagonist of *Two for the Seesaw* finally abandons his Gittel Mosca, Jewish em-bodiment of impulse and sexual generosity, to return like a good American to the Gentile wife he left behind.

But beside the nightmare of the Jew's alluring daughter flanked by the castrating father, there exists for the Ameri-can imagination a dream of the "little Jew," too, enduring and forgiving under abuse—a kind of Semitic version of "Uncle Tom." Unfortunately, this is to be found nowhere in our serious writers and is, I suspect, an English importa-

[73]

tion where found, a spreading out and down of George Eliot's hortatory philo-Semitism. There appeared, at any rate, in the 1868 volume of the children's magazine called *Our Young Folks*, a poem which begins:

> We were at school together,
> The little Jew and I.
> He had black eyes, the biggest nose,
> The very smallest fist for blows,
> Yet nothing made him cry.

and which ends, after the speaker has thrust an apple under that "biggest nose" on Yom Kippur, mocking the child for his fast, and has then repented:

> Next day when school was over,
> I put my nonsense by;
> Begged the lad's pardon, stopped all strife.
> And—well, we have been friends for life,
> The little Jew and I.

A second-hand nightmare is answered by a borrowed dream.

The Jewish writer himself was engaged with these half-felt stereotypes in the latter half of the nineteenth century, and his responses seem as unreal, as far from the center of American psychic life, as those stereotypes themselves. Up to the end of the last century (and in a certain sense that century did not end for us until the conclusion of World War I), Jewish-American literature, the stories and poems written out of their own experience by those willing to call themselves Jews, or descended immediately from those so willing, remains not only theoretical but parochial. In this regard, it is like all the sub-literature which we customarily call "regional"—writing intended to represent the values and interests of a group which feels itself penalized, even threatened, by the disregard of the larger community. From one side, such writing constitutes a literature of self-congratulation and reassurance, intended to be consumed by an in-group which knows it is abused and suspects that it is hardly noticed by those who abuse it; and from another, it aims at becoming a literature of public relations, intended to "sell" that in-group to certain outsiders, who, it is assumed, will respond favorably only to "positive," i.e., innocuous or untrue, images of the excluded group.

Regional writing ceases to be sub-literary, however, not when those it portrays are made to seem respectable, but when they are presented as representative (in all their particularity) of the larger community: the nation, an alliance of nations, all of mankind. But this only begins to happen when regional writers stop being apologists and become critics, abandon falsification and sentimentality in favor of treating not the special virtues of the group from which they come, whether those virtues be real or fancied, but the weaknesses it shares with all men. Such writers seem often to their fellows, their very friends and parents, traitors—not only for the harsh things which they are led to say about those fellows, friends and parents in the pursuit of truth, but also because their desire for universality of theme and appeal leads them to begin tearing down from within the walls of a cultural ghetto, which, it turns out, has meant security as well as exclusion to the community that nurtured them.

The plight is particularly difficult for those who are not even psychically exploited, not even used to represent certain deep uncertainties and guilts in the undermind of the larger community, but only psychically ignored, which is to say, blanked out of the range of vision of that larger community. They may, indeed, congratulate themselves on their social invisibility, taking it for a result of their own firm resolve not to be assimilated to the ways of strangers. Mythically invisible men, that is, tend to confuse their essential peculiarity, to which they are resolved to cling, with the psychic walls that make them invisible and which they know they must someday breach. They are, therefore, likely to think of those who first begin to breach these walls, in quest of the freedom to become the selves of their own imagining, as apostates from their ancestral identity and the values which sustain it.

[75]

The breakthrough to such psychic freedom and to the cultural assimilation which is its concomitant requires, then, a series of revolutionary acts at a critical point in the history of a minority group; but that critical point is determined not by the revolutionary writers alone. It is no more a mere matter of a certain number of heroic individual decisions than it is of the simple growth in size and prestige and power of the mythically non-existent community. The mass immigrations of Eastern European Jews to the United States was over by 1910, and, some decades before that, a novelist who called himself Sidney Luska had attempted single-handed to transform various aspects of Jewish immigrant life in New York, which he had observed at first hand, into fictions capable of moving all Americans. Even the names of his novels, however (*As It Was Written*, *The Yoke of the Thorah*, etc.), are by now forgotten; for he had begun by imposing on the facts, as he knew them, a vision of the Jew as the infinitely sensitive artist and the herald of the future, compounded out of George Eliot's portrait of herself as a young Jew in *Daniel Deronda*, and the dreams of the Ethical Culturists of his time. And "Sidney Luska" was not really a Jew, only a disaffected white Anglo-Saxon Protestant who had affected what he took to be a "Jewish" beard as well as a "Jewish" name; and who, when confronted by the pettiness and weakness of actual Jews, returned to his own name, Henry Harland, and ended as an expatriate and editor of the *Yellow Book* and the author of a fashionably Catholic, anti-Semitic best-seller called *The Cardinal's Snuffbox*. It is the comic-pathetic catastrophe fitting to one hubristic enough to have attempted single-handed to give to Jews the status that only time and history could bestow.

The creation of Jewish characters able to live in the American imagination cannot be the work of Jewish writers, real or imagined, alone. As the Jewish writer goes out in search of his mythical self, he is bound to encounter the Gentile writer on a complementary quest to come to terms with him, the stranger in the Gentile's land. As collaborators or rivals, wittingly or not, Jewish author and Gentile must engage in a common enterprise if either is to succeed. The presence of talented Jewish writers concerned with Jewish life, and of a rich and complex Jewish life itself, are essential preconditions of the Jewish breakthrough into the deep psyche of Gentile America; but there is a necessary third precondition, too. At the moment of such a breakthrough, the Jew must *already* have become capable of projecting psychological meanings with which the non-Jewish community is vitally concerned, must already have come to represent in his mode of existence, symbolically at least, either a life lived and aspired to by those others—or at least (and more probably) one passionately rejected and secretly regretted by those others. But this is the job of non-Jewish writers, and for this reason we must look to such writers, rather than to the Jewish writers of the period, to understand just how the Jewish character became mythically viable during and just after World War I.

There were, to be sure, Jewish writers of varying degrees of talent who not only published during this period but were, in certain cases, widely read. In fiction, for instance, there were the mass entertainers: Fannie Hurst and Edna Ferber; middlebrow wits like Dorothy Parker; and even quite serious novelists like Ben Hecht (before his removal to Hollywood) and Ludwig Lewisohn (before his surrender to Zionist apologetics). The nineteenth-century "poetesses" from good Sephardic families, chief of whom was Emma Lazarus, were giving way to high school teachers with social consciences: Louis Ginsberg, James Oppenheim, Alfred Kreymborg. The minor achievements of such poets were preserved, along with the brittle verse of F.P.A. and Arthur Guiterman, the efforts of certain Village Bohemians of the Twenties (e.g., Maxwell Bodenheim), and the verses of Jewish prodigies like Nathalia Crane in the pages of Louis Untermeyer's earlier anthologies. In a time when poetry was in the process of becoming what was read in classrooms, certain Jewish journalists and educators compiled the standard classroom anthologies. Though these Jewish-American writers thus controlled American taste to some extent, they did not—in verse any more than in prose —succeed in making images of even their own lives that

[77]

were capable of possessing the American mind. In any case, the writers anthologized by Untermeyer and others had little consciousness of themselves as Jews, were engaged, in fact, in assimilating themselves to general American culture by pledging allegiance to social or cultural ideals larger than their Jewishness, whether Bohemianism or socialism or humanism in its broadest sense.

No, the compelling images of Jews were made by writers who were not merely Gentiles but anti-Semites, interested in resisting this assimilationist impulse and keeping the Jews Jews. It is important to understand, however, the precise nature of their anti-Semitism. Quite different from working-class or populist, economic anti-Semitism, that "Black Socialism" of the American factory hand or poor farmer which identifies the Jews with Wall Street and international bankers, theirs was the cultural anti-Semitism of the educated bourgeois seeking status through a career in the arts; and it was, therefore, aimed not at expelling the money-changers from the Temple, but at distinguishing the Jewish exploiters of culture from its genuine Gentile makers, at separating the pseudo-artists (naturally, Jews) from the true ones (of course, Gentiles). This cultural anti-Semitism was the inevitable result of certain provincial Gentile Americans' moving toward the big city (Theodore Dreiser, for instance, and Sherwood Anderson) and discovering that the Jews had beat them to the artists' quarters of Chicago and New Orleans and New York; and it was exacerbated when still other provincial Gentile Americans, attempting expatriation (Pound and Eliot, Hemingway and Fitzgerald, and E. E. Cummings), found Jews even on the Left Bank, in the heart of what they had always dreamed of as Heaven. What the expatriates discovered in fact when they arrived at the Paris of their dreams was most vividly sketched not in a book by any one of them, but rather in one about all of them, Wyndham Lewis's *Paleface*: "Glance into the Dôme, anyone . . . who happens to be in Paris. You would think you were in a League of Nations beset by a zionist delegation, in a movie studio, in Moscow, Broadway or even Zion itself, anywhere but in the mythical watertight America . . ."

[78]

And when, in the Thirties, Henry Miller belatedly arrived in the same city, abandoned now, as far as Americans went, to the second-rate and the shoddy, he found the same overwhelming proportion of Jews in the expatriate community and exploded with baffled rage:

> He is a Jew, Borowski, and his father was a philatelist. In fact, almost all Montparnasse is Jewish, or half-Jewish, which is worse. There's Carl and Paula, and Cronstadt and Boris, and Tania and Sylvester, and Moldorf and Lucille. All except Fillmore. Henry Jordan Oswald turned out to be a Jew also. Louis Nichols is a Jew. Even Van Norden and Chérie are Jewish. Frances Blake is a Jew, or a Jewess. Titus is a Jew. The Jews then are snowing me under. I am writing this for my friend Carl whose father is a Jew. All this is important to understand.
>
> Of them all the loveliest Jew is Tania, and for her sake I too would become a Jew. Why not? I already speak like a Jew. And I am ugly as a Jew. Besides, who hates the Jews more than the Jew?

No wonder the German occupation forces in Paris made Miller a favorite author, finding in him not only sex but their favorite obsession with the Jew as the absolute Other. And, meanwhile, Miller's fellow German-American writer of the Thirties (one is almost tempted to say Nazi-American), Thomas Wolfe, was finding in New York City similar occasions for anti-Semitic outbursts, reacting with hatred and fear, and a lust of which he was ashamed, to the young Jewesses at New York University, forerunners of later Jewish coeds, who, a short generation later would be writing (under Jewish advisors) theses about the very anti-Semites of the decades before.

Even Jewish writers of the Thirties were more likely than not to produce hostile travesties of their own people, especially if—like Michael Gold, for instance, whose *Jews Without Money* was the first "proletarian novel" of the period—their Messiah was a Marxian rather than a Jewish one. The anti-Semitism so deeply implanted in Russian Communism during the Stalin regime was reflected in the American Communist Party, largely Jewish though it was, and in the literature which followed its line. Indeed, the presence of such anti-Semitism was taken as evidence that American Jewish Communists were emancipated from parochialism and chauvinism. In Michael Gold, at any rate, only the *yiddishe mamme*, the long-suffering maternal figure, comes off well; the Rabbi, the landlord, the pawnbroker are treated as egregious villains, and Gold's portraits of them disconcertingly resemble both those of European Jew-baiters like Julius Streicher, and native American provincials like Thomas Wolfe.

There are ironies involved here disturbing to both sides; for the anti-Semite, intending merely to excoriate the Jew, learns eventually that he has mythicized him. And the offended Jew realizes, after a while, that before the Jewish character could seem to author and reader in the United States an image of the essential American self, he had first to seem the essential American enemy. Nevertheless, it is depressing for the Jewish American to think how many of our most eminent and central writers in the decades during which we entered fully into world literature produced anti-Semitic caricatures, not from mere habit or tradition, but from conviction and passion. What a black anthology lives in his head: out of Cummings ("and pity the fool who cright/ god help me it aint no ews/ eye like the steak all ried/ but eye certainly hate the juse."); and Eliot ("And the jew squats on the window sill, the owner,/ Spawned in some estaminet of Antwerp,/ Blistered in Brussels, patched and peeled in London."), and Pound ("the yidd is a stimulant, and the goyim are cattle/ in gt/ proportion and go to saleable slaughter/ with the maximum of docility . . ."), and Hemingway ("No, listen, Jake. Brett's gone off with men. But they weren't ever Jews, and they didn't come and hang about afterward."), and Fitzgerald ("A small, flat-nosed Jew raised his large head and regarded me with two fine growths of hair which luxuriated in either nostril. After a moment I discovered his tiny eyes in the half-darkness. . . . 'I see you're looking at my cuff buttons.' I hadn't been looking at them, but I did now. . . . 'Finest specimens of human molars,' he informed me."), and Michael Gold ("The landlord wore a black alpaca coat in the pawnshop, and a skull cap. He crouched on a stool behind the counter. One saw only his scaly yellow face and bulging eyes; he was like an anxious spider."), and Thomas Wolfe (". . . Jews and Jewesses, all laughing, shouting, screaming, thick with their hot and sweaty body-smells, their strong female odors of rut and crotch and armpit and cheap perfume . . .").

How hard it is, after Hitler, for any man of good will, Gentile or Jew, to confess that the most vivid and enduring portraits of Jews created in the period are not works of love and comprehension, but the products of malice and paranoia: Robert Cohen of Hemingway's *The Sun Also Rises* and the multiformed Jewish usurer of Ezra Pound's *Cantos*, Boris of Miller's *Tropic of Cancer* and Abe Jones of Wolfe's *Of Time and the River*—anti-*goyim* and anti-artists one and all. And yet they are not all quite the same; though Hemingway and Pound, for instance, were motivated by a similar malice, and though both moved through the salons of Paris just after World War I, learning, as it were, their anti-Semitism in the same school, their ideologies must be sharply distinguished.

For writers like Pound and Eliot, on the one hand, it is European culture, particularly of the Middle Ages and the Renaissance, which represents the essential meaning of life when it is more than just "birth, copulation and death." And to them the Jew, excluded from the culture in the days of its making, is the supreme enemy; for as merchant-tourist and usurious millionaire, he desires now to appropriate what he never made, to buy and squat in the monuments of high Christian culture, fouling them by his mere presence. He is, therefore, felt and portrayed not only as the opposite to the artist but also to the aristocrat, who, traditionally, sustained the artist in his days of greatest glory.

To writers like Hemingway, on the other hand, to the devotees of raw experience who went to Europe to fish rather than to pray (though also, of course, to make books), the Jew stands for the pseudo-artist. Along with the homosexual, he seems to them to travesty and falsify their own real role; to help create in the public eye an image, from which they find it hard to dissociate themselves, of the effete intellectual, the over-articulate, pseudo-civilized fake. For them, too, the Jew represents the opposite of the Negro, Indian, peasant, bullfighter, or any of the other versions of the noble savage with whom such writers, whether at home or abroad, sought to identify themselves. When either the cult of the primitive or a genteel tradition is in the ascendancy, the Jew is likely to be regarded as the Adversary; for he is the anti-type of Negro and Indian, a projection of the feared intelligence rather than the distrusted impulse, and "genteel" equals Gentile in the language of the psyche. Neither paleface nor redskin, neither gentleman nor genital man, to what can the Jew appeal in the American imagination, which seems to oscillate helplessly between these two poles? Is he doomed to remain merely the absolute un-American, everybody's outsider?

This seems an unanswerable question at first; but it answers itself with the passage of time, and in the very terms in which it is posed. When Americans have grown tired of the neo-gentility, the selective ancestor worship and high-churchly piety of Eliot, and when they are equally sick of the white self-hatred and the adulation of blood sports and ignorance, but especially when they are sick and tired of the oscillation between the two, they can find in the Jewish writer and the world he imagines a way out. Through their Jewish writers, Americans, after the Second World War, were able to establish a new kind of link with Europe in place of the old paleface connection—a link not with the Europe of decaying castles and the Archbishop of Canterbury, nor with that of the Provençal poets and Dante and John Donne, nor with that of the French *symbolistes* and the deadly polite *Action Française*—for these are all Christian Europes; but with the post-Christian Europe of Marx and Freud, which is to say, of secularized Judaism, as well as the Europe of surrealism and existentialism, Kafka, neo-Chasidism—a Europe which at once abhors and yearns for the vacuum left by the death of its Christian god.

[82]

And through the same intermediaries, Gentile Americans discovered the possibility of a new kind of vulgarity unlike the old redskin variety, the when-the-ladies-are-out-of-the-room grossness of works like Mark Twain's *1601*, which depended upon naïveté and simplicity in writer and audience alike. The special Jewish vulgarity exemplified with greater or lesser skill from Ben Hecht through Michael Gold and Nathanael West to Norman Mailer and Philip Roth, is not merely sophisticated, but compatible with high complexity and even metaphysical transcendence. The Semite, someone once said (thinking primarily of the Arabs, but it will do for the Jews, too), stands in dung up to his eyes, but his brow touches the heavens. And where else is there to stand but on dung in a world buried beneath the privileged excretions of the mass media; and where else to aspire but the heavens, in a world whose dreams of earthly paradises have all come to nothing?

Moreover, the Jewish-American mind, conditioned by two thousand years of history, provides other Americans with ways of escaping the trap of vacillation between isolationism and expatriation, chauvinism and national self-hatred. Jewish-American writers are, by and large, neither expatriates nor "boosters"; and they do not create in their protagonists images of the expatriate or the "booster." More typically, they have begun to produce moderately cynical accounts of inpatriation, the flight from the quasi-European metropolis to the provincial small town. This flight they have, indeed, lived, moving in quest of more ultimate exile not out of but *into* America, moving from New York or Chicago, Boston or Baltimore, to small towns in New Mexico, Oregon, Nebraska, and Montana.

After all, if it is a *difference* from what one is born to that is desirable, there is a greater difference between New York and Athens, Georgia, than between New York and Athens, Greece, or between Chicago and Moscow, Idaho, than between Chicago and Moscow, Russia. Within the past couple of years the first fictional treatment of this new migration, a comedy involving an urban Jew in a small university community in the West, has appeared in the form of *A New Life*, the novel by Bernard Malamud which we have already noticed. But though Malamud's book begins with exile, it ends with return; for, like the expatriates of the past, the in-patriate of the present also ends by going home, returning East as inevitably as his forebears returned West.

All flights, the Jewish experience teaches, are from one exile to another; and this Americans have always known, though they have sometimes attempted to deny it. Fleeing exclusion in the Old World, the immigrant discovers loneliness in the New World; fleeing the communal loneliness of seaboard settlements, he discovers the ultimate isolation of the frontier. It is the dream of exile as freedom which has made America; but it is the experience of exile as terror that has forged the self-consciousness of Americans.

Yet it is the Jew who has best been able to recast this old American wisdom (that home itself is exile, that it is the nature of man to feel himself everywhere alienated) in terms valid for twentieth-century Americans, which is to say, for dwellers in cities. The urban American, looking about him at the anonymous agglomeration of comfort-producing machines that constitutes his home, knows that exile is what one endures, not seeks, and he is willing to believe the Jewish writer who tells him this. That the Jewish writer be his spokesman in this regard is natural enough, for he descends from those whose consciousness had already been radically altered by centuries of living in cities; and he stands at ease, therefore, in the midst of the first generation of really urban writers in the American twentieth century. Unlike those who made up the first waves of the movement in the United States, replacing the representatives of proper old Boston and old New York, he is no provincial, no small-town Lewis or Anderson or Pound come to the big city to gawk; he is the metropolitan at home, though expert in the indignities, rather than the amenities, of urban life.

Therefore the American-Jewish writer chooses, characteristically, to work in neither the traditional tragic nor the traditional comic mode; for he feels both modes to be aristocratic, that is, pre-industrial, pre-mass-culture genres, reflecting the impulse of a reigning class to glorify its own suffering and to laugh at the suffering of others postulated as inferior to them, to treat only its own suffering as really real. The Jew, however, functions in his deepest imagination (influenced, of course, by the Gentile culture to which he aspires) as his own other, his own inferior; and he must consequently laugh at himself—glorify himself, if at all, *by* laughing at himself. This is the famous Jewish humor, rooted in a humility too humble to think of its self-abasement as religious, and a modesty too modest to think of its encounter with pain as really real. But this is also the source of a third literary genre, neither tragedy nor comedy, though, like both, based on the perception of human absurdity—a genre for whose flourishing in recent American literature certain Jewish-American writers are largely responsible, though with thanks to Mark Twain as well as Sholom Aleichem.

We have similarly witnessed, over the last thirty years or so, the recasting in terms of second-generation American urban life certain American archetypal heroes and the re-rendering of their adventures in an American English affected by the rhythms of Yiddish and shot through with a brand of wit conditioned by the Jewish joke. These great figures out of our deepest imagination, whom we had thought essentially American, we now learn are—or at least can be made to seem—characteristically Jewish as well. It is not a matter of cultural kidnaping, but of the discovery of cultural resemblances. What, for instance, has happened in the middle of the twentieth century to Huckleberry Finn: loneliest of Americans; eternally and by definition uncommitted; too marginal in his existence to afford either conventional virtue or ordinary villainy; excluded, by the conditions which shape him, from marriage and the family; his ending ambiguously suspended between joy and misery; condemned to the loneliness which he desperately desires? Reimagined by Saul Bellow for the survivors of the thirties, he comes now from northwest Chicago, works for petty Jewish gangsters, reads Kafka and Marx, goes to live with

Leon Trotsky, and is called Augie March. Or re-invented yet again by J. D. Salinger for a younger and more ignorant audience, he comes from the west side of New York, a world of comfortably assimilated and well-heeled Jews (though his name cagily conceals his ethnic origin), plays hooky from an expensive prep school, slips unscathed through a big-city world of phonies and crooks, and is called Holden Caulfield.

Meanwhile what has happened to the most typical of all the heroes of American poetry? Conceived so deeply and specifically, expressed so passionately and intensely out of the self of the poet who first invented him, this mock-epic hero, crying the most pathetic and lovely of American boasts, "I was the man, I suffered, I was there," once seemed doomed to remain forever what he was to begin with— Walt Whitman, who was born of Quaker parents and moved through a world without Jews. But now, improbably reborn, he remembers listening beside his mother to Israel Amter, idol of the Jewish-American Communists of the Thirties, scolds America for what it has done to his Uncle Max, howls his rage at his father's world (the world of Jewish high-school-teacher-poets memorialized by Louis Untermeyer), and when he has symbolically killed it, writes a volume called *Kaddish*, title of the Hebrew prayer for the dead and tenderest of pet names by which a Jew calls his son. Walt Whitman, that is to say, becomes Allen Ginsberg.

Not only on the highbrow level of Bellow and Ginsberg, however, but on all levels of our literature, archetype and stereotype alike are captured by the Jewish imagination and refurbished for Gentile consumption. Norman Mailer and Irwin Shaw, for instance, have conspired to teach us that no platoon in the United States Army is complete without its sensitive Jew to suffer the jibes of his fellows and record their exploits, while Herman Wouk has made it clear that the valiant virgin beset by seducers, whom female Anglo-Saxondom once thought of as the pale projection of its own highest aspirations, is really a nice Jewish girl who has misguidedly changed her name. What Shaw and Wouk teach, the movies and *Time* magazine transmit to the

[86]

largest audience; and who is to say them nay in a day when all rightminded men approve the fact of Israel and detest the memory of Hitler, a world in which Anne Frank, our latest secular saint, looks down from the hoardings on us all. Even the crassest segregationists sometimes combine their abuse of Negroes with praise for the Jews. "From the days of Abraham . . ." writes a certain Reverend G. T. Gillespie of Mississippi, "the Hebrews . . . became a respected people . . . and they . . . have made an invaluable contribution to the moral and spiritual progress of mankind." So the occasional anti-Semitic crank who still sends through the mail a cry of protest ("Every book that goes into print . . . is either written by, edited by, advertised by, published by—or what is common, all four—Jewish people . . . these publishers are at war with the American intelligence, as well as its Christian morality.") seems scarcely worth our contemptuous notice.

And there is no end. Very recently, for example, there has been an attempt, in the screenplay for *The Misfits* written by Arthur Miller, to adapt the classical American Western to new times and new uses. It is not merely a matter of making the Western "adult," as certain middlebrow manipulators of the form like to boast of their efforts on television, but of turning upside down the myth embodied in such standard versions of our archetypal plot as *The Virginian* and *High Noon*. In both of these, a conflict between a man and a woman, representing, respectively, the chivalric code of the West and the pacificism of Christianity, ends with the capitulation of the woman, and the abandonment of forgiveness in favor of force. In *The Misfits*, however, the woman is no longer the pious and pretty but flat-chested schoolmarm that Gentile Americans know their actual grandmothers to have been, but the big-busted, dyed blonde, life-giving and bursting with animal vitality; she is all that the Jew dreams the *shiksa*, whom his grandmothers forbade him as a mate. In Miller's film, that archetypal blonde was played by Marilyn Monroe (at that point Miller's wife and converted to Judaism), who, under the circumstances, was bound to triumph over the male Old West:

[87]

the Gentiles' Saturday-matinee dream of violence and death, personified by Clark Gable, tamer of horses and females. What remained for Gable, after so ignominious a defeat, except, aptly, to die? Only the author lived on, though his marriage, too, was doomed by the very dream out of which he made a movie in its honor.

Generation after overlapping generation, American-Jewish writers continue to appear: Bellow and Malamud, Irwin Shaw and Arthur Miller and Karl Shapiro, followed by J. D. Salinger and Norman Mailer and Grace Paley, after whom come Philip Roth and Bruce Jay Friedman and Norman Fruchter, on and on, until at last Gore Vidal, himself a white Anglo-Saxon Protestant, writes in mock horror (but with an undertone of real bitterness, too) in the pages of the *Partisan Review*, where, indeed, many of these authors first appeared: "Every year there is a short list of the O.K. writers. Today's list consists of two Jews, two Negroes and a safe floating *goy* of the old American Establishment (often Mr. Wright Morris) . . ."

But it is the whole world, not merely *our* critics, who list, year after year, the two new Jews, plus the two Negroes and the one eternally rediscovered *goy*. The English boy in the sixth form of the Manchester Grammar School digs Norman Mailer; and his opposite number in the classical *liceo* in Milan sees himself as Salinger's *giovane Holden*. At the moment that young Europeans everywhere (even, at last, in England) are becoming imaginary Americans, the American is becoming an imaginary Jew. But this is only one half of the total irony we confront; for, at the same moment, the Jew whom his Gentile fellow-citizen emulates may himself be in the process of becoming an imaginary Negro. "Do we have to become Gentile Jews before we can become White Negroes?" an impatient and reasonably hip youngster from a college audience I addressed recently asked me; and he was only half joking.

6

JEWISH-AMERICANS, GO HOME!

In any case, the Jewish-American writer is likely to view with detached amusement (and the younger he is, the more likely this is to be the case) the fact that his Jewishness is currently taken as a patent of his Americanism, and that he is, willy-nilly, the beneficiary of a belief that in their very alienation the Jews were always mythically twentieth-century Americans—long before the twentieth century and even, perhaps, America itself had been reached. Quite simply, he does not know in what his Jewishness—so symbolically potent—consists; he is only aware that it is on the point of disappearing. This disappearance he may celebrate or deplore when he is called on to take a stand in the symposia on the subject which have tended to become staple items in the Jewish press (we have seen them recently in *Commentary*, *Judaism*, and *Midstream*); and, indeed, he is free in this regard, so long as he is willing to suffer criticism and reproach, to plump for persistence or annihilation as his principles or instincts incline. But when he functions as a writer, when he pledges himself, that is to say, to describe in fictional form the kind of Jew he most probably is and the kinds of Jews he most probably knows, these *must* be, if not terminal Jews, at least penultimate ones: the fathers or grandfathers of (barring always some horrific or miraculous turn of events) America's last Jews.

Such are the inhabitants of Philip Roth's re-created suburban America: vestigial Jews who find the appearance in their midst (as recounted in "Eli the Fanatic") of a Chasidic Jew, garbed still and believing still as their ancestors were garbed and believed, quite as disturbing as Dostoevsky's Grand Inquisitor found the return of Christ; and such, too, are the inhabitants of J. D. Salinger's New York west side, those parents and friends of Holden Caulfield whose Jewishness has faded and paled until it could be proved against them in no court. But the portrait of the terminal Jew *in extremis* has recently been drawn in the title character of Bruce Jay Friedman's wicked and veracious short novel, *Stern;* a man whose Jewishness has lost all ideological content, positive or negative, and survives only as a psychological disease (strong enough to create an ulcer and motivate a breakdown), kept alive by an equally vestigial and almost equally impotent anti-Semitism.

Moreover, the Jewish writer begins to be influenced by the responsibilities he feels implicit in the recognition accorded him. Quite as the work of certain Nobel Prize winners is altered, even falsified, by the award, and they are tempted to respond imaginatively not to the world of their own making, but to another, more "real" world of whose existence the applause and the prize money reminds them, the Jewish writer's work is altered, even falsified: he has, it is borne in on him, an unsuspected *noblesse* which begins to *oblige* him. If, indeed, the particular experiences into which he happens to have been born have come to seem archetypal to Gentiles, if it is he who must "forge the conscience" of his nation in his time, he must attempt to become worthy of the role (he is likely to think) by guarding himself against the parochial and eliminating from his books all merely local and chauvinistic concerns.

Like the Negro, the homosexual, the southern author who has left the literature of protest and apology behind, he starts to feel uneasy about eternally projecting characters who are images of himself and his people: Jews, Jews, Jews, Jews! He is not, of course, in the situation of those early Jewish (or Negro or homosexual or southern writers) who wanted only to *pass*, to mingle unnoticed in the world of northern, white, Anglo-Saxon Protestants. That is to say, he wants to be not a Jewish writer who is less than Jewish, but one who is more than Jewish. And the devices open to him are many, ranging from the quite simple (and patently false) to the quite devious (and complexly true). He can, like Arthur Miller, for instance, and Paddy Chayefsky, create crypto-Jewish characters; characters who are in habit, speech, and condition of life typically Jewish-American, but who are presented as something else—general-American say, as in *Death of a Salesman*, or Italo-American, as in *Marty*. Such pseudo-universalizing represents, however, a loss of artistic faith, a failure to remember that the inhabitants of Dante's Hell or Joyce's Dublin are more universal as they are more Florentine or Irish. The works influenced by pseudo-universalizing lose authenticity and strength.

Or the Jewish writer can, like Herman Wouk in *The Caine Mutiny*, reverse the stereotypes of popular art: set in opposition a hyper-articulate intellectual, who ought to be a Jew but is disguised as a *goy*, and a hard-bitten fighting man, dedicated to the armed forces and loving authority, who ought to be a *goy* but is given a Jewish name and face. This kind of stereotype-inversion, however, merely substitutes falsification for falsification, sentimentality for sentimentality, even when, as in Leon Uris's *Exodus*, the Jewish military heroes are presented as Jews already become, or in the process of becoming, Israelis. The work of both Wouk and Uris represents, in fact, a disguised form of assimilationism, the attempt of certain Jews to be accepted by the bourgeois, Philistine Gentile community on the grounds that, though they are not Christians, they are even more bourgeois and philistine so that one is not surprised to find Uris appearing in court in the role of *all-rightnik* and enemy of literature, to cry out that Henry Miller's *Tropic of Cancer* "goes beyond every bound of morality I've ever known in my life—everything I've been taught. And I'm not ashamed to say I have morals."

On a more serious level, it is possible to create characters who are specifically half-Jewish, like Salinger's Glass family, those witnesses against the general corruption of a society who appear in story after story in the *New Yorker* and seem

[91]

always on the verge of becoming the actors in a full-fledged novel, which, alas, never materializes. That the Glasses are Irish as well as Jewish is especially attractive to a public the older members of which have been conditioned by *Abie's Irish Rose* on the stage and the Cohens and the Kellys in the movies; but Salinger seems bent on making more of the popular contrast than its earlier commercial exploiters. In a similar way, I have attempted to pass beyond the Philistine uses of stereotype inversion, as practiced by Herman Wouk, reversing in my *The Second Stone* the traditional roles of accepted Gentile and excluded Jew in order to raise the disturbing question: who in this time of semi-required philo-Semitism is the *real* Jew, the truly alienated man?

It is possible, too, to experiment, as Bernard Malamud has in *A New Life*, with writing a book about Jewish experience that scarcely mentions the word Jew, presenting a character Jewish in name and background, but not identifying him as a Jew until the book's final pages, and then only indirectly. Even more daring, and finally, I think, more successful, is Malamud's attempt in *The Assistant* to create a Jewish Gentile in Frankie Alpine: a man who moves from a position of vague hostility to the Jews, through exclusion and suffering, to the point where he is ready to accept circumcision—to become *de jure* what he is already *de facto*, one of the ultimately insulted and injured, a Jew: "One day in April Frank went to the hospital and had himself circumcised. For a couple of days he dragged himself around with a pain between his legs. The pain enraged and inspired him. After Passover he became a Jew." It is one of the oldest and (from the vantage point of 1789) one of the most unforeseen happy endings in a literature of strange happy endings; and it could only have happened in 1957, at the high point of the movement we have been examining.

This solution of Malamud's already begins to look a little old-fashioned, appearing as it does in a book which seems a belated novel of the Thirties, a last expression of the apocalyptic fears and Messianic hopes of those terrible but relatively simple times. Certainly *The Assistant* is a book which reminds us of ancestors, rather than suggesting to us progeny, like, say, certain works of Saul Bellow and Norman Mailer, a book, for all its desperation, not quite desperate enough to be in tune with the more post-apocalyptic fears and hopes of our bland but immensely complex times. Nowhere in Malamud's pages, for instance, do we find allusions either to Zen Buddhism or the psychology of Wilhelm Reich; and this is an important clue. For not only in Bellow and Mailer, but in Paul Goodman and Isaac Rosenfeld and Allen Ginsberg and Karl Shapiro, there is felt the influence of Reich, one-time brilliant exponent of Freudian insights, and later independent *magus* and healer, who taught that through full genitality man could conquer the ills of the flesh and the corruptions of society; and who died—convicted for quackery under the Pure Food and Drug Act—in jail, an ambiguous martyr. A flirtation with Zen, and especially a commitment to Reichianism, however, often indicates a discontent with simple or conventional plot resolutions and hence a deeper awareness of the contradictions in the situation of the Jewish-American writer than that possessed by Roth or Malamud or Salinger (who has played with Zen but avoided Reich), much less Uris and Wouk.

It is not enough merely to know that at the moment serious Jewish writing comes to play a central part in American life, the larger Jewish community is being assimilated to certain American values which are inimical to everything for which that serious writing stands, pledging allegiance to belongingness and banality and sociability while condemning abberration and intellectual concern and dissent. One must also be aware (as perhaps even a belated Forties writer like Philip Roth is not sufficiently aware) that the opposition to belongingness and banality and sociability has been itself kidnaped by suburbia. Anti-conformism has become a comfortable slogan of the well-to-do middle-aged with B.A. degrees, and intellectual concern itself has been transformed into academic diligence: standard equipment for teaching jobs at the colleges to which more and more young Jewish people go to sit at the feet of professors, more and more often Jewish, too; not City College any longer—but Amherst or Princeton or Vassar.

Similarly, the radicalism of the Thirties has, with the passage of time, become a polite, accepted leftism—in whose name certain well-meaning Jews, along with their Gentile opposite numbers, twice worked hopelessly to elect Adlai Stevenson President of the United States and then accepted, with a sigh, John F. Kennedy. Meanwhile the great sexual revolution of the Twenties has turned into a vaguely Freudian broadmindedness toward masturbation in the very young and casual copulation in the somewhat older; and the search for sources of cultural strength in the European avant-garde has become the frantic quest for prestige in the pursuit of the chic.

To some contemporary Jewish writers, therefore, the effort simultaneously to exploit a vestigial Jewishness (never quite understood) and to satirize the American-Jewish Establishment (pitifully easy to understand) seems itself an outworn convention, conformism once removed. Such writers are driven, in their attempt to preserve what seems to them the essential Jewish tradition of dissent, to attack the academy in which the second degree Philistinism of the sub-Freudian pseudo-left especially flourishes. Their heroes are likely to be boys running away from school, perpetually "on the road"; and revolt for them tends to be defined as high-level (involving prep school at least, and preferably the university) hooky playing. Such an attack on school and professors inevitably becomes an attack on the kind of literature and criticism which such schools and professors foster, and then an attack on literature and criticism themselves—finally an onslaught against and a rejection of intelligence: the very quality for which, in the deepest American imagination, the Jew has traditionally stood. Imagine living in an age when, with whatever reservations and ironies, an American-Jewish novelist has founded a magazine called *The Noble Savage*, and an American-Jewish poet has collected certain of his essays under the title *In Defense of Ignorance!*

[94]

Astonishingly, the literary and cultural ideals of many younger Jewish writers (and these by no means the worst among us) appear no longer to be conceived primarily in terms of the European avant-garde, but rather to be modeled after the examples of certain nativist hyper-American authors of the immediate or remote past. To be sure, no American, not even a Jew in pursuit of a Utopian Americanism, can escape European culture completely; after all, Reich himself was a European before becoming an American and shreds and scraps of existentialism play an important role in the works of the writers in question. But it is Walt Whitman who most deeply possesses the imagination of such writers, along with Henry Miller and William Carlos Williams; and from them is derived the dream of a literature native as well as unbuttoned, untidy, intuitive, and passionate. Indeed, there are some Jewish-American authors (most notably Karl Shapiro) who have tried to argue that in Judaism itself there are to be found grounds for a revolt against the academic, formalistic, and genteel, that our tradition has been all along more Whitmanian than Eliotic.

At any rate, certain Jews now stand in the forefront of the newest American revulsion from Europe and the life of the intelligence which Europe represents to the popular imagination in the United States. Under the aegis of such publishers as Grove Press, and in such magazines as *Big Table* and the *Evergreen Review*, the Jewish offspring of Twenties schoolmasters and Thirties Communists have oddly banded together with Gentile ex-athletes and junkies to make the movement called "beat," and to define for that movement a program advocating the rediscovery of America and the great audience via marijuana and jazz, more and better orgasms, and a general loosening of literary form. Some of the bright young Jews currently producing first novels and early poems are "beat" or "hip" as their parents were once Stalinists or Trotskyites, only in their larval stage; with maturity (i.e., marriage or a graduate fellowship), they are likely to shave off their beards and settle down to doctoral dissertations or new publishing ventures. And some of the older writers who have climbed on the bandwagon in search of a second youth may have been driven less by their conviction that youth is an absolute good, to be repeated as often as possible, than by a sense of flagging powers, sexual or creative; and they may not preserve their new-found allegiances past the next turn of fashion. But the new Jewish anti-intellectualism cannot be wholly explained away by an analysis of its psychogenesis; the works produced in its name will survive the allegiances behind them, and the critic must deal with them in their own terms.

In their own terms, they are marked by the abandonment of the Jewish character as a sufficient embodiment of the Jewish author's aspirations and values, and by the invention, beside him or in his place, of characters who are not merely non-Jewish, but are, in fact, hyper-*goyim*, super-Gentiles of truly mythic proportions: specifically, sexual heroes of incredible potency. Such characters represent a resolve on the part of certain Jewish writers to invent (reversing the traditional roles) mythical Gentiles with whom they can identify themselves. But even here, they were anticipated by a non-Jewish writer, Henry Miller, who enjoys the special distinction of being the first Gentile author in our literature to see himself not directly as an American, but defensively as a Gentile, the Jew's *goy*—even as certain white writers now begin to see themselves as the Negro's *o'fay*. "I sometimes ask myself," Miller writes in *Tropic of Cancer*, "how it happens that I attract nothing but crackbrained individuals, neurasthenics, neurotics, psychopaths—and Jews especially. There must be something in a healthy Gentile that excites the Jewish mind, like when he sees sour black bread." It is perhaps because Miller has already provided them with a living imaginary Gentile that American-Jewish writers did not turn, as one might have expected, to the Negro as a model for their re-invented selves. Certainly the Negro is the Jew's archetypal opposite, representative of the impulsive life even as the Jew is the symbol of the intellectual; and the Negro is everywhere in these times at the center of our concern. Indeed, there were tentative efforts

[96]

in this direction: the account, for instance, written by Bernard Wolfe along with Mezz Mezzrow, of how the latter had passed, or almost passed, by way of the world of jazz, into the deep world of the Negroes; and the manifesto, or more properly pre-manifesto, of Norman Mailer in which the life of the "hipster," the White Negro, is more sighed for than advocated.

Mailer, however, when he dreamed his mythical *goy* in the character of Sergius O'Shaughnessy (who moves through the novel *The Deer Park*, is hinted at in the story "The Man Who Studied Yoga," and reappears heroically in "The Time of Her Time") created a protagonist who seems less White Negro than Jew's Hemingway and, in this respect, improbably resembles the Eugene Henderson of Saul Bellow's *Henderson the Rain King*, though Bellow, for all his commitment to Wilhelm Reich, is not "hip" or "beat" at all. Both writers at any rate, have recently projected similar versions of the good life: passionate, genital, anti-intellectual, impulsive, though the one has lived a life of risk, daring drug-addiction, and even jail, while the other is a professor at the University of Chicago, daring only boredom and the dangers of security.

While the general American reader is still eager to identify himself with the mythical Jews of the Forties and the Fifties, alienated intellectuals like Mailer and Bellow, who began by portraying such Jews, have moved on to imagine themselves as mythical Gentiles: paleface Protestant noble savages, great muscular conquerors of women and jungles, aging athletes, who, to the parents of those writers, would still have represented the absolute Other.* Where, then,

* There is a fascinating apology for this strategy in a little poem of Mailer's which reads:

If
Harry Golden
is the Gentile's
Jew
      can I be-
come the Golden
Goy?

has he come from, this Anglo-Saxon hero-monster, the "Golden Goy," with which certain hitherto dutiful Jewish-American boys insist on confusing themselves? Appropriately enough, out of the ambivalence stirred in the minds of these writers by the public image of Ernest Hemingway: inventor—out of anti-Semitic malice—of the first notable Jewish character in American fiction, Robert Cohen. Committed to Hemingway insofar as they are Americans of a generation that learned its speech and its life-style from his books, but cut off from him insofar as they are Jews and, therefore, to Hemingway embodiments of the fake artist, the fake lover, the fake outsider—they constructed, in irony and desperate love, portraits of the elder novelist at the moment of his artistic defeat and just before his death.

Norman Mailer's Sergius O'Shaughnessy is portrayed in "The Time of Her Time" as giving bullfight lessons in a loft in Greenwich Village: a bullfighter without real bulls, though surrounded by real enough women whom he actually possesses, in the place of imaginary conflict. It all amounts to a strange yet somehow tender travesty of the images of Eros and death and of Hemingway himself as connoisseur in both areas which run through *The Sun Also Rises* and *Death in the Afternoon*. In Bellow's *Henderson the Rain King*, the same author is evoked by a hulking giant of a protagonist whose initials are E.H., and who seeks in the heart of Africa, in an encounter with savages and wild beasts, the answers to questions he is not articulate enough to formulate; and for all its mannered irony and outright burlesque, Bellow's book, too, seems—especially now—a memoir and a tribute. But Hemingway, as we have noticed earlier, could never tell the difference between himself and Gary Cooper, who came to play on the screen so many of the roles projected by Hemingway out of his own anguish and vanity, while Gary Cooper is finally an up-dated Natty Bumppo, perhaps the last Natty we can afford. And Natty was to begin with, of course, the American Indian in whiteface.

The Jewish writer, trying to imagine the *goy* he longs to

[98]

be, or at least to contemplate, succeeds finally in re-inventing the mythical redskin out of James Fenimore Cooper, which is amusing enough. But it is not the whole story; for Henderson and O'Shaughnessy are half-breeds, and the Indian in them, which is to say, their American component, is improbably crossed with a legendary horror out of the deep Jewish past, a component rooted in the life of the *shtetl* and memories of that life: a world the first Cooper surely never made and the second never acted. There are clues to the true nature of this second component in both Bellow and Mailer, though in Bellow they are few and obscure. Nonetheless, before Henderson became fully himself, turned loose in Africa to flee dark princesses and mate chastely with African kings who tame lions and read Wilhelm Reich, he was tentatively sketched as the Kirby Allbee of Bellow's earlier novel *The Victim*: a seedy Anglo-Saxon anti-Semite, bound to Asa Leventhal, his Jewish victim (or victimizer) with a passion like that which binds the cuckold to his cuckolder. That passion is rendered in terms of an appalling physical intimacy: "Leventhal . . . was so conscious of Allbee . . . that he was able to see himself as if through a strange pair of eyes: the side of his face, the palpitation of his throat, the seams of his skin. . . . Changed in this way into his own observer, he was able to see Allbee, too . . . the weave of his coat, his raggedly overgrown neck . . . he could even evoke the odor of his hair and skin. The acuteness and intimacy of it astounded him, oppressed and intoxicated him." And its consequences are violence, a final scene in which Leventhal thrusts Allbee from his apartment, though not until they have been joined in the embrace of struggle, an even closer contact of the flesh, and a kind of consummation in horror. Allbee, Bellows makes clear, is Leventhal's beloved as well as his nightmare, just as Leventhal is Allbee's beloved as well as his nightmare; and the climax of such ambivalence is a kind of rejection scarcely distinguishable from rape. What Bellow leaves unclear, perhaps deliberately, is the order of generation of these nightmares. We suspect that Leventhal (closer to his author in origin and tempera-

[99]

ment, though by no means a self-portrait) is dreaming All-bee dreaming him, but Bellow does not tell us this.

Mailer, on the other hand, has placed the question of the genesis of the mythical *goy* at the center of his most recent work, commenting on it editorially and including it inside his fictional framework as well. Originally, he tells us, for instance, the two Sergius short stories preserved in *Advertisements for Myself* and the one Sergius novel were to be part of a larger, immensely ambitious scheme: a study of how an inadequate Jew, baffled sexually and artistically, invents, in his troubled sleep, the synthetic *Ubermensch*, Sergius O'Shaughnessy. "I woke up in the morning," Mailer writes in *Advertisements for Myself*, "with the plan for a prologue and an eight-part novel in my mind, the prologue to be the day of a small, frustrated man, a minor artist manqué. The eight novels were to be eight stages of his dream later that night, and the books would revolve around the adventures of a mythical hero, Sergius O'Shaughnessy . . ." The "artist manqué" is not identified in these notes as a Jew, but we are not surprised to discover, reading the novella into which Mailer's "prologue" turned, that his name is Sam Slabovda, and that he is given to making statements beginning, "You see, *boychick* . . ."

Mailer's scheme has fallen apart in his hands, as his view of the world and himself has fragmented perilously; and surely one of his basic problems has been a temptation to believe that, after all, he himself is the *goy* O'Shaughnessy rather than the small Jew, Slabovda, who, in defeat and distress, has dreamed O'Shaughnessy. Hemingway had the same difficulty in keeping himself, brown-eyed poet and laureate of impotence, distinct from the *Amerikanski* heroes of his later works; yet in Hemingway no ethnic-mythic gulf separated him from his Gentile protagonists. And he was never driven, even in his moment af acutest anxiety, to imagine a mating, brutal as an evisceration, between his passive self and its more active projection. Such a mating, however, constitutes both the action and theme of Mailer's most successful piece of fiction, the short story "The Time

[100]

of Her Time." At once a confession of terrifying candor and a parable of our times, "The Time of Her Time" imagines an encounter between O'Shaughnessy and a Jewish coed from N.Y.U., whom we might well take for his *anima*-figure did we not know that she represents the Jewish author, and O'Shaughnessy the *animus* of his fantasies. No wonder the "heroine" is possessed completely and at last, not as a woman may be but as a man must, through what Mailer calls "love's first hole."

Mailer opens his tale in a Negro hash-house, but cannot keep it there. Ill at ease in that theoretically preferred milieu, he returns quickly to the pseudo-Hemingwayesque Village loft and his true subject: the long struggle between his mythic, beloved hero and his equally mythic but hated heroine, called Denise. Denise seems at first glance the Temple Drake of the Sixties, as archetypal a coed for our troubled days as Temple for the Twenties. Like her prototype, she is hot for love but incapable of submission to it, and therefore incapable of an orgasm; but, unlike Temple, she is no decadent last product of Anglo-Saxon gentility—only the black-haired offspring of a hardware merchant from Brooklyn (out of, presumably, one of those sexually aggressive Jewesses who terrified and allured Thomas Wolfe in the Thirties); and she is not driven, but committed to bohemian freedom, T. S. Eliot, and Sigmund Freud, or at least to her own analyst.

The blow-by-blow description of the sexual combat between her and O'Shaughnessy threatens momentarily to turn into an allegory of the cultural plight we have been examining, but it is saved by the vigor of Mailer's language and the acuteness of his senses, especially his nose. We are not surprised to discover that it is rape, on either the literal or symbolic level, which Mailer's coed demands before she will pay any man the tribute of her orgasm; though we may not have been as prepared as is Mailer's O'Shaughnessy to understand just what sort of rape she had all along required. And why not, since Sam Slabovda (who is Mailer, who is Denise) invented him? ". . . and then she was about to hang again," Mailer makes his protagonist say, "and I said into her ear, 'You dirty little Jew.' That whipped her over . . ." And whipped Mailer over with her; for precisely here, I think, *he* made it, too, for the first time in his life, made it artistically as his heroine made it sexually; and he has been more or less peacefully writing *midrashim* on Buber's retelling of Chasidic tales ever since.

What is finally clear in Mailer as well as in Bellow, though clearer in the former, is that the other half of Henderson-O'Shaughnessy, the non-Hemingway half, is the *pogrom-chik*, the Cossack rapist of the erotic nightmares of the great-grandmothers of living American Jews and that the great-grandchildren respond to him precisely as their archetypal female ancestor in the not-very-funny old Jewish joke, who whispers over the shoulder of her assaulter to the child indignantly screaming and attempting to tug him away, "Quiet, Rosalie, a pogrom is a pogrom." Adopted to our needs of today, however, it seems funny enough: a joke both very American and very Jewish this time around; not merely one more but perhaps the greatest, as well as the latest, Jewish-American joke. Yet there is one more: the Jew who thinks he is an American, yet feels in his deepest heart an immitigable difference from the Gentile American who thinks he is a Jew, need only go abroad to realize that, in the eyes of non-Americans, the difference does not exist at all.

"*Americans go home!*" the angry crowds cry before our embassies; and hearing them, the Jew knows not only that he is quite as American as his Gentile fellow-tourist, but also that the fellow-tourist along with him, that *all* Americans, are the Jews of the second half of the twentieth century: refused (outside of their own country, at least) any identity except the general one contained in a name which is an abusive epithet. "*Americans go home!*" the crowds roar again, while the rocks fly, the police-lines buckle; and running for cover, the Jewish-American keeps imagining that he hears behind him (as, running from the schoolyard once, he heard the cry, "You killed our Christ!")

[102]

the shout, "You killed our Julius and Ethel Rosenberg!" "Your Rosenbergs?" he wants to yell back, "*your* Rosenbergs?" as once he had wanted to holler, "*Your* Christ?" And remembering the childhood indignity in the midst of adult ones, remembering when it was as difficult to be a Jew as it has become to be an American, he finds himself laughing too hard to be dismayed.

7

INDIAN OR INJUN?

It is finally, however, foolish for the Jewish-American writer
to try to re-imagine himself as a redskin, for the paleface
reader to whom he has appealed over the past two or three
decades demands of him quite another legendary role. And
it is no more use for him to penetrate, with Bellow's Henderson, the heart of Africa, or, with Mailer's O'Shaughnessy,
the black ghettos of the United States, in search of Negro
models on which to refurbish himself. If America has turned
west again from Europe in search of the passage to India,
the dream of which ends now, as in 1492, with discovering
our own "Indians," ourselves as "Indians," this means that
the fictional Jew is becoming irrelevant; and to daub him
with warpaint will make him as little a genuine redskin as
Al Jolson's blackface made him a genuine Negro. Mythically
speaking, the Jew is neither redskin nor paleface, neither
black nor white; and his current attempts to pass as a colored man in order to keep up with shifting literary fashion,
represent as vain a pursuit as his earlier efforts to qualify as
a white one in order to get into country clubs. No indig-
enous or pioneer American, the Jew represents to the
American imagination an interloper, an alien who was
never on that raft, either as Jim or Huck, nor in that
primeval forest, either as Natty Bumppo or Chingachgook,
and in whom other Americans therefore find an image not
of their belonging in their own land, but of their alienation
from their parents and their past.

On the other hand, the most profoundly mythical levels of our literature do not have to be parodied or ironically altered to provide fables capable of representing even the most recent relations of black and white as well as Indian and white. How much more nostalgia and less travesty there is in Faulkner's recasting of Huck as Ike McCaslin in "The Bear" than in Saul Bellow's reworking of that archetypal figure as Augie March, or J. D. Salinger's transmutation of Huck into Holden. And Faulkner, of course, is a link both to a later generation of white writers and a still later one of Negroes.

We need only to evoke in our minds the face of Julie Harris to realize how close the Hucks of, say, Carson McCullers are, not only ethnically but in the ambiguity of their sex, to the Huck of Mark Twain. It makes no difference that, in Mrs. McCullers's books, the "worst boy in town" is reborn as a boyish girl called Mick or Frankie, who finds comfort in the arms of a Negro woman; in this respect, the more things change, the more they are the same. Mrs. McCullers is surely the most accomplished of the neo-Faulknerians, her talent more versatile and durable than that of Truman Capote, for instance, who takes up many of her cues and moves the transmogrification of Huck to a more ultimate state. Standing as she does on the border between the Lady Faulknerians and the boy exploiters of homosexual sensibility, she can project with some detachment the image of the homosexual as a symbol of alienation quite as satisfactory as, and, in a sense, more authentic than, the Jew. Yet in her work, the homosexual is still in hiding, disguised as a prepubescent girl, reaching out—in the author's stead—to touch in love the equally alienated Negro. And even when that girl becomes a boy, as in Capote, the nature of the redeeming love which we, as a nation, have so long dreamed is still not quite candidly confessed.

It has been a Negro writer who has recently dared to take the final step by turning the implicitly, tentatively, innocently homosexual romance of colored man and white into a frank account of overt homosexuality crossing ethnic lines and healing interracial strife. But James Baldwin's *Another Country* has failed to have the impact which might have been expected from a book which reveals our long-kept secret—not only because it happens to be technically inadequate to its task, but because it has attempted that task too late. Even so, Baldwin moves the popular mind at the moment when white violence begins to abate or, at least, to proffer itself with an uncustomary shamefacedness, and black violence, long stored up, begins to fill the vacuum of tolerance and self-righteous indifference left by its disappearance. Baldwin has, however, attained the precision of language and feeling appropriate to a first-rate novelist only in his essays, while his three novels have represented (along with their growth in scope and ambition) a decline in control and accomplishment. *Another Country* has, indeed, broken through to best-sellerdom and a kind of prestige among certain liberal academics, but only at the price of the admiration of Baldwin's earlier and more discriminating readers, who have been busy ever since explaining to each other the grounds of his failure. To understand that failure adequately, however, it must be set not only against Baldwin's personal difficulties with his talent and his role, but against certain larger contexts: first of the shifting place of the Negro writer in our culture; and second, of the most recent developments in the history of the dream of a great love between white and colored men.

Already, in the Forties and Fifties, the onerous privilege of mythicizing the relations of black and white had begun to pass to the Negro writer, to the descendants of Jim rather than those of Huck; and some of these, at least, have, from the start, struggled to escape the Huck Finn-Nigger Jim archetype which they have dimly felt as an imposed restraint. Richard Wright, for instance, sought to avoid, by means of realism and social documentation, all versions of the Negro provided by traditional myth; but though he moves out from under the shadow of Jim, he becomes the victim of other more dangerous and, perhaps, less relevant legends. His Bigger Thomas, for instance, the sullen protagonist of *Native Son*, is identified by his very name as a

[106]

reaction to Uncle Tom, the imaginary Negro who has seemed to most Negroes the most offensive travesty of their long history and current plight.

In any case, Wright has come to seem to us a belated writer of the Thirties; his novels mere "protest literature," incapable of outliving the causes that occasioned his wrath. And though Baldwin, after an initial critical onslaught on Wright, has tried to make peace with his ghost, for most readers Wright's books have begun to seem of less and less importance, especially as the number of books by and about Negroes grows with astonishing speed. Recently we have been almost overwhelmed with new novels by younger Negro writers (most impressive among them, the Faulknerian *A Different Drummer* by William Melvin Kelly), as publishers have sought to fill the hunger they perceive in the mass audience for first-hand accounts of Negro experience and new myths derived from that experience.

Nonetheless, no new Negro writer—not Kelly, certainly, nor even John Williams, who has had a somewhat longer career—has seemed so much the spokesman of his people as Baldwin, whose political manifesto, *The Fire Next Time*, has profited by, and perhaps also reinforced, the popularity of his last novel, and whose portrait appears in the press side by side with those of Bayard Rustin and A. Philip Randolph, as if, like them, he too set large masses of Negroes into action in sit-ins and demonstrations. There is, to be sure, Ralph Ellison, whose *Invisible Man* has been justly admired in many quarters; but he is the author of only that single book, though he is working patiently and slowly, we are assured, on another. In any case, *The Invisible Man*, whatever its merits, is a book which technically speaking looks backwards rather than forwards, being a Kafka-esque allegory very much in the mood and manner (though its matter is specifically Negro) of the Jewish novels of the last decades; and Ellison's invisible protagonist, however convincingly specified, reminds us disconcertingly of Kafka's K., i.e., seems a secondhand version of the black man in America, based on a European intellectual's version of the alienated Jew.

[107]

Like Baldwin's characters, Ellison's reflect the experience of Negroes not in that South which at the moment stirs with their awakening, but in the great cities of the North, where they confront a terror much like West's or Bellow's or Malamud's. Baldwin, however, precisely because he is a homosexual as well as a Negro, manages to establish living connections with a pastoral American archetype older than our cities. And if we would understand him, as we must, since he stands at the center, if not in the vanguard, of Negro writing now, we must move back to the very beginnings of our literature and beyond, to a place where legend exists, though serious literature has not been invented. And to find that place, let us turn to Henry David Thoreau, who not merely imagined, like James Fenimore Cooper, the role of a white Indian, or lived it, like Daniel Boone, but imagined *and* lived that role. The most illuminating of Thoreau's books, for our purposes, is his earliest—a very odd, very duplicitous, and hence very American work called *A Week on the Concord and Merrimack Rivers*. Pretending to be the day-by-day account of a vacation jaunt, a short excursion, it turns out to be an elegy for a lost love, a praise of friendship, and a compendium of a young man's reactions to his current reading—chiefly in Oriental philosophy. It contains also (and here it is of critical importance to us) the record of what certain seventeenth- and eighteenth-century encounters between white men and Indians had come to mean to the romantic American imagination in the mid-nineteenth century. It represents, that is to say, the moment at which the meeting of white race and red on the North American continent was passing from history to myth.

Let us begin, then, with the entry for a Wednesday in Thoreau's discursive journal. He has been traveling, he tells us, between Manchester and Goffstown, and has been reflecting on two subjects, somehow linked in his mind: the satisfactions of friendship, and the problem of whether America has "antiquities" of its own worthy of being compared with those of the Old World. Friendship and antiquity—no wonder Indian history rises in the mind of Thoreau as he idles in the boat carried downstream through

Connecticut by the peaceful flowing of water. It is an incident from the chronicles of the trapper Alexander Henry which he recalls in particular, the account of Henry's idyllic friendship with an Indian called Wawatam:

> The Friendship which Wawatam testified for Henry the fur trader, as described in the latter's *Adventures*, so almost bare and leafless, yet not blossomless nor fruitless, is remembered with satisfaction and security. The stern, imperturbable warrior, after fasting, solitude, and mortification of body, comes to the white man's lodge, and affirms that he is the white brother whom he saw in his dream, and adopts him henceforth. He buries the hatchet as it regards his friend, and they hunt and fish and make maple sugar together . . .

"Dream" is the key-word, the white man's dream of reconciliation, which he presents here as if it were the dream of the red man, and next "satisfaction and security," for only if he believes the hatchet is really buried with the red man can the white man be at peace with himself. But Thoreau's reconstruction of Henry's story continues:

> If Wawatam would taste the "white man's milk" with his tribe; or take his bowl of human broth made of the trader's fellow countrymen, he first finds a place of safety for his Friend, whom he has rescued from a similar fate.

Once more the wish-theme recurs: "place of safety"; but this time it becomes clear that the reconciliation is not for everyone. Only a chosen few, only the chosen *one* (with whom the lonely American artist finds it easy to identify himself) is loved and preserved, while his fellows are slaughtered, even consumed. And even for the one, the exceptional idyll does not continue long:

> At length, after a long winter of undisturbed and happy intercourse . . . it becomes necessary for Wawatam to take leave of his Friend. . . . "We now exchanged farewells," says

[109]

Henry, "with an emotion entirely reciprocal. I did not quit the lodge without the most grateful sense of the many acts of goodness which I had experienced in it. . . . All the family accompanied me to the beach; and the canoe had no sooner put off than Wawatam commenced an address to the Kichi Manito, beseeching him to take care of me, his brother, till we should next meet . . ." We never hear of him again.

Like a dream, the idyll in the lodge cannot last; and like a dream, it has no consequences, no future, but exists out of time. (Notice how Thoreau has moved it out of Henry's past tense into a timeless present.) Yet it has continued to possess us, this old dream of peace, appearing and reappearing everywhere in our greatest verse and prose, though it has never had the wide, popular appeal, nor won the schoolroom approval, of that other deep American legend of race relations, the story of Pocahontas and Captain John Smith.

That story, ending with a marriage, a conversion, and the possibility of a family, exists in time as the story of Alexander Henry and Wawatam does not. It is a tale passionate and domestic and Christian; which is precisely why it does not appeal to Thoreau, and would not to Cooper or Melville, Walt Whitman or Mark Twain. Thoreau is aware of this, and wants us, his readers, to be so, too. "Friendship . . ." he remarks in the paragraph immediately following his retelling of the story of Wawatam, "has not much human blood in it, but consists with a certain disregard for men and their erections, the Christian duties and the humanities . . . We may call it an essentially heathenish intercourse, free and irresponsible . . ." We can take it, I think, that Thoreau knows just what he is saying and does not merely by accident suggest the possibility of "intercourse" without "erections." The sexual language of this anti-sexual idyll is deliberate; and we are expected, I am sure, to recall it when we read Thoreau's account of a contrasting episode out of the past: an episode containing elements passionate and domestic and Christian, as well as "much human blood." But how different is the tale he tells of Hannah

[110]

Dustan from that of Pocahontas, and how differently he tells it, even to keeping its tenses historically in the past. We find it in the midst of the ruminations headed "Thursday":

On the thirty-first day of March, one hundred and forty-two years before this, probably about this time of the afternoon, there were hurriedly paddling down this part of the river . . . two white women and a boy. . . . They . . . handled their paddles unskillfully, but with nervous energy and determination, and at the bottom of their canoe lay the still-bleeding scalps of ten of the aborigines.

So much for the "human blood." But Thoreau goes on with an identification and the sort of circumstantial narration to which he was not moved at all in recounting the relations of Henry and Wawatam:

They were Hannah Dustan, and her nurse, Mary Neff . . . and an English boy, named Samuel Lennardson, escaping from captivity among the Indians. On the 15th of March previous, Hannah Dustan has been compelled to rise from child bed, and half dressed . . . commence an uncertain march . . . through the snow and the wilderness. She had seen her seven elder children flee with their father. . . . She had seen her infant's brains dashed out against an apple tree. . . .

So much for matters domestic, "the Christian duties and the humanities." The story continues:

When she reached the Wigwam of her captor . . . she had been told that she and her nurse were soon to be taken to a distant Indian settlement, and there made to run the gauntlet naked . . .

And now the passionate note suggested by "half dressed" above is repeated full-voice: the threat of rape suggested, though not quite spoken. We are in the realm of "men and

[111]

their erections." The threat of naked gauntlet or rape is never fulfilled, however; for Hannah Dustan, Thoreau tells us, succeeded in outwitting her captors, using the small boy to gather information on the best methods for dispatching an enemy and killing "them all in their sleep, excepting one favorite boy, and one squaw who fled wounded with him to the woods."

The story seems finished at this point, but it is not, since Hannah and her nurse, having made good their escape in a canoe, then turn back into danger to take the scalps of those they had killed. It remains a little unclear, at first, just why they ran such risks to indulge in an exercise clearly unsuitable to ladies of breeding, but Thoreau's last paragraph, his explicit happy ending, makes it all quite transparent:

> According to the historian, they escaped as by a miracle all roving bands of Indians, and reached their homes in safety, with their trophies, for which the General Court paid them fifty pounds.

Commerce has entered into the list of the "humanities" at the rate of five pounds per scalp, and the picture is complete, the tale really done. But Thoreau will not let things go even yet, for he has wanted not merely to retell an old story but to mythicize it, and he continues:

> The family of Hannah Dustan all assembled alive once more, except the infant whose brains were dashed out against the apple tree, and there have been many who in later times have lived to say that they had eaten of the fruit of that apple tree.

It is, of course, no mere actual tree to which Thoreau refers (though one still stood in his time); but lest it not be sufficiently clear what he means by *eating the fruit of the tree*, he hastens to add immediately: "This seems a long while ago, and yet it happened since Milton wrote his Paradise Lost."

[112]

What we have been reading, then, is a special American version of the fall of man, an account of original sin in the New World. And in light of this, we must interpret not only Thursday's story but Wednesday's as well; for if the adventures of Hannah Dustan signify the loss of paradise, the idyll of Wawatam describes for us the paradise lost. His wigwam represents the earthly paradise of the American imagination, a Garden of Eden, be it noted, for men only —and for one chosen out of many, to boot. Once the female enters the wilderness, it ceases to be heaven and becomes hell, since she brings with her the nurse, the child, the homestead, the family, the courts and bounties on scalps: all, that is to say, the compounded evils bred of sex and money. In her presence, the dream of reconciliation between the races turns into the nightmare of miscegenation, not a promise but a threat.*

It is clear, at any rate, that deep in the mind of America, if not actually below, at least at the lowest level of consciousness, there exist side by side a dream and a nightmare of race relations and that the two together constitute a legend of the American frontier, of the West (when the second race is the Indian), or of the South (when the second race is the Negro). In either case, it is the legend of a lost Eden, or, in more secular terms, of a decline from a Golden Age to an Age of Iron—as America moves from the time of the trapper to the days of the settler, the era of the great plantations to the days of Reconstruction. What makes the Golden Age golden, is, in the case of the Indian, as we have observed, an imagined state of peace between white man and red man, transplanted European and aboriginal at home: love, innocence, a kind of religious, even other-worldly calm, preside over this peace. And what makes the Iron Age iron is a state of war between redskin natives and paleface invaders: a burden of hatred and guilt, a history of scalpings and counter-scalpings, revenges and counter-revenges, make this war ultimate hell.

* This complex subject is treated at length, and from a somewhat different point of view, in my *Love and Death in the American Novel*, published in 1960.

[113]

In the end, though both of Thoreau's waking visions are based on events which actually happened, are matters of record, we are asked to accept them on quite a different level of belief. The vision of peace is presented to us as anomalous, rare, exceptional, almost a miracle while the vision of war is proffered as usual, customary, the rule. It is not, that is to say, treated purely as a myth, like the former, but as history: one episode in what James Joyce calls the nightmare from which we all try vainly to awake. For a long time, indeed, it seemed not only a peculiarly but an *exclusively* American nightmare; for though the history of every nation may be, as Joyce suggests, a bad dream from which it cannot wake, each has its own nighttime fantasies, as each has its own fate. With the rise of the dark-skinned peoples everywhere, however, a peculiar white American experience (shared, up to now, perhaps, only by white South Africans) may become the common experience of all the whites of the world. I am talking about our sense of acting out our national destiny in the presence of *witnesses* involved in that destiny (through fear and hate, we know; through love as well, we hope) by virtue of their color, but by the same token detached from it. It is this special experience which has bred our special nightmare, as well as our special dream; and it is this which lies behind the two anecdotes brought to the surface of Thoreau's mind, not by chance but by necessity, as he and his brother drifted along the quiet rivers of New England in 1839.

If we would know, then, not merely what the two visions of Thoreau meant at the moment he wrote them down, but what they can mean to us still, we must remind ourselves over and over of the fact, too omnipresent to be visible at all, perhaps, certainly too familiar to be remembered easily: the white, largely European settlers of America have had, from the earliest times, to work out their personal fates and national destiny in the presence of two alien races. This situation is not ·a creation of Americans, but a precondition of their existence as Americans, a heritage from the Europeans who settled on our continent before America itself was invented. With the darker races, white

[114]

Americans have, of course, inevitably mixed, mingled, even mated, in friendship and in furtive lust; but *they have not assimilated to them*. The three races remain distinguishable in America today, though there are few Indians, and perhaps even fewer Negroes, without some admixture of white blood, and though culturally, even psychologically, as we shall see, differences once quite real begin to blur and disappear. Indeed, the distinction seems to become, for most white men and some colored ones, too, more and more psychically important to maintain, as it becomes more and more difficult to do so. At any rate, the majority of white Americans at the moment seem unwilling to surrender a distinction it pains them to maintain. What satisfaction would it be, in any case, to reach a time when lines between colored and white can no longer be drawn, if there are no colored people around to applaud it—as there have always been colored people to suffer under and deplore discrimination?

To the two darker races, with whom he must in many places live, the white American is, then, bound by bonds of guilt older than his national identity itself; and of those bonds he and those races are *both* aware. The white man knows his guilts have long been mitigated by law and statute, as well as by kindness and love; but they will not disappear, cannot, he suspects, short of the moment of total assimilation, which he rejects for reasons he does not ever clearly understand. And when he has persuaded himself that somehow they do not matter, he sees in the eye of the Negro or Indian watching him (or fancies he sees, it scarcely matters) evidence that they do. The intelligent white man's burden of guilt consists not merely in knowing himself an oppressor, but in knowing the oppressed know this, too.

Indeed, in our latter-day, liberal world, the weight of reflexive guilt has become greater than that of direct guilt (and it is to this that a recent writer like James Baldwin has learned to appeal): we are aware that the Negro is aware of his long sexual and economic exploitation; we are aware that the Indian is aware of his expropriation and the

[115]

disruption of his communal life. And it is their awareness from which we have now come to flinch. For this, we know, even the most rapid advance of reform and amelioration in race relations cannot change; as long as the Negro remains a Negro, the Indian an Indian, a part of his self-consciousness must be the consciousness of our offenses against him. And so long as we are able to recognize him as someone distinctly other from us, we are convinced he must feel himself an other, too. But without a hatred equal to our guilt, he would not know himself for what he is, that is, what we have made him.

This is why we have long not merely dreamed a dream and a nightmare, but dreamed that the colored man dreamed them, too. This is why Thoreau's "satisfaction and security" depend on the myth that Wawatam dreamed of his "white brother," as his white brother dreamed of him, and that their love is "entirely reciprocal." What is harder to understand is that we have also dreamed the black man and red dreaming our nightmares: that black rebellion and red massacre we have portrayed for decades in popular fiction and films. We long for an accounting, which we pray we may be spared, and need somehow to believe the oppressed peoples among us long for it, too. If only they dreamed it, perhaps that would be enough; or if, alternatively, they dreamed with us figures of forgiveness like Harriet Beecher's Uncle Tom. If only in fantasy we were united, no matter whether in fantasy of reconciliation or revenge, then we could forgive ourselves. But we do not forgive ourselves. And, indeed, it is hard to know which comes first in the logic of the psyche, which, on that level, is the cause of which: our not forgiving ourselves, or our not being quite able to imagine the dark-skinned people we oppress forgiving us.

Our greatest literature has always understood what we are just beginning to come to terms with in the realm of social action: that the white Americans have, from the first, hopelessly confused the real Negroes and Indians, with whom they must for the sake of social survival and civil peace learn to live, with certain projections of their own deepest minds, aspects of their own psychic life with which precisely they find it impossible to live. Here is the deepest sense in which the oppressor suffers equally with the oppressed, enslaves himself along with those who are his slaves. But to understand it adequately we must be willing to risk a detour (from which some have never returned) into the No Man's Land between politics and psychology.

8

THE JIG IS UP!

What we customarily call the "oppressed minorities" (and the same is true when the oppressed are, in fact, majorities) are exploited not only economically and politically, but also *psychologically*, though this latter fact is less noticed in election speeches, newspaper editorials, or even serious analyses of class and race relations, whether pro or con. Oppressors, that is to say, project upon the oppressed certain of their own psychic dilemmas, elements of their own mental life of which they are ashamed, or toward which they are deeply ambivalent. And such projection, it is worth noting, *does not work both ways*—only from the more favored group to the less favored one, from, say, white to Negro, but not, in a white-controlled society, from Negro to white. So, in the Middle Ages, males projected upon females their own longings for lust and treachery, their unconfessable fear and hatred of marriage; so, under Hitler, Germans projected upon Jews their own self-hatred and resentment of their demonic leaders, as well as their own most secret erotic impulses—particularly toward children. So adults project upon schoolchildren and adolescents their own denied desire for irresponsibility and sheer dirt; so masters project upon servants their suppressed wish for more disorderly sex lives, less devotion to honor, etc. etc. So, finally, heterosexual males in our society, project upon homosexuals their own unconfessed dream of aping, and competing with, women, of turning the other cheek. But in all of these cases, a one-way psychic transaction is involved; there is no equal and opposite projection possible for females or Jews, children, servants, or homosexuals.

Meanwhile the psychically oppressed flounder in their attempts to come to terms with the burden imposed upon them: the obligation—clearly understood or dimly felt or unwittingly suffered—to act out, in addition to their own authentic roles, secondary ones corresponding to the inner necessities of quite alien others. The culture they share with their oppressors demands duplicity of them; and, like all who lead double lives, they are troubled by anxiety and guilt. To allay this, various strategies are available to them, all aimed at mitigating or destroying the unendurable doubleness of their lives by denying either their authentic selves or their projective roles.

In the first instance, we are dealing with the strategy called by American Negroes "passing": the attempt of the psychically exploited to remake themselves in the image of those who exploit them, to assimilate to those exploiters, or at least to seem to do so. With such an end in view, homosexuals marry and beget children, Jews join the Episcopalian Church, the Irish send their children to finishing schools, and Negroes take out hunting licenses. But "passing" is, alas, impossible for those of the psychically underprivileged who are as clearly distinguishable from the group that imposes its fantasies upon them as, say, women and children; for they cannot, in ordinary course, disguise themselves as males or adults. Indeed, total assimilation is difficult in America even for Negroes and Jews, conventionally identified by certain quasi-mythical physical traits: kinky hair, thick lips, great hooked noses, etc. etc.

Yet there are, of course, businesses and professions which flourish precisely on the basis of attempts to change or conceal such identifying traits: the producers of skin bleaches and hair-straighteners, or those doctors who specialize in bobbing noses. Where names serve as an additional device for segregating the unfavored group, name changing becomes a convention: those with conspicuously non-Anglo-Saxon family names, for instance, applying to the courts for

[119]

others, or at least bestowing on their children given names derived from ancient English castles or more recent English poets. So, in the nineteenth century, women eager to write books rather than appear in them as archetypal characters rechristened themselves as males (usually choosing, for obscure reasons, to call themselves "George"); and so, in the twentieth, Indians eager to be done with reservation restrictions depend on some conveniently French name to make them seem more *Canadien* than redskin. Finally, however, only intermarriage does the trick, actual physical assimilation, though in cultures where inter-racial psychic exploitation still flourishes, the children of such mixed marriages have still to make the choice of "passing" or not. The unions which produce them may, indeed, be motivated by mythical pressures as well as love (the hunger of one partner for what he has cast out of himself onto the people of the other); and choosing between Mother and Father, the children take sides—or are chosen for one side or another before they have a chance—in the most desperate of psychological games.

There is, however, another order of assimilation, a kind of "passing"-once-removed, in which the psychically exploited emulate in the privacy of their own excluded world, and for no eye other than their own, the behavior patterns of their exploiters. It is as if they sought to prove to themselves their absolute immunity to all the impulses and desires projected upon them by those exploiters, as well as demonstrate their complete identity with those who consider them completely other—whether those others ever acknowledge it or not. So, for instance, Jewish boys gather in fraternities and dedicate themselves to athletics, hard drinking, and sex, to make clear that they are by no means the joyless scholars, the bodiless "brains" that Gentile fantasy would make them. So, too, the members of all-Negro P.T.A.'s in more prosperous neighborhoods gather to discuss juvenile delinquency or the threat of comic books—the ladies in fur scarves, the gentlemen in rimless glasses, to prove their lives are as earnest, well-regulated, and gray as that of any white Philistine. So, finally, high school kids, even from

[120]

Indian reservations, gather in jackets and ties at Boys' States and mock U.N. meetings to second motions and pound gavels, as if they never "made out" in parked cars, or wallowed drunkenly on illegitimately bought whisky, or sat with their parents around the bonfires at peyote "picnics."

Such "passing"-once-removed often results in parody rather than genuine emulation: an unconscious parody of the solemn idiocies of the social world of the psychic exploiters, which those exploiters find it easy to take as a joke on the exploited. Certainly, for generations now (up to the recent moment when the N.A.A.C.P. decided to impose its veto on such traditional literary condescension), white American humorists, from Mark Twain to Octavius Roy Cohen and the writers of "Amos and Andy," have delighted in mocking the Negro's attempts to re-enact the mores of white society and white business—not realizing how double-edged the ridiculousness of such travesty in fact is. The most hilarious example of such parody (and, in its undertones, the most bitter) is to be found not in mockery of Negroes, but in Hemingway's account of the exclusive Indian Club, which Yogi Johnson, ill-starred hero of his *The Torrents of Spring*, tries vainly to crash. Yogi is being shown about, near the opening of the scene, by a guide, who has not yet spotted him as white:

> "Our committee room," Red Dog said. On the walls were framed autographed photographs of Chief Bender, Francis Parkman, D. H. Lawrence . . . Jim Thorpe, General Custer . . . Mabel Dodge, and a full-length oil painting of Henry Wadsworth Longfellow.

> Beyond the committee room was a locker room with a small plunge bath or swimming-pool. "It's really ridiculously small for a club," Red Dog said. "But it makes a comfortable little hole to pop into when the evenings are dull." He smiled. "We call it the wigwam, you know. That's a little conceit of my own."

At this point, Yogi is moved to ask to join but is quickly exposed as an impostor trying to pass.

[121]

"I'd have sworn you looked a bit on the white side," Red Dog said. "Damned good thing this came out in time. There'd have been no end of scandal." He put his hand to his head and pursed his lips. "Here, you," he turned suddenly and gripped Yogi by the vest. Yogi felt the barrel of an automatic pistol pushed hard against his stomach. . . .

A second strategy of the oppressed, generally called "Tom-ism" after Harriet Beecher Stowe's much admired and much maligned Uncle Tom, represents a resolve on the part of the underprivileged to be done with doubleness by becoming entirely what it pleases their exploiters to think them, thus abandoning any attempt to establish an authentic identity. So Anglo-Saxon women, for instance, not merely endured but enthusiastically embraced the symbolic virginal role imposed on them by male guilts and fears from the mid-eighteenth to the early twentieth centuries; they not merely read but wrote the books which defined for their fellows such archetypal functions. The scornful term "Tom" has been conventionally used to designate only those willing to turn themselves into the images of humility and forgiveness dreamed by their oppressors; but similar satisfactions are provided by those who agree to become the bogeymen of terror and revenge also dreamed by those oppressors. Uncle Tom and Bigger Thomas, Tom and anti-Tom, are not very different in the end: wooly-haired sniveler and black bully both sacrificing the possibilities of authenticity and full humanity in order to provide "satisfaction and security" for those bound to them by ties of mutual terror. To play the black rapist of D. W. Griffith's *The Birth of a Nation* is as abject a surrender as to play the hero (really an Anglo-Saxon good woman in blackface) of Mrs. Stowe's *Uncle Tom's Cabin.* And precisely such a surrender we see these days in the "beat" young (really bad Negroes in whiteface) who act out the repressed fantasies of their middle-aged parents in a profitless and self-betraying charade.

Indeed, the woman who turns herself into the pale embodiment of virtue, the young man who assumes the role of mother's helper, the pious black advocate of understanding and non-resistance, are likely to seem in the end more disturbingly ambiguous and more truly dangerous to husbands and parents and white segregationists than the dark, passionate vamp, the run-away young rebel-without-a-cause, or the sullen, insolent Negro. For the professional good darky, like the good girl and good boy, the psychic oppressor cannot help suspecting, may be putting him on, pulling his leg; and, indeed, there is a wavering and uncertain boundary between true "Tom-ism" and what homosexuals call "camping": the flagrant exaggeration of characteristics attributed to the excluded minority by unsympathetic insiders —in order to disarm and mock those outsiders.

Who can tell the moment at which the bluff and hearty stage-Irishman, the obsequious and hand-rubbing Jew, the mincing, wrist-flapping fairy, the blond, blue-eyed, dependent girl, the faithful black servitor crying "Yassuh, massah!" cease genuinely trying to become the humble roles in which they have been cast and begin to exploit those roles subversively. A recent book by Elia Kazan, finally published under the title of *America America*, was originally called *The Anatolian Smile*—with reference to the placating, insidious show of teeth common to all those who flaunt before their oppressors the humility demanded of them, yet somehow make it a threat. Such a smile represents a first level of slave-revolt—a psychic counter-attack which presages social and political action, but which can be proved against those who practice it in no court. Thinking of all that smile means, James Baldwin has written to Kazan in praise of his book, "Gadg, baby, you're a nigger, too,"; recognizing that not only the Greeks, like Kazan's forebears, but all the psychically underprivileged, including Negroes, have learned to tread the dangerous line between being "Tom" and playing "Sambo," between, that is to say, genuine self-abasement and self-denial, on the one hand, and the secret freedom of mad, mocking "camp," on the other.

"Camping," however, is an activity less than fully human: a slave's secret revolt that leaves him (even in his own deepest self-consciousness) a slave still; and the joke of composing manifestoes of freedom in code, a language of

[123]

gesture and speech really comprehensible only to the in-group, soon runs out. What final satisfaction is there in Emancipation Proclamations written in *Yiddish*, which the Gentile exploiters cannot read; or of songs of contempt in a jive-talk which the square white masters do not understand? The point is ultimately, of course, to make them understand; and all minorities dream of the day on which they will be able to declare openly their freedom not only from archetype and stereotype, but from the devious strategies with which they have long had to come to terms with their double existence—the day on which they will be able to boast that they have begun to invent themselves.

American Negroes have in fact reached that point during the last decade or two, not only on the level of mass culture and popular propaganda through the political movement which calls itself the Black Muslims, but also in the fiction of Richard Wright, Ralph Ellison, James Baldwin, John Williams, and William Melvin Kelly. It was, however, in a prophetic little story by a white author which first appeared in *Partisan Review for* May-June 1943, in H. J. Kaplan's "The Mohammedans," that the New Negro, the Negro as his own mythologist—comic and terrible at once —entered our literature. And the younger Negro writers who have followed him have not been able to start from scratch but have had to construct their images of themselves on models provided by white writers, European and American—by Faulkner, for instance, or Franz Kafka. Nevertheless, Negroes in the United States are coming to exist at last *in their own minds,* not reflectively but directly, despite the images of Aunt Jemima which beam out at them from the boxes of pancake flour, or the pictures of Little Black Sambo that grin up at them out of children's books.

And this is perhaps why the old ladies of Harlem, however little they may be able to formulate such an idea even to themselves, hail James Baldwin as he walks along the street—quite as if he were a leader in their political struggle like, say, Martin Luther King. But at the moment that he invents himself, the Negro begins to invent the white Amer-

[124]

ican, *his* white American, too; *must*, indeed, invent him out of the scraps he has left over, the human elements he has chosen—painfully or in apparent relief—to discard from his own image. And already there are white Americans who begin to see themselves as "fay" or "o'fay," as everything the Negro thinks them when he names them so in contempt; just as all Negroes once, and many still, thought and think of themselves as "niggers."

One nail, however, has not yet quite driven out the other; for still in our greatest books, and in our deepest imaginations, we find the old archetypal images of Negro and Indian, and we still turn to those images eagerly, though with diminishing psychic returns. What, then, have and do the darker peoples (not only Indians and Negroes, but Polynesians and Orientals, too—even Mediterranean Europeans, who are half-Negroes to the pallid, Anglo-Saxon-Celtic-Scandinavian-Germanic blend that makes up the legendary *Amerikanski*) represent to our paleface majority? Two things chiefly, closely linked but still distinguishable: nature itself, which is to say the romantic's nature—the wilderness, anti-civilization, anti-culture; and the impulsive life—the extra-rational part of the mind, which earlier Americans liked to call "the heart," but which I prefer to call instinct or *libido* or *id*.

Ask any American for his attitude toward Indian and Negro, and you will discover his attitude toward his own impulsive life; or conversely, find how any American deals with his own basic drives, and you can guess his attitudes toward our colored minorities. The man who "whops niggers" or "shoots injuns" is, symbolically, trying to kill the savage in himself, though he may, perhaps must, at the same time lust for dark flesh. Mrs. Stowe, much more acute than anyone ever seems quite to remember, knew all this when she made Simon Legree a son of the Puritans to begin with, and portrayed him as pursuing black females when not tormenting black males. But maybe both, after all, are forms of exorcism congenial to the Puritan mind: whipping and rape—a double assault on the despised natural. There is a curious pessimism in Mrs. Stowe; for though her book may have provided an ideology for abolitionism, it does not really foresee such a solution, but closes just short of any happy ending, even the rescue of Uncle Tom by the white boy who loved him. For her, love comes too late, here on earth at least; and the reconciliation of black and white must be remanded to heaven.

Other Americans have, however, if not quite hoped, at least imagined more; for they have known how much depended upon our making peace with the Indian and Negro, on the symbolic level as well as the literal one; and Thoreau, as we have seen, was one of these. His idyll of Wawatam and Alexander Henry represents first of all, of course, a desire we all share to achieve social peace and a united nation; but on a second level, it stands for our need to come to terms with the wilderness, into which emigrating Europeans were thrown with a rude suddenness which created perhaps the greatest culture shock of human history: the shock out of which our image of ourselves has exploded. And on a third, the deepest, perhaps the ultimate level, it represents the need of men divided against themselves by the heritage of the Puritans (which alone enabled them to survive that culture shock) to join together their sundered selves: the impulsive self identified with the hostile forest and its inhabitants, the moral self identified with the best they had rescued from the Old World and hoped to preserve in the New.

In the very greatest American writers, in Melville, for instance, and Mark Twain, even (despite his embattled political position as a latter-day Southerner) in William Faulkner, we discover the full realization that until the American solves what he calls the "Negro" or "Indian problem," the white American cannot be a whole man. The Emancipation Proclamation we long for is the proclamation of our own emancipation from a genteel rigidity of spirit, the *rigor mortis* of Anglo-Saxon rigidity; and it is in search of this that Ishmael yields himself to Queequeg, Huck embraces Nigger Jim, and the boy of Faulkner's "The Bear" makes himself the foster-son of the half-Indian half-Negro Sam Fathers. Yet none of our greatest writers, however

[126]

idyllic their celebration of the union of white and colored, is without ambivalence. In Twain, typically, the murdering Indian is balanced off against the loving Negro, while in Melville the loving Polynesian is answered by the treacherous black; and in Faulkner the representatives of instinct and nature are sorted out not by tribe or race, but by age: post-menopausal colored women and aging colored men playing saintly or even Christ-like roles, in contrast to young and potent Negroes who are cast as demi-devils.

But this we expect, and, indeed, find everywhere until very recent times, when political liberalism and the cult of the primitive succeed in driving the dark side of our ambivalence deep, deep underground. Traditionally there have been two contradictory attitudes toward nature at work in the American mind, the "Rousseauistic" and the "Puritan," the first, as we have seen, expressed in the dream of Alexander Henry, the second in the nightmare of Hannah Dustan. Not only in our literature but in our lives, we have shuttled back and forth between a romantic nature cult and a Philistine anti-nature religion: on the one hand, becoming enthusiastic advocates of nudism, and the world's warmest supporters of Freudian psychology; on the other, joining movement after movement against whatever pleasures the flesh—alcohol, meat, tobacco, drugs. In fact, we maintain these two polar attitudes not alternately but simultaneously, choosing duplicity rather than compromise; and this, indeed, is the essence of the American way.

Corresponding to each attitude, there is, moreover, a program, a kind of politics which creates divisions more fundamental and real than the purely nominal ones which separate Republicans from Democrats among us. One program urges us to *stamp out nature*: chop down trees, kill off buffalo, slaughter whales, rape and ruin the wilderness, join the Christian Science Church. The second cries in answer, *disappear into nature*: preserve our primitive areas, guard our natural resources, provide summer camping grounds with real live bears, strip to the buff and lie in the sun. And each of these approaches, of course, entails a corollary program in respect to the Negroes and Indians: the first, *stamp out the coloreds*; the second, *blend with them*. In its most extreme form—as in the case of the Indians, for instance, who have always seemed to us economically dispensable—the negative program is simply: *kill them off*, an American version of the Nazis' Final Solution. And certainly there rings deep in the mind of anyone who has ever seen an old-fashioned Western movie, or read an old-fashioned Western story, the folk-saying: "The only good Indian is a dead Indian."

But the advance of civilization quite soon mitigated the naïve program of total suppression with which we began; and *pen them off* replaces *kill them off* as official policy. Especially if there are economic advantages, as with the Negroes, in keeping the underprivileged alive, but, for enlightenment's sake, too, in other cases, it seems preferable to isolate the oppressed in segregated communities, in colonies abroad or ghettos at home, on reservations, in slave quarters or red-light districts. The last has always appeared to us an especially attractive solution. In the West, for instance, the early brothels were stocked largely with Indian girls; and even when the gun-fighters we honor had begun to bring in and protect their white replacements, a longing for more local fare remained. Similarly, the slave quarters on southern plantations were notoriously private brothels for the master and his sons; and a taste for Negro women survived their abolition. To make a woman a whore is like making any human a slave; it denies her identity, even reality (especially in a bourgeois world, where the human is defined almost wholly by the family group), and ends by making her a thing, a device for pleasure.

The ghetto has, then, two purposes: to force upon the ghetto-ized conditions of squalor which seem to verify the grounds of discrimination against them; and to make them if not unreal, at least invisible. We affect surprise at how "invisible" the German concentration camps were to many Germans; but precisely as "invisible" are the Negro ghettos of New York and Chicago to those who never walk that way; for to be thus "invisible" is precisely the point of their existence. And if, in the United States, poverty has in recent years become "invisible," too, this is because it has tended to become more and more exclusively the lot of those already penned off for their skin color or cultural backwardness. But this is the final triumph of Puritanism: to have ghetto-ized the unsuccess it fears as the outward sign of sin, along with the dark-skinned people who symbolize its deepest guilts and fears.

Alongside the Puritan program of annihilation and segregation, however, there has always flourished a sentimental counter-program of conciliation and love. Beside the figure of the Indian killer, there lives in our imagination that of the Indian lover: and if the former is likely to be, like Hannah Dustan, a woman, and the latter, like Alexander Henry, a man, this is because we have always sought to keep distinct the notion of a comradely union (which our deepest mind approves) and miscegenation (which our deepest mind abhors). Though we have continued to tell each other in the schoolroom the tale of the love of Captain John Smith and Pocahontas, we have traditionally distrusted the squaw man, the renegade; and the notion of the woman who goes over to the wigwam has, until recently, stirred on the popular level nothing but horror. In the past, at least, it has been only the dream of a Garden of Eden with two Adams—one colored, one white—and no Eve, that has given us the illusion of "satisfaction and security"; though, as early as the Twenties, Sherwood Anderson and D. H. Lawrence had begun to express overtly an envy of, and a longing for, the presumed superior pleasures of dark-skinned heterosexual love. In the Sixties, the "spade chick" begins, at last, to replace Chingachgook and Nigger Jim as a typical figure of reconciliation in the novels of, say, Jack Kerouac and Robert Gover.

The recent popular success of the latter's *Hundred Dollar Misunderstanding* marks, perhaps, a critical point in the evolving mythology of the Negro in the United States. Certainly few would have predicted, even a year or two ago, best-sellerdom for a book which tries to turn Topsy into the sweetheart of teen-age America by glorifying her as a fourteen-year-old black whore, who understands orgasms

E

and drugs, but despises fast cars, television and war. Gover's is, finally, a false book, motivated less by a desire to tell the truth than by white-self-hatred and self-abnegation (his chief white character is a cartoon version of what the "o-fay" imagines the Negro imagines him). But it is not untypical of a moment in the history of our culture when at a point in the United States as remote from the world in which and for which Gover speaks, a young white Montanan can write and believe, after a night of peyote-eating at the bonfires of the Cheyenne:

> The Indians are colossal downmen (they are too lazy to write). While we have been playing checkers they have been playing give away. As a result they have nothing but poverty, anonymity, happiness, lack of neuroses, wonderful children, and a way of life that is free, democratic and in complete fulfillment of the American dream. . . .

Yet the myth of an earthly paradise for males only has died hard. Not so long ago, in fact, it was for the first time expressed without camouflage or disguise in a popular movie: a film called *The Defiant Ones*, which closes on a scene in which a white fugitive finds peace in the arms of the Negro comrade he has begun by despising, after both of them have been betrayed by an evil white woman. And in Saul Bellow's novel *Henderson the Rain King*, his white hero flees the world of female love to find satisfaction in the company of an affectionate, preternaturally well-read black prince. Not only from the white side, but from within the Negro community, too, come refurbishings of the old myth; as if Thoreau had been right, after all, and the colored men *had* all along dreamed the dream we dreamed he was dreaming: a dream which, with the advance of literacy and the breaking down of segregation, he is finally able to confess in literature. Certainly Thoreau's dream plays a major part in James Baldwin's *Another Country*, in which it is demonstrated that the hatred between black and white, only exacerbated by attempted inter-racial unions of men and women, can in fact be resolved in homosexual love.

[130]

And Baldwin has been nominated, by popular acclaim, a spokesman for his people: his cover portrait on *Time*, and the action shots of him in *Life*, confronting us in doctor's office and barbershop to insist that we are hated one and all—and to hint that our salvation, if it is not already too late, lies in "love."

Even the Indian improbably returns to the American scene, in literature as well as in visions over the bonfires of the Native Church of America. In John Barth's *The Sot Weed Factor*, the legend of Pocahontas is debunked, on the one hand; and, on the other, the legend of red-white male comradeship is tenderly (though comically) revived. Jack Ludwig's *Confusions* contains a character called Flamand, who is an Indian disciple of Thoreau *and* Wilhelm Reich; and in Ken Kesey's *One Flew over the Cuckoo's Nest*, a redheaded Irish-American rebel-bum joins forces with a psychotic Indian giant to defeat "Big Nurse," guardian of the nuthouse to which they have been committed, as well as the biggest-breasted, whitest mama-figure in all American literature. And even Allen Ginsberg, reflecting ironically on the conflict between Red Russia and white America, finds himself turning red man and beginning to speak Saturday-matinee Indian:

> The Russia want to eat us alive . . .
> Her wants to grab Chicago. Her needs a Red Readers' Digest.
>> Her wants our auto plants in Siberia. Him big bureaucracy running our fillingstations.
> That no good. Ugh. Him make Indians learn read . . .

The red man, whose disappearance is symbolically memorialized in Robert Frost's "The Vanishing Red" ("He is said to have been the last Red Man/ In Acton. And the Miller is said to have laughed—/ If you like to call such a sound a laugh."), will not stay vanished, but returns to have his own last laugh.

Yet there is a sense, especially among the very young and those who may have been interested in or disturbed by my attempt to demonstrate this theme in my *Love and Death in the American Novel*, that the myth of two races becoming reconciled in homosexual companionship is no longer quite viable. A reviewer in a little magazine, for instance, has recently cried out against Baldwin's *Another Country*, insisting that: "The trouble lies in Baldwin's mythology. . . . He appeals with Walt Whitman to the open road on which the holy marriage of males (Ishmael and Queequeg in Fiedlerland) is celebrated. But that era is over, and if Baldwin is going to write the social novel he is capable of, he will have to avoid it like a plague." And Jack Ludwig, who has—by way of immunization or as a spell—included the critics, under the name of the Devil, in his novel, makes his critic-Devil warn, "Think what Fiedler will say if you write a scene starring yourself and this red man?"

The dream which began with trapper Henry and flowered into the mid-nineteenth century cult of male friendship seems to many contemporaries too sentimental, or wrongly sentimental—too blandly liberal, perhaps, at any rate too easy, to sustain us now. And in certain of our latest books, in the whole cluster of works, for instance, called "hip" or "beat," we have seen the emergence of a new dream, a new Edenic ideal, pointed toward the future, rather than, as in Thoreau's case, toward the past.

Yet the new dream begins with the old, in fact, presupposes it; but it goes further, for it not only imagines joining with Indian or Negro in pseudo-matrimony, or being adopted by some colored foster-father, but being reborn as Indian or Negro, *becoming the other*. The *locus classicus* of this altered archetype is Norman Mailer's essay "The White Negro," reprinted in his *Advertisements for Myself*. "In such places as Greenwich Vilage," Mailer writes, "a ménage-à-trois was completed—the bohemian and the juvenile delinquent came face-to-face with the Negro, and the hipster was a fact in American life." Mailer is not a notably clear writer, and it seems at first reading as if he were merely talking about yet another sexless union of the races, in which, as he tells us, "marijuana was the wedding ring," and "it was the Negro who brought the cultural dowry," i.e., jazz, "the music of orgasm." But he is trying

[132]

to tell us about something else: about the child born at long last out of that union, about the hipster himself—rebel-without-a-cause, pseudo-psychopath, drug addict, and pursuer of danger; in short, the white Negro.

Here, then, finally is the justification of Thoreau's boast about the friendship he describes, "so almost bare and leafless, yet not blossomless nor fruitless": the strange fruit not of the physical miscegenation so long feared by white supremacists, but of the innocent union of Huck and Jim on the raft. And here, indeed, may be the solution to our deepest guilts and starkest quandary (making possible, without further ado, even physical assimilation, to which not skin color but cultural and psychological differences have always been the real impediments), the resolution we scarcely dared hope for in actual life, however often we imagined it in books. In light of this, it scarcely matters whether the Negro whom the hipster becomes in his imagination ever really existed at all; for it is with the projection of our rejected self which we have called "Negro" that we must be reconciled. Moreover, a new generation of Negroes is presently learning in Greenwich Village, or in Harvard College, to be what the hipster imagines it to be, imitating its would-be imitators. It is the kindest joke our troubled white culture has played on them; and, one hopes, the last.

In any case, the "savage" proposed by Mailer as a model for the hipster is, though he calls him a Negro, quite as much an Indian; which represents a further reach of absurdity, considering that even some forty years ago D. H. Lawrence was already able to say, "The Red Man is dead, disbelieving in us," and that today, certainly, few of his remaining representatives ever penetrate the bohemias of America's big cities. But Lawrence knew, too, that, contrary to folk-belief, even the dead Indian is not a good Indian; quite the contrary. "The moment the last nuclei of Red life break up in America," he wrote, "then the white men will have to reckon with the full force of the demon of the continent." It is not merely that the hipster's beloved marijuana is rather the gift of the Indian through the Negro, than of the Negro himself, but that, as Mailer reports, those

[133]

two imaginary Indians, D. H. Lawrence and Ernest Hemingway, are among his "intellectual antecedents," and that, therefore, he feels himself "a frontiersman in the Wild West of American night life." Somehow it has been necessary for white Americans to be reborn as imaginary Indians before they could become imaginary Negroes; and, indeed, Americans were imaginary Indians from the start, our national destiny beginning when certain New England pale faces, eager to demonstrate they were no longer Europeans, put on feathers and warpaint to celebrate the Boston Tea Party.

From the beginning, there have been in myth, if not in fact, white Indians among us, Crèvecoeur, for instance, asking in his *Letters from an American Farmer*, "By what power does it come to pass that children who have been adopted when young among these people [the Indians] can never be prevailed upon to readopt European manners?"; and crying out in astonishment, "There must be something in their social bond singularly captivating . . . for thousands of Europeans are Indians, and we have no examples of even one of those aborigines having from choice become European. . . ." Even in the movies, Tom Mix and Gary Cooper (spiritual offspring of Natty Bumppo and Chingachgook) preceded Marlon Brando and Elvis Presley (cultural sons of Huckleberry Finn and Nigger Jim). If the frontiersman was a mock Indian, and the Western movie star a mock frontiersman, what is Hemingway but the white Indian twice removed, out of whose union with the imaginary bad Negro, the black rapist of the *Birth of a Nation* recast as a hero, the hipster, or at least Mailer's version of the hipster, has been born?

In our very lives, we have come to repeat this pattern, individual biography recapitulating cultural history. Born theoretically white, we are permitted to pass our childhood as imaginary Indians, our adolescence as imaginary Negroes, and only then are expected to settle down to being what we are told we really are: white once more. Even our whiteness, however, threatens to become imaginary, as the Negroes we have long mythicized begin to mythicize *us*; and

[134]

we think of the embattled whites of the Reconstruction days in the South, attempting to assert counter-myths of themselves against those of their former slaves and the abolitionist ideologues. How comically-pathetically that experiment worked out we cannot forget; intending to appear white knights out of Sir Walter Scott, the imaginary white men of the Ku Klux Klan in fact revealed themselves as the gibbering and sheeted dead, anonymous ghosts of nameless fathers, able to ride only in malice and in the dark. The white Anglo-Saxon Protestant, appalled at such a prospect, has had, as we have seen, the alternative option, in the last couple of decades, of becoming in late youth or early middle-age an imaginary Jew—modeling himself, in accordance with his politics and taste, on Herman Wouk or Leon Uris, Irwin Shaw, Saul Bellow or Bernard Malamud. But that option, too, begins to wear out.

In any case, for a long time now we Americans, white or black, Gentile or Jew (and the rest of the world oddly follows our example, though without the deep impulses which motivate us), have been somehow pleased to see our children, at four or five and ten or twelve, dressed, if not actually like Indians, at least like the frontiersman, the trapper, the cowboy: all those who learned from Indians to dress in the skins of beasts, to carry a weapon, stalk the woods, and present to the world the bronzed, stolid face, the inarticulate hero's gaze common to Sitting Bull and Gary Cooper. Wherever jeans go in the world, and they go everywhere that Coca-Cola goes, the dream of the West goes with them; and wherever that dream goes, the drugs we have learned to use from the Indians follow after. First, of course, came tobacco, carried back with them by the sailors of Columbus, and introduced by Sir Walter Raleigh to the English bohemians of the Age of Elizabeth—wild young Indians, like Christopher Marlowe, who added smoking to atheism and homosexuality to round out their sum of sins. And ever since the series has continued without flagging: marijuana, mescalin, the Mexican mushroom—all moving from tepee to high school or college or young man's "pad," as our youngsters at least begin the shift from a whisky culture to a dope culture; and carrying with them cancer, hallucinations, addiction, madness; the red man's revenge.

But the boy who smokes "tea" is an adolescent, not a child, which is to say, no longer an imaginary Indian but an imaginary Negro; and, indeed, nowadays, it is the black man rather than the red who is likely to have introduced him to the red man's "medicine." But it is not merely a matter of dope, this affinity of the young and the Negro. There is scarcely a father of an adolescent in the United States who is not presently becoming aware (though he may feel it as a pain, rather than know it as a fact) that his son is, in his whole life-style, his speech, his gait, the clothes he wears, the music he loves, as well as the vices he emulates, closer to the life-style of Negroes than *he* could have foreseen on the day of his son's birth. He may find him, in fact, in posture and in gesture, in intonation and inflection, perhaps even in the deepest aspirations, which, after all, control such outward behavior, closer to the great-grandfathers of his Negro friends, or at least to what those great-grandfathers have meant to the white imagination, than to their own great-grandfathers—Anglo-Saxon or Italian, Jewish or Greek, Scandinavian or German, Irish or Slav. It is what we have really longed for from the first, perhaps, what the story of Alexander Henry has all along meant; but we have scarcely begun to acknowledge it to ourselves, much less come to terms with it. And if we are awaiting the artist who will make poetry of the pathos and comedy it entails, we scarcely know this.

Certainly Baldwin has not—in his concern with the Negroes' inability to transcend their hatred of the whites, and his war on the white man's God—been able to notice how rapidly both colored and white are becoming, in the United States, a *tertium quid*, more closely related to white myths of the black man than to the actual lives of either. And even those contemporary white writers who have made a mystique of jazz, "pot," and the Negro life-style have failed to recognize how their own revolt joins them to, rather than separates them from, a majority of the restless young, who may not always know that they chafe against the color of

[136]

their skins, but are most often aware that they hate the school system which is an invention of their paleface ancestors. That school system they reject at the moment when their elders are considering imposing it on all Americans, not for eight or twelve, but for sixteen years; and are busy exporting it to Africa and Asia, to the very heart of the colored world. But who can imagine Huck's Jim or Ishmael's Queequeg or trapper Henry's Wawatam behind a desk?

9

THE WAR AGAINST
THE ACADEMY

Indeed, it is the revolt against school, and in particular against the university, which most clearly distinguishes the generation of the Sixties from those which immediately preceded it. Given the opportunity, that generation prefers (theoretically at least) to go on the road rather than into school; and even, if forced so far, would choose the madhouse over college, prison over the campus. Yet, at the very center of the generations immediately before them, there stands a group of novelists bound together, whatever their social origins, by a common social fate: that is, by a commitment, primary with some of them, secondary with others, to the university. Among distinguished recent American writers of fiction who have taught, or are teaching, in universities are Saul Bellow, Isaac Rosenfeld, Bernard Malamud, Philip Roth, Mary McCarthy, Randall Jarrell, John Hawkes, John Barth, Wright Morris, Walter Van Tilburg Clark, Robert Penn Warren, Peter Taylor, Robie Macauley, Herbert Gold, Lionel Trilling, Vladimir Nabokov, and a host of others.

As a matter of fact, its role as teacher in the university may seem in the long run the truly distinguishing characteristic of the generation of the Forties-Fifties, more critical even than its urban origins, or the particular flavor lent it by the Jewish writers who constitute so large a part of it. Naturally, the writers of that generation have distilled out of their experience a kind of fiction new at least in theme, a sub-genre of the novel which treats the academic community as a microcosm reflecting the great world, an adequate symbol of our total society. The college novel is a form as clearly defined for us as the historical romance or the tale of terror; and, indeed, it usually *is* a tale of terror, with appropriate comic overtones. In this respect, it resembles the war novel of the Twenties, and especially the Hollywood novel of the Thirties: that other product of the American writer's dream of finding a job not wholly at odds with what he is driven to do, whether it pays or not. The encounter between such a dream and reality is bound to eventuate in a catastrophe at once comic and horrible, a pratfall from which the comedian does not rise again; and models for such pratfalls are provided in Fitzgerald's unfinished *The Last Tycoon*, as well as Nathanael West's *The Day of the Locust*.

Fitzgerald's book provides, in addition, suggestions for introducing into such new versions of Gothic Burlesque, elements of the class struggle. And, indeed, the college—or more properly, anti-college—novel of the Forties-Fifties is distinguished from earlier American books with academic settings by its quasi-Marxian or Popular Front view of the relationship between professors and administrators. As early as Hawthorne's *Fanshawe*, there had been novels in which college-educated authors returned in imagination to the scenes of their youth; but unlike *Fanshawe*, and the scores of middlebrow entertainments with campus settings which followed, from *Fair Harvard* to *Stover at Yale*, or even such works of serious novelists as Fitzgerald's *The Beautiful and and the Damned* and Faulkner's *Sanctuary*, recent academic novels deal primarily with professors rather than students. When students enter at all, they enter briefly to seduce, or be seduced by, their teachers, thus providing erotic relief from the struggle of faculty and administrative officers at the barricades. In this light, George Stewart's *Doctor's Oral* seems a transitional book, representing, as it were, the American author in the process of getting his Ph.D., and thus graduating from the distillation of undergraduate reminiscence to the dispensing of post-graduate gossip.

[139]

Yet despite the large number of talented writers who have taught in college and have been willing to tell the tale (Robert Penn Warren, Randall Jarrell, Mary McCarthy, Bernard Malamud, Howard Nemerov, and Robie Macauley come to mind), we do not yet have a college novel to compare with West's account of the artist in Hollywood or with Hemingway's of the writer at war; perhaps because, in the university, tragedy tends to be reduced to the pathetic, and the comic to stir a titter rather than a belly-laugh. Or perhaps it is the incestuous nature of the academic novel, the apparently irresistible temptation implicit in it that makes its practitioners abandon their administrator villains in favor of writing about those most like them in the university. Randall Jarrell's *Pictures from an Institution* typifies the genre, being a book about a writer writing a book about a college; and beyond it we imagine a counter-counter-novel about a writer writing about a writer writing about a writer in the academy.*

Or perhaps the failure of the anti-college novel has to be explained on the grounds that failure is its very subject, and that its authors typically cannot maintain enough distance between their protagonists and themselves to keep the inadequacies of the former from seeming their own. As accounts of the writer's continuing doomed battle with the establishment in its manifold forms, latter-day academic novels tend to fall into self-pity or self-exculpation, since they are inevitably histories of defeat, a defeat which the institution the writer berates may consider his, but which he asserts (without final conviction) is the institution's. In any case, the feelings which motivate such books are primarily frustration and impotent rage—secondarily the desire to strike back and be revenged by making a last-

* Most recently Jack Ludwig has witten, in *Confusions*, a college novel intended to end all college novels. At least his protagonist, contemplating one of his own (surely the one in which he appears), attempts to make a pact with the Devil to help him achieve so improbable an end. "Devil, tell me," he says, "if I merge with you will you guarantee . . . That this book will kill off, once and for all, the Jewish novel *and* the campus novel?" To which the Devil answers, "What, what? Should I bargain away my primary vehicles?"

minute success out of failure, i.e., a best-selling or critically acclaimed novel. And precisely such successes wrested from such failures have been achieved in books which present the writer's case against the army, or even Hollywood.

Why not then in the anti-college novel? Is it because such novels are often too circumstantial, too much *romans à clef*, or personal justifications, ripped unaltered from the diary, or directly transcribed from the complaint to the American Association of University Professors? But once more, precisely such undisguised apologies have survived the occasions they bewailed, and outlived the friends and enemies they travestied or praised, Hemingway's *The Sun Also Rises*, for instance, or Henry Miller's *Tropic of Cancer*—so why not academic novels, too? Is it simply that no one has ever succeeded in making typical university events seem at once as banal and surreal as they actually are? Most college novels are, in fact, not nearly grotesque enough for their subjects, and end up seeming not the descents into hell their authors had surely intended, on one level or another, but merely descriptions of obstacle courses devised by minds more apt at tedium than terror. They are, that is to say, hopelessly middlebrow, muted where they pretend to be moderate, melodramatic where they pretend to be tragic, commonplace where they pretend to be wise. And this is, surely, their essential flaw, the clue to why they inevitably end by falling into the very attitudes they begin by satirizing. Certainly most of them seem not so much transcendent explorations of the failures of institutions of higher learning as depressing symptoms of the way in which such institutions subserve the flight from excellence and the parody of high art represented by the triumph of midculture in our lives.

Some literary forms appear to be born middlebrow, while others have to be radically debased to suit middlebrow ends; and the college novel, like, say, the earnest exposé of advertising in such sub-novels as *The Big Ball of Wax*, or attacks in satirical science fiction on organized religion, is an innately vulgar form. Certainly two of its major themes which we have already noticed—the teacher as liberal and innocent victim of social repression, and the teacher as lecher and guilty seducer of the young—belong respectively to the stock subjects of sentimental, popular-front politics and to garden-variety pornography. Both of these demand cliché rather than truth, since their end is titillation rather than insight; and both are hard to avoid, since they are as old, or older than, the form itself.

Long before the kind of college had been invented to which the writer can come to be disillusioned, the archetypal story of Abelard and Héloïse had been adapted to novel form by Jean-Jacques Rousseau in his *Julie, or the New Eloise;* and the notion of the teacher burning with lust behind his pretense to detached wisdom has continued to excite the popular imagination on levels progressively more and more debased. The truth is, of course, that the relationship of teacher and taught is a passionate one in essence, though no official theory of education has taken this into account since the collapse of the Greek synthesis of pedagogy, gymnastics and pederasty expounded in Plato's *Symposium*. But middlebrow writers have never forgotten it, taking advantage of relaxing taboos to make more and more explicit the aura of sex which the mass mind connects not only with teachers but with coeds as well, even when quite unencouraged.

Lowbrow fantasy has always conceived of college as a place where atheism and communism are taught, while middlebrow liberalism has thought of it rather as one where those two challenges to orthodoxy are persecuted; but both have agreed that within its walls good girls are likely to be deflowered by their mentors as well as their fellow students. And the writers of college novels have done much to sustain this view. Herbert Kubly's recent *The Whistling Zone* is a case in point, not only describing a pair of professorial love affairs and an academic cuckolding, but culminating in a campus orgy dripping with more sperm than has flowed in any American book since *Moby Dick;* but Kubly intersperses his sex with pious exhortations to political tolerance, and righteous sermons about freedom in the classroom. More sophisticated, and consequently more frankly pornographic, though not without some satirical intent, is the

[142]

account of the adventures of a particularly luscious college girl (saved from her lubricious teacher only by the intervention of a boy lover of that teacher) in "Maxwell Kenton's" *Lollipop,* one of the latest books to have passed from a first publication by the Olympia Press, which launched *The Ginger Man* and *Lolita,* to the list of a respectable American publishing firm.

If, however, the relationship of teacher to student in the university is unconfessedly passionate, his relationship to the administration is avowedly political; and since the time of Senator McCarthy, at least, has been seen in the light of the middlebrow liberals' defense against all attacks on the intellectuals' flirtation with communism. For serious writers, however, the mass of obtuse clichés associated with that defense have seemed as formidable an obstacle to art and truth as those which have grown up around campus love life; and they have sought to redeem the former, as they have the latter, by ambiguity and parody and inversion. Their models in this regard have been Nathanael West's *A Cool Million,* which attempted to rescue Horatio Alger for literature by standing him on his head, and Saul Bellow's *The Victim,* which succeeded in refurbishing the liberal-sentimental novel about anti-Semitism by dissolving into ambiguity the relationship which joins anti-Semite and Jew.

So more ambitious and subtle novelists have tried to free the academic novel from the limitations of erotic reverie and ritualistic liberalism, by making, on the one hand, a sexual victim rather than an aggressor of the professor, and, on the other, by turning him from the guileless butt of reaction into a disingenuous exploiter of the clichés of the politically enlightened. Quite early on, Faulkner had portrayed Temple Drake, the University of Mississippi student in *Sanctuary,* as more seduced than seducing, but no teachers were numbered among her prey; and not until Robie Macauley's *The Disguises of Love* was there a detailed, self-conscious study of the seduction of a professor by a coed, in that ironic mode which we are likely to associate these days with Nabokov's *Lolita.* So extraordinary, however, did this pursuit appear at first to one critic, conditioned by conventional notions of who pursues whom in the classroom, that he accused Macauley of having fallen back on what that critic called the "Albertine strategy," of having, like Proust, presented a really homosexual relationship in the guise of a heterosexual one.

In an analogous way, Mary McCarthy's *The Groves of Academe* parodies the political platitudes of the academic world by portraying a grossly inefficient professor, a monster of self-pity and self-adulation, who hangs on to his job by pretending to have been a communist—thus becoming the beneficiary of the stereotype propagated by a hundred middlebrow novels and ten thousand middlebrow tracts proving that a commitment to the radical movement (at the proper moment, of course) was the noblest of human errors. *The Groves of Academe* is a witty and satisfying book; but it is essentially a parasitic one, its satisfactions, like those of parody always, depending on a knowledge of, and contempt for, the kind of literature which it inverts and mocks. Finally, that is to say, it does not transcend its occasion, though in its failure it provides many more incidental pleasures than most books of the genre to which it belongs. In no case, at any rate, has a fictional work of independent power and enduring appeal been created against the drag toward middlebrow banality that besets even the most wary writer of academic fiction.

Nevertheless, we keep trying. The number of academic novels turned out in the Forties and Fifties exceeds many times over the number of Hollywood novels produced in the Thirties, in part because the professor, and even the administrator, is driven to turn writer in emulation of the writer turned professor (think of Carlos Baker, one-time chairman of the Princeton English Department and then anti-academic novelist, or of Stringfellow Barr, first president of St. John's at Annapolis and then author of *Purely Academic*), in part because so many writers have sought the numerous college posts opening wholesale in a time of academic expansion. Is it an accident that Hollywood shrinks as the academy grows, or is it an essential part of the comedy of our cultural life? Driven from one kind of cover, the writer seeks another, the ironic prayer of Melville always on his lips, "Oh time! Oh cash! Oh patience!"

In any case, we must be careful to understand the precise nature of the joke which the community plays on the professor-author at the moment he believes he is playing a joke on it; and to understand this, we must disabuse ourselves of all conventional notions of the "academic" writer and the kind of "academy" he inhabits, particularly those sponsored by Europeans. The American writer who teaches in a university and lives in a college town necessarily inhabits neither a cultural center nor an "ivory tower." Rather than being protected from the bourgeois world, he is plunged into it, immersed in its small politics and petty spites, its institutionalized hypocrisy, its self-righteous timidity, and its endless bureaucratic ineptitude. If it is a refuge from the pressures of real life he is after, he can find that more easily in the artificial paradises of North Beach or Greenwich Village; the world he inhabits may be artificial, too, but it is likely to be a small artificial hell, in which not only the demons who torment him (i.e., deans and administrators) but even his fellow damned are likely to be members of the local Rotary Club.

It must be remembered that the presence of the intellectual in an American university community is bound to be an anomalous one, even when he is a full-fledged Ph.D., but more especially when he is a writer-in-residence without the customary academic degrees. His appointment is likely to represent (quite like the Hollywood producer's quest for big-name writers) the tribute middlebrow vice pays to highbrow virtue, a tribute inevitably withdrawn when cultural shame feelings yield to hostility and suspicion. And, after all, this is fair enough, for the writer is likely to regard his non-writing colleagues with a certain amount of genial contempt, based on his sneaking conviction that all their differences are to his advantage. The difficulty of his position is compounded in cases where he is not merely an intellectual among anti-intellectuals, but also, say, a Jew among Gentiles, an Easterner among Westerners, a radical among conservatives, a European refugee among the native-born, or simply an urban type among defensive provincials.

Two recent attempts to deal with the tragi-comedy involved in such situations (though in each a tribute has also been paid to the standard middlebrow problems of sex and politics) are Bernard Malamud's *A New Life* and Vladimir Nabokov's *Pale Fire*: the former, Malamud's valedictory to one college he was about to leave for another; the latter, Nabokov's farewell to teaching. But there is no way out for the teacher-writer in the end. Even when he has exchanged a less sympathetic set of colleagues for a more amiable one, or has fled all academic colleagues forever, he hears still his own hectoring voice demanding: *Why were you there to begin with? What on earth did you think you were after?* And this voice is not really appeased by the answer: *I went to make a book, to turn the very experience in question into art—like Mary McCarthy in* The Groves of Academe *or Randall Jarrell in* Pictures *from an Institution, or John Barth in* The End of the Road; *to show how funny it all is, to make clear the joke on everyone, including myself.* To which the first voice answers: *Not funny enough!*

Indeed, there have been some who have found the whole adventure, the entry of the free intellectual into the university, and his future there, not funny at all; but most of these have feared self-pity and have camouflaged their pathos with quips and funny sayings (like Malamud and Barth and Nabokov), though a few have tried to reveal the naked horror behind the superficial humor. The suicide of F. O. Matthiessen, late professor at Harvard and author of that astonishingly non-academic critical work, *The American Renaissance*, has twice over tempted novelists to try their hands (more successfully in May Sarton's *Faithful Are the Wounds*) at academic tragedies in which his self-destruction and the betrayals that presumably prompted it are made parables of the intellectual's defeat in the university. Unfortunately, in America no fictionist with the gifts and sensitivity of the Italian Cesare Pavese has been moved as Pavese was moved by the death of Matthiessen; and for Pavese no possible novel seemed an adequate response to his feelings about that death. What followed for him was his own suicide—cued, doubtlessly, by many other things beside the example of the American critic he loved, though his suicide note was, like Matthiessen's, the quotation from Shakespeare that had been underlined for them both by Herman Melville: *We must endure our going hence even as our coming hither. The ripeness is all.*

For a younger generation of Americans and their spokesmen, however, those who represent the final horror of academic life are not the defeated intellectuals who fled the campus or died on it, but those who have adapted to the demands of the university and stayed in the classroom— most usually to teach literature, and, presumably, to write novels on the side. The viewpoint of the latest generation is not, in any case, that of the professor, licked or victorious, but that of a bright and skeptical student looking *at* the professor, particularly at the kind of professor who, for over two decades now, has helped create the new academic novel. Sometimes, as in William Goldman's *The Temple of Gold*, the eye that looks and the voice that speaks belong to an actual child of the university, a professor's son, whose values, unlike his father's, are derived from popular culture rather than the classics, from the screen version of *Gunga Din* rather than the plays of Euripides.

More usually they are the voice and eye of a sensitive freshman, unattached to the academy except by wavering choice; and what he sees or hears is rendered by some recent college graduate or by one moved in sympathy and love to emulate the undergraduate role, as Salinger is moved to play Franny in the story called by her name. But here is Franny's version of the "section man," the kind of young teacher, proud, as she does not even trouble to note, of his difference from the old-fashioned scholars who taught him, and of his intimate knowledge of recent or currently prized books, and likely, as she has no way of knowing, to end by writing a conventional anti-academic novel.

. . . where *I* come from, a section man's a person that takes over a class when the professor isn't there or is busy having a nervous breakdown or is at the dentist or something. He's usually a graduate student or something. Anyway, if it's a course in Russian Literature, say, he comes in, in his little button-down-collar shirt and striped tie, and starts knocking Turgenev for about a half hour. Then, when he's finished, when he's completely *ruined* Turgenev for you, he starts talking about Stendhal or somebody he wrote his M.A. on. Where I go, the English Department has about ten little section men running around ruining things for people, and they're all so brilliant they can hardly open their mouths . . .

Only Lionel Trilling has attempted to treat a similar situation from the teacher's, which is to say the adult, point of view, though there is an anticipation of such an approach —much confused by overtones of anti-Semitism—in the section of Thomas Wolfe's *Of Time and the River* which deals with his relationship at N.Y.U. with an undergraduate whom he calls Abe Jones. Trilling, more sure of what he is after, has made of his attempt his only wholly successful piece of fiction, the short story "Of This Time, of That Place," which has won an extraordinary kind of fame for so brief a work. Indeed, a recently inaugurated television series based on campus life has as its hero a young instructor, called Joseph Howe after the protagonist of Trilling's story, though the actual shows since the pilot program, which was an adaptation of that story, have had nothing to do with Trilling's vision or the actual plight of the universities. Worthy of much better treatment, Trilling's story invites, by virtue of its subject matter, middlebrow degradation and dilution, despite the fact that it first appeared in the almost archetypically highbrow pages of *Partisan Review*.

And how much more easily is the fiction of Salinger assimilated to the same level; for his earlier stories appeared in *Good Housekeeping, Colliers*, and *The Saturday Evening Post* while, at the height of his career, he has been content to write for the kind of reader to whom the *New Yorker* represents ultimate sophistication. Yet even if the young for whom Salinger means most come out of the social circles to which the readers of the *New Yorker* aspire when they do not belong, this does not make them unrepresentative, nor the stories which appeal to them untypical. His audience consists, it is true, of the cleanest, politest, best dressed, best fed, and best read among the disaffected youth—and his protagonists reflect (or explain) that fact. Not junkies or faggots, nor even upper bohemians, his chief characters travel a road which leads from home to school and from school either back home again or to the nuthouse, or both. They have families and teachers and psychiatrists rather than lovers or friends; and their crises are likely to be defined in terms of whether or not to go back for the second semester to Vassar or Princeton, Dana Hall or St. Mark's. Their *angst* is improbably motivated by such questions as: "Does my date for the Harvard weekend *really* understand what poetry is?" or "Is it possible that my English instructor hates literature after all?"

I do not mean by reduction to mock the concerns of Salinger's characters; they cannot in any case be reduced, and I should only mock myself making fun of them. For better or worse, a significant number of young Americans live in a world where politics is meaningless, words in the newspaper repeated by the solemn old; and sex unreal—a threat or a promise, a compulsion or a curse, but never a pleasure; and in that world, the classroom and the football game provide adequate arenas for anguish and joy, both to the dull majority who go to them, and to the more sensitive minority who stay away from them. To that world, at any rate, Salinger has been more faithful than it perhaps deserves; more faithful than one would have expected of a writer who, far from remaining in it, with whatever ambivalence, like Trilling, for example, was busted out of it for good early in his college career. For this reason, Salinger, unaffiliated as he is, must be understood as an academic novelist, though one fixed forever in the student's stance at the point he had reached when he flunked out; and in this regard, he resembles such other notable flunkees, returning forever in the imagination to the sophomore year they never quite attained, as Faulkner and Fitzgerald.

If Faulkner's Temple Drake stands as the classic coed of the Twenties, the Franny of Salinger's Glass stories bids to become her equivalent for the Fifties, her only rival Denise, the young lady in search of an orgasm who shuttles back and forth among T. S. Eliot, her psychoanalyst, and two lovers in Norman Mailer's short story, "The Time of Her Time." Mailer's story preserves much of the brutal impact of Faulkner's novel; and if there is a decline in terror and intensity in Salinger's, this is not only because of the markets for which he writes, but also because he is more faithful to the general experience of the middleclass young in our cushy times. Not the orgasm, as Mailer would theoretically insist, but madness, as Salinger instinctively knows, what politer circles call a "nervous breakdown," is the fatal Cleopatra of the young; for they are fighting now new enemies in new wars, not the Anthony Comstocks with whose ghost Mailer still jousts, but precisely the most enlightened of their elders. And this, of course, those elders find harder to understand in direct proportion to their enlightenment. Indeed, the females among them, earnest readers of the *New Yorker* one and all, revealed the depth of their incomprehension, when "Franny" first appeared in that magazine, by interpreting her collapse in the face of impending insanity as a symptom of pregnancy.

The revolt they remember, and are braced to understand and forgive in the young (as their parents did *not* understand and forgive it in them), is the sexual revolt, the attack on vestigial Puritanism and obsolescent chivalry which had set Temple in motion and had led her to take up the weapons of booze and promiscuity and getting away from home to college. But Franny's is a revolt against literature and the New Criticism, and her weapons are the "Jesus prayer" and the quick retreat from school to home. Certainly this is fair enough, for in the thirty years that separate the two coeds, the culture religion of western Europe has replaced Christianity as the orthodox faith of those most eager to send their children to college, at least if they are urban, middleclass Americans; and the pastors to whom our

[150]

hungry sheep look up in vain are not ministers of the old-time religion, but Ph.D.'s in literature and those section men who serve as their acolytes. In a society presided over by this new clergy, to play with Vedanta or Buddhism, or even Christian orthodoxy, except as reflected in certain poetic texts like Eliot's *Four Quartets*, i.e., to seek a salvation beyond the reach of art, is considered heresy or insanity, or some particularly blasphemous compound of both, for which the recommended cure is psychiatry.

Franny, at any rate, who will not write the proper critical papers or go out for the next college play, seems, not only to her elders and her more submissive peers, but even to herself, a heretic guilty as charged and therefore self-condemned to a "nervous breakdown." Certainly, she enters the scene in which Salinger asks us to be interested as an academic "drop-out": one of that group of quiet protesters who adapted passive resistance to American conditions long before it was taken up by CORE, and who have managed to shake our society—or at least to impress it to a point where the President himself had begun to set up committees to study the problem. Certainly the suggestion that college has failed our young men and women stirs in us feelings of guilt and confusion. The specter that haunts a world, secure economically, but culturally uncertain to the point of panic, is precisely this threat; and Franny, in her own way, embodies it.

Despite her final submission to that unspeakably false *guru*, her brother Buddy, with his pop-culture dogma that "Christ is the Fat Lady," she remains a sister in rebellion, a fellow traveler, at least, to Ferdinand R. Tertan of Trilling's "Of This Time, of That Place," the student always right in his literary judgments, of whom his poet-instructor is nonetheless forced to decide: "Oh, the boy was mad. And suddenly the word, used in hyperbole, intended almost for the expression of exasperated admiration, became literal . . ." Yet that instructor must finally prefer, at the same time he must inevitably betray, Tertan's madness to the sanity of his "well-adjusted" and "well-rounded" classmate, bound for success in the same world in which the instructor seeks to be recognized, though the latter will publish poetry, while the former sells insurance or real estate.

Interestingly enough, Tertan was modeled in part, at least, on a leading member of the generation of the "beats," who had turned up in Trilling's own classes and has survived to tell much of his own story, though he has never treated his college years in any detail. Such self-conscious devotees of un-reason, to whom the phrase "to flip," i.e., to go out of one's head, represents a supreme achievement, do not ordinarily write about classroom experience, for they are likely to be well out of it, and immune to nostalgia, before they have begun to define themselves. It is their teachers, therefore, loved for having, with whatever doubts, protected the right of others to "flip," but despised for not having dared cross that frontier themselves, for having preferred academic security to insanity, who must write the record as best they can. Such teachers can, moreover, in baffled affection and unconscious desire for revenge, invite their madder students back to the campus to lecture or read from their works; but it does not really help, for such occasions are likely to end in frustration and scandal. In any case, even after we have seen him in an academic auditorium, we cannot imagine Jack Kerouac, for instance, in any relationship to the college community except one of mockery and evasion; and the brief valedictory of Allen Ginsberg's *Howl* remains in the mind ("who passed through the universities with radiant cool eyes hallucinating Arkansas and Blake-light tragedy among the scholars of war, who were expelled from the academies for crazy & publishing obscene odes on the windows of the skull . . ."), no matter how often he has returned since to read it to undergraduates in scheduled class meetings.

We have come full circle to the Twenties and the attitudes of Ernest Hemingway: the centrifugal young, once more running away from school to strange lands, if not to strange wars, in search of salvation, instead of the centripetal young going to school to sit at the feet of the writer-in-residence. And the former is, alas, the more typical American way. Though enormous numbers of novelists and poets are still sustained by the colleges and still make themselves visible there to the less enlightened young who seek them still, we begin to feel that we have reached the end of an era; begin to see that it was perhaps only a single generation which tried, against the grain of our tradition, to bring about a marriage of literature, at its freest and most advanced, with the university.

Yet it was not an utterly ignoble dream, this hope of compromising yet another of the polarities that have disrupted American life, and the generation of the Forties and Fifties could not have foreseen how soon it would be disavowed. Certainly that generation continues to consider naïve and ignorant the contempt for the professor so rampant in the Twenties (and so attractive once more in the Sixties); just as that generation tends still to despise the cult of raw experience, which usually accompanies such contempt, and which has for so long helped keep American literature callow and immature. It was not just in search of security (which in any event they did not find) that the children of the Depression turned to the colleges, but also in pursuit of the long-delayed adulthood of American culture, and of a kind of independence never possible in bohemias.

Isolated in small academic communities hundreds of miles apart, seeing each other rarely at brief, ritual, and often drunken gatherings, it was possible for writers in colleges to remain lonely eccentrics, protected from each other by precisely the lonely crowd which surrounded and despised them.

Finally, the most terrible threat to the freedom of the writer is the chumminess engendered by the ghetto life of bohemian refuges, the rubbing up against each other of flocks or schools with common dogmas, easily represented or travestied in the popular press. Early or late in their careers, it has been in universities that such anti-flock writers as Walter Van Tilburg Clark, Wright Morris, John Hawkes, and John Barth have found sustenance and protection; and if Barth seems at the moment the most promising novelist of those now in the neighborhood of thirty, it is because he has, like the generation before his, found in the provincial college that vacuum which nature abhors and art loves.

With the publication of *The Sot Weed Factor*, his third novel, which begins in English academia and ends in the American wilderness, Barth has passed from seeming merely the most promising of a new generation to seeming the best, the most achieved. But the very disciplined intelligence, which, along with his wild invention and outrageous wit, constitutes his strength, isolates him from his contemporaries. To be a trained philosopher in a time of required misology is, like being neither Negro nor Jew in a time of required ethnic roots, to be isolated, indeed. But where, really, is the new center against which such a new eccentric as Barth defines himself? What are the essential experiences that influence the generation of the Sixties, besides the lust for madness and the aversion to school? What public events, for instance, move them as the generation of the Forties-Fifties was moved by the Depression and the war in Spain, and that of the Twenties by the first great prosperity and World War I?

10

THE ALTERATION
OF CONSCIOUSNESS

Though some members of the latest generation are old enough to have lived through the Korean War, this oddly peripheral conflict still remains as non-existent for them as for the American imagination in general. The one notable attempt at portraying it seriously, Francis Pollini's *Night*, has been published abroad by a press accustomed to printing banned books, and hence has had a small atypical circulation. Richard Condon's *The Manchurian Candidate*, on the other hand, a middlebrow rendition of similar themes, has found its appropriate reward in a movie version which compounded all its falsities, and turned its hero into Frank Sinatra, who, whatever his talents, is able somehow to play only himself, a figure sufficient unto an age when popular entertainment is linked not merely, as it has been always, to the underworld, but also to the culture-hungry world of upper-middlebrow politics symbolized by the wives of the Kennedy regime. Symptomatically enough, both books are less concerned with combat than with the undermining of conscious ego ideals, that deliberate alteration of morality and allegiance which the press calls "brain-washing." In this sense, they are more closely related to political-psychological novels like Arthur Koestler's *Darkness at Noon* than to the genre practiced all the way from *The Red Badge of Courage* to *The Naked and the Dead*. Perhaps the last war novels are being written out of the aftermath of World War II, since World War III, in anticipation at least, breeds only science fiction.

Yet for most of the younger writers today, the only war that *counts* is World War III, the war that does not happen, may indeed never happen, but which remains all the same the war for which they long, as all generations long for the *Götterdämmerung* they most fear. To be sure, they have the Bomb that *does* happen with sufficient frequency, though in their time only for the purposes of drill and deterrence. Yet they are shaken by the tests in which no one dies, as the earlier generations, which lived through the invention of the Bomb and its dropping on Hiroshima, oddly are not; and they read eagerly the reports on rising radiation in milk to assure themselves that their terrors are less symbolic than real.

More disturbingly than the Cold War or the Bomb, the Great Prosperity, which most of them endure willy-nilly, touches the imaginations of the new young. Against that prosperity they cannot protest, or even pretend that lacking it they would not have prayed it for themselves. Unlike their less honorable and more furtive desires (for violence and the destruction of all they have not made), this cannot be concealed from their conscious selves; and the young men of the Sixties know that even when they dream of choosing poverty, they dream of seeking a state costing someone (usually their absentee parents) somewhere in the neighborhood of three or four thousand dollars a year, i.e., a sum equal to that demanded for fairly comfortable living in the years of the depression.

And where can they flee except from one suburb to another, from the kind of suburb where the show of well-being is demanded to one where (in the decaying heart of an old city, or close by a great university) the semblance of indigence is *de rigueur*? They can, to be sure, move from city to country, from country to city, from small town to large, or large to small; but what does such shuffling about mean? The America they inhabit is a society where country and city, small town and large, melt into indistinguishable hyper-urban agglomerations, sharing a vulgar, gray, standardized sub-culture; and when they flee America, they court disappointment.

Any one of three major illusions may have induced their flight. The first is simply the very American desire to escape America and other Americans, when the one has come to seem a travesty of its own dream, and the others caricatures created by those who hate them most. The second is an equally American tendency to confuse some particular place with an imagined Utopia. And the third is the identical hunger for an absolute freedom which brought the first Americans across the Atlantic and sent later generations trekking West after what, after all, can only be sought but never found. All three impulses obviously are self-defeating, as well as authentically American and more than a little naïve; and the young these days are born knowing that fact, as even James and Eliot and Pound did not.

No more than the trapper or the cowboy can the American artist escape his countrymen. As the national park springs up in the footsteps of the cowboy, the Hilton Hotel rises on the heels of the artist. There is no use in the highbrow seeking in the Sixties a Europe the tours have not yet reached. His fellow-countrymen will scent him out; and the middlebrow hounds run fast and true. Let him leave Athens for Mykonos, Mykonos for Skyros; sooner or later the hordes will follow. Let him leave Naples for Capri, Capri for Ischia; busloads of uncomfortable worshipers at the shrines of culture will track him down. Americans cannot leave their artists alone, but having presumably driven them into exile, insist on following them there.

Similarly, in the long run, they incline to ape the opinions of the avant-garde, which in the short run they have despised. Let the wary highbrow try to assert his independence by despising the Parthenon in favor of the Erechtheum in Athens, by preferring the San Clemente to St. Peter's in Rome, or the Sant' Ambrogio to the Cathedral in Milan—the next generation of middlebrows will be taught his preferences by *Time* magazine, and the generation after by its guidebooks. And in the meanwhile, the Europe which the highbrow prefers to the America he remembers is

[157]

remaking itself as fast as it can in the image of that America. The comics, picture magazines, electric refrigerators, bad American movies, and television await him everywhere. For it is true that the Riviera becomes Miami Beach, true that most Europeans *want* it Miami Beach. For transatlantic middlebrows and lowbrows, this is the next best thing to the emigration which has been denied them.

How, then, can the intellectual-artist-highbrow continue to believe Paris or Rome or Athens to be the earthly embodiment of the invisible Republic of Letters, the long-lost spiritual homeland to which he owes an allegiance beyond the patriotism demanded of him by an America which nurtured his body but starved his spirit? The portable radio held by the European beside him plays Frank Sinatra or Elvis Presley; the girl who, bending to tie her sandal, looks like the stone statue of Nike in a similar pose, chews gum, and dances the twist. There is no Utopia made of stone and wood, only a shabby world moving toward mass industry and mass culture—only a score of pseudo-Americas whose various pasts blend into a dismaying future.

All the same, there are various possibilities open to the writer who aspires to exile. The first is to deceive himself more or less deliberately, even as his middlebrow parents at home deceive themselves, though about another country: to make his slogan, "My non-country, right or wrong!"; and to refuse, for instance, to be vaccinated when leaving the United States, on the grounds that there is no smallpox in Greece or Turkey or France, only in America, to which he is determined never to return!

A second possibility is to move beyond Europe to ever more remote and alien lands. Even now, one sees in Athens and Instanbul the highbrow hordes, bearded and sandaled like traditional pilgrims, and bearing the holy books of William Burroughs to countries whose chief industries have always been mysticism and the "alteration of consciousness." They have thus reached the borders of Europe in their quest, and beyond the marches of Greece and Turkey the way lies open to the Orient, to India and on to Japan. It is Japan, of course, which has already become the

[158]

favorite meta-European haven of the highbrow. But Japan is, alas, precisely the most American country in the Far East. Since 1860, it has been available to our ships and our imaginations; and we are linked to it by Lafcadio Hearn, *Madame Butterfly*, and hundreds of *haiku* produced at the turn of the century by genteel New England ladies. Even the atom bomb beat the first large wave of expatriates to Japan; and, indeed, both they and the bomb represent aspects of a continuing chain reaction: extensions of the Americanization more mildly begun by Deanna Durbin and Gary Cooper movies. How is it possible ever to forget the images of the new Hiroshima out of Alain Resnais' *Hiroshima Mon Amour*, its portrayal of the atrocity after the final atrocity—as Coney Island rises on the ruins we have made, a parody of America out of the cold cinders?

A final possibility is to go, as some of them like to say, "on the road," but the road leads to no place where they have not been before, and to remain perpetually in flight between nowhere and nowhere is not possible for very long, even for the very young. Perhaps this is why the generation of the Sixties characteristically attempts to escape to that other globe, to their own head: not to Europe or to the provinces of America, though they would as soon be there as any place else—sooner than in the places, usually urban, in which they happen to have been born—but to the unexplored reaches of their own sub-minds. This world they enter with the help of dope, particularly the hallucinogens, marijuana or mescalin or the Mexican mushroom, or with stroboscopic lights or the exercises of various mystical sects; with, that is to say, the help of a discipline traditionally called *magic*. Like all magic, that of the young has often a shabby and disreputable, even a grotesquely comic or shockingly Satanic air; though perhaps in the end their favorite drugs will be socialized and neutralized, just as in Western culture the once-potent magic of cocoa, tea, coffee, and tobacco has been reduced to the level of polite titillation.

Meanwhile, however, something really new has been attained, or at least the end reached of something old: the uses of the cult of sexual freedom and that of alcohol have been at long last exhausted. Twice discovered for America (just after World War I, and again after World War II), Freud has come to seem too timid, too puritanical, and above all too *rational* for the second half of the twentieth century. His notion of the reclamation of the unconscious ("where *id* was, *ego* shall be!") strikes the present age as beside the point; and his celebration of sublimation as the basis of civilization seems to that age a cowardly concession. It is Wilhelm Reich who moves the young, with his antinomianism, his taste for magic, and his emphasis on full genitality as the final goal of man. The cult of the orgasm developed in his name has won converts in recent years, even from members of the generation of the Forties and Fifties, approaching middle-age and disillusioned with orthodox Marxism and Freudianism. Isaac Rosenfeld, Saul Bellow, Paul Goodman, and especially Norman Mailer, trying to live a second, menopausal youth, have chosen to live it, for longer or shorter periods, under Reichian auspices; and Mailer at least has seemed to the young a model and leader in this respect. Indeed, "The Time of Her Time" speaks with almost scriptural authority to the newest generation. But the cult of the orgasm is a *reductio ad absurdum*, even when its communicants are unaware of the fact; and like all parodies, it simultaneously connects with and destroys the tradition it mocks, however unwittingly.

There are signs everywhere that the by-now-almost-old-fashioned celebration of "full genitality" will continue to exist only on the middlebrow juvenile level, in more and more obvious novels and movies derived, via Jack Kerouac, from the last, mad efflorescence of the dream of utopian sex. But what lies beyond the sexual revolution through which we have lived from the beginning of the Twenties to the verge of the Sixties? On the one hand, a revolt against the orgasm, based on a concept of a universal fleshly love without penetration and consummation; and on the other, an attack on heterosexuality, either frankly homosexual in nature or, more politely, committed to some shadowy ideal of "bisexuality." Norman O. Brown, in his *Life Against*

Death, has engaged directly with Wilhelm Reich on both of these fronts, insisting—in the name, he claims, though not quite convincingly, of Freud and Marx to boot— that "mankind is unalterably, in the unconscious, in revolt against sexual differentiation and genital organization"; and proposing in their place the "infantile" ideal of the "polymorphous perverse."

Oddly enough, he has won acclaim for this extraordinary, though not unprecedented, doctrine from many genteel academics as well as certain mass-circulation magazines: the former gratified and the latter dazzled by the erudition with which he connects his advocacy of bisexual *coitus reservatus* with an impressive array of mystics, Christian and oriental; and both, presumably, pleased to be able to take a stand on such a lofty plane against indiscriminate boy-girl copulation and the pursuit of the orgasm. Yet similar theories have moved the advanced young as well, apparently because they realize that where there is orgasm, there is limitation and exhaustion; and that, therefore, the hope of unlimited promiscuity, of hypergamy, which is to say polygamy raised to the ultimate power, demands the contact of bodies not only without procreation (oral contraception has now put that in the power of everyone), but without the expenditure of seed. A young lady writes in this vein, in the pages of an ephemeral little magazine issued by the City Lights Bookshop, official publisher to the so-called "beats": "But it is not sexual union the soul is after. It is some chemical interchange from skin to skin . . . from sleeping in the same bed. From the clasping of hands, from the touching of skins." And she does not realize that she has re-invented (though Norman O. Brown might have told her) the *amor purus* of Andreas Capellanus: "This kind consists in the contemplation of the mind and the affection of the heart; it goes so far as the kiss and the embrace and the modest contact with the nude lover, omitting the final solace . . ."

And, after all, such "pure love" is a more satisfactory ideal than that other post-Freudian revolt, the revolt against heterosexuality, which has meant in fact (or at least in theory) the celebration of male homosexuality and the

F

[161]

exclusion of more than half the human race from the prom-ise of bodily joy. To have fun without becoming Father is more than just another form of birth control; and the homo-sexuality of the "beats" is not like that of the southern dandies, a last, slightly provincial version of European-style aristocratic pederasty, a kind of social climbing. It is revolu-tionary in its own right, in its resolve to be democratic even at the risk of seeming *lumpen*—a kind of homosexuality for the millions—but it still leaves that baffled more-than-fifty-percent-of-us-all merely sweeping up the joint, laundering the towels, and preparing an occasional hot meal. Yet in the world presided over by Kerouac and Gregory Corso and Allen Ginsberg, it is the boast of being queer that is flaunted as the last sexual excess capable of shocking an emancipated and hopelessly understanding bourgeoisie.

Homosexuality implies, moreover, a certain contempt for whisky ("They do not shout or fuss, they do not contain too much alcohol," writes an elderly exponent of the homosexual sensibility in praise of stories of a younger com-peer) and a complementary taste for dope. The nexus between dope and uranian love has been analyzed deftly and convincingly by Elémire Zolla in his *Eclissi dell' Intel-letuale*. "Dope," he writes, "is an object which penetrates the body and modifies its state, giving joy and threatening to impregnate what it penetrates with itself. [How can we not recognize from this description a correlation with the sexual act seen from a passive point of view?] . . . An uncertainty about one's proper role in the sexual rite obliges one to play out the comedy of taking drugs . . ."

But though, psychologically speaking, the drug-taking of the young may begin with the rejection of the male role at the bar and in bed, and though, from the point of view of sociology, it may arise from the same panic in the face of the collapse of traditional theories of "free will" which has led to a drift toward brain-washing in all modern soci-eties, these "causes" do not count in the literature devoted to its defense. To be sure, Madison Avenue and the Military High Command of Communist China share with the "beats" a desire to "alter consciousness," and if the former has not yet embraced chemical means to facilitate the process, perhaps time will bring them to it. The essential difference between advertising and psychological warfare, on the one hand, and the dream of "flipping," on the other, lies elsewhere: in the fact that one advocates a method of psychological reconditioning, responsible and socially induced, whose aim is the well-being of a particular social order; while the other sponsors a method, irresponsible and self-induced, whose aim is to render impossible the existence of any imaginable social order. This difference has not always been clearly understood, and the confusion has led to an uneasy alliance between certain laboratory scientists (whose superiors have assumed their experiments in psychochemistry to be dedicated to social conditioning and mental health) and such arch-junkies as Burroughs himself. But the end of such alliances is scandal, as we have seen during the recent blow-up in the Department of Psychology at Harvard.

In any case, it is the rationalization rather than the genetic cause, the myth rather than the fact of addiction, which works in certain contemporary novels of special interest, particularly those of William Burroughs. The theory of the "alteration of consciousness" is largely the invention not of Burroughs, however, but of Allen Ginsberg, a poet who has played an extraordinary role in the development of both the myth and the fact of the newer novel (or more properly, I suppose, anti-novel) in the United States. It is Ginsberg who is reported to have gathered together the scraps of narrative, protest, and hallucination which make up William Burroughs' first novel, *The Naked Lunch*, and to have given them what semblance of shape—approximate only, even after Ginsberg's ministrations—the book has.

But he has not only played, as it were, the Ezra Pound to Burroughs' T. S. Eliot, collating and editing what the madness of another had created but could not organize; he has also invented the legend of Jack Kerouac, this time with the collaboration of certain photographers from *Life* and the ladies' magazines, transforming the ex-Columbia

[163]

University athlete, the author of a dull and conventional *Bildungsroman* remembered by no one, into a fantasy figure capable of moving the imagination of rebellious kids with educations and literary aspirations, as his more *lumpen* opposite numbers, Elvis Presley, Marlon Brando, and James Dean, were moving their less literate and ambitious contemporaries. The legend of Kerouac is, to be sure, much more interesting than any of his books, since it is the work of a more talented writer; but the young confuse the two, as, I presume, do Ginsberg and even Kerouac. Much more important, however, than Ginsberg's rescue of Burroughs' crumpled notes from himself to himself, is Ginsberg's invention of a theory to justify both Burroughs' work and his own, for it constitutes the nearest thing to a program possessed by our own quite un-programmatic young.

Two comments, however, are in order, I think, before we pass to a consideration of the theory of the alteration of consciousness itself. The first is simply this: that Kerouac, Burroughs, Ginsberg, and company, though spokesmen for the young, are not themselves young,* not so young, for instance, as John Barth, or even John Updike, that *New Yorker* writer much touted recently by those who want the illusion of vision and fantasy without surrendering the kind of reassurance provided by slick writing at its most professionally *all right*.

Like J. D. Salinger, who speaks for the disaffected young in the better prep schools and colleges, or Norman Mailer, who is spokesman for extra-academics who never made it from New York to San Francisco, Burroughs and his associates are much closer in age to the generation of the Forties and Fifties than to the twenty-year-olds whom they now address. In a certain sense, their books are fake adolescent books as certain pretended kids' books are fake children's books (I think of *Winnie the Pooh*, for instance, or, for that matter of *Tom Sawyer*), works intended to be read by

* But now they begin to have genuinely young imitators, like John Rechy, whose *City of Night* might well be subtitled *Burroughs in the U.S.A.*, wandering as it does among our great cities, and ending, American style, with a return to Mom and Texas.

[164]

adults over the shoulders of their presumed sub-adult audience.

Yet it would not be true to say that the young do not read Burroughs (or Salinger or even Mailer); having nothing else to read, since they have not yet produced out of their own age group a sympathetic ideologue, they turn to the aging leaders of the youth. As a matter of fact, any American abroad has come to expect to see the hordes of the new young descending on Athens or Paris or Florence or wherever, bearded and sandaled and carrying beneath their arms the holy books, *The Naked Lunch, The Soft Machine*; and if they do not sing, "Burroughs is our leader, we will not be moved," they might just as well.

Now there is nothing strange or reprehensible, after all, about the fact that a generation of twenty-year-olds must look to comparative oldsters for books to move it; what is, if not strange, truly reprehensible is a tendency on the part of those oldsters to pretend they are youths, to make themselves into full-fledged youth impersonators. It is, perhaps, easier for the homosexual, pursuing the phantom of youth and immune to the responsibilities of a family, to play this game than it has been for writers otherwise committed in the past; and, I am tempted to believe, what is easiest must be most resisted.

There is, moreover, a second irony which should be appreciated if one is to relish the full comedy of the relationship between our youngest readers and their not-so-young spokesmen. The irony is implicit in the fact that, if Ginsberg invented Burroughs and Kerouac (in some sense, to some degree), Ginsberg himself (in a similar sense, to a similar degree) is the invention of the man who was his teacher, and who has become the dean of the generation of the Forties and Fifties, as well as the center of the new establishment that generation has created around Columbia University, the Mid-Century Book Society, the *Partisan Review*, and certain other journals in Europe and America. His teacher was, of course, Lionel Trilling, in whose story "Of This Time, of That Place," Ginsberg, as we have already observed, appeared as a character before existing as an author in print. First portrayed as a mad student with whose madness his genteel but intellectually committed teacher learned finally to identify himself, Ginsberg sprang to a kind of mythic life. And if it is not a third irony, certainly it is an academic footnote to the second that Trilling's only wholly successful piece of fiction is this story, rather than his more ambitious novel, *The Middle of the Journey*. In the latter, Trilling tried gallantly to become the laureate of the Thirties, the novelistic recorder of the experience of two generations of American writers with the Communist Party, as well as of their consequent disillusionment. Though certain actual prototypes of his characters, Whittaker Chambers, for instance, moved and baffled (sometimes enraged and dismayed) us all, the book itself remains strangely inert. No, whatever Trilling's merits as a critic, and they are considerable, as a writer of fiction, Trilling will survive chiefly as the prophet of a movement with which he could never sympathize completely, but in whose inception he played an important role. The bestower of the blessing sometimes does not know whom or what he has blessed.

It is not, however, the student Ginsberg, whom Trilling evoked in "Of This Time, of That Place," the victim of his own language and imagination, but the poet Ginsberg, master of his own destiny and expert in public relations, who has developed the theory of the alteration of consciousness. Ginsberg's theory is rooted deeply in the shift we have already noticed as it works in the youthful subcultures of America and threatens to impinge on the centers of our social life: the shift from a whisky culture to a dope culture. And it has connections with current experiments in the field of psycho-chemistry, experiments aimed at assessing objectively the effect of certain still-unacceptable drugs on the mental life of normally functioning men and women, as well as the seriously disturbed. Meanwhile, other drugs, barbiturates and tranquillizers, "sleeping tablets" for the aging neurotic and airplane glue sniffed surreptitiously by the young, have come to give the deliverance and "kicks" until recently sought almost exclusively in alcohol.

There is a political, or meta-political side to the theory,

too, the dream of an ultimate revolution against all previous revolutions as well as against all hitherto conceivable *status quos*. In the period of the enlightenment, an advocate of alteration of consciousness might argue, men began to believe that by extending the range of consciousness, by accepting into the conscious mind (and there *understanding* them) certain experiences earlier thought of as external phantasms, man could triumph over his own weaknesses and the difficulties of his environment. The technique of psychoanalysis is, I suppose, the supreme manifestation of this faith that to know is, if not to have conquered, at least to have moved into the position from which one can begin to conquer.

But at the end of the nineteenth century, various revolutionary philosophers, most notably Karl Marx, had begun to insist that the point was to change the world, not to understand it. No matter how clearly seen, such thinkers argued, poverty was an offense, man's alienation from his work a scandal, and only action rather than consciousness was capable of mitigating the offense and the scandal. Even religious credulity and superstition, the Marxists argued, had survived the onslaught of reason because they were sustained by a social system which the rationalist philosophers had not challenged at all. However, we have now lived through more than a century of attempts to change the world by assaulting the social structure and have only learned what some from the first tried to tell us, namely, that the more it changes, the more it is the same—*so long as a particular way of perceiving and understanding, bred by science out of scholasticism, persists.*

In Russia and America alike, the alterationists would plead, men study physics and build the bomb, worship the ego and fear their own bodies, ban heroin and drink alcohol, so what is there to choose? The world apparently cannot be changed by fiat or force of arms, by understanding or revolution, but what can be altered is the range of our perception and its mode. We can *see* a different world without firing a shot or framing a syllogism, merely by altering our consciousness; and the ways to alter it are at hand:

[167]

drugs, on the one hand; the techniques of oriental adepts on the other. To be 'sure, at the very moment some voices in the West cry out in favor of hashish and yoga, heroin and zen, the East has opted for the reality principle: science and work, and the conversion of id into ego.

No matter. There *is* a weariness in the West which undercuts the struggle between socialism and capitalism, democracy and autocracy; a weariness with humanism itself which underlies all the movements of our world, a weariness with the striving to be men. It is the end of man which the school of Burroughs foretells, not in terms of doom but of triumph. Let the experiment be over; let the focused consciousness blur into the cosmic night; let the hallucinatory monsters bred of fragmented consciousness prowl that night again; let the perilously sustained absurdity' of the "soul" be abandoned; yet let the demons who once trafficked in souls thrive anew.

William Burroughs is an extraordinarily naïve man, naïve artistically (he takes the warmed-over Proustianism of Lawrence Durrell for a great new esthetic discovery), naïve ideologically (he is just now discovering William Reich), naïve philosophically (I suspect he believes he can kick the demonism he has embraced when he kicks the drug to which he is addicted); but he has written a terrible and deeply moving group of books—a single book, actually, padded-out even in one volume, and varied with childish ingenuity and unendurable tedium in the later two. Sometimes he is funny, sometimes earnest (much of his *Naked Lunch* and *The Soft Machine* is dull protest literature, manifestoes against cops and in favor of junkies or homosexuals), but always he is nauseating. And the nausea he produces is not so much in his compulsive images of anal assault or of the meaningless orgasm of the hanged man, but in an authentic cosmic vision of the end of man, total death. There is no playing with the shocking in Burroughs, no affectation, no falsification; only a stupidity monumental enough to be called holy. Reading him, the disaffiliated bourgeois young (bohemians we used to say, "beats" we call them now) can believe that their own affectless lives, their endless flirtation with failure, their repulsion from their failed selves, and their pride in that repulsion, are neither specific and particular disasters, nor mere by-products of the life of a leisure class in a high-standard-of-living society, but symptoms of a more general cosmic catastrophe.

We have a name for this kind of writing when it is middlebrow, for at that level too, men demand legends which begin with the end of humanity, the prevision of a future in which robots, or humanoids, or monsters from remote planets, or our unrecognizably mutant children will inherit the earth we have failed to hold. I am talking, of course, about science fiction; and in terms of technique, what technique Burroughs occasionally attains and holds is precisely a technique of science fiction—as Burroughs himself is a character out of science fiction. His dreams are compounded not of simple desire, but are gimmicked, artificially induced by heroin or stroboscopic lights, then not merely written down, but rearranged by the methods he calls "cutout" or "fold-in": mechanical devices for scrambling a text entirely his own or combining it almost randomly with someone else's text. Expectedly enough, one of his favorite "fold-in" texts is *Pincher Martin* by William Golding, himself an expert in the highbrow manipulation of science fiction form; and there are sections from *Thuvia, Maid of Mars,* by Edgar Rice Burroughs (Burroughs' namesake) in *Naked Lunch.* Obviously, Burroughs' methods for culling material and composing novels will someday be carried out with greater efficiency by a computer. Meanwhile, he is willing to carry on himself in his role of pioneer mutant; for if he is not already a child almost any family (his own, of course, are the manufacturers of adding machines!) would be willing to disclaim as human, much less their own, he is pledged to becoming one.

11

THE END OF THE NOVEL

And what is there for Burroughs to do with the novel in his present future, his anticipation of non-human times? Nothing, of course, but to destroy it; or rather, to make clear that it has already destroyed itself; for it is a form which realized itself in the mid-eighteenth century, precisely at the moment that men become conscious of their unconscious minds and resolved to redeem them. And it is hard to see how it can outlive the faith of the first novelists in the power of reason to know even the irrational. There are various ways to declare the death of the novel: to mock it while seeming to emulate it, like Nabokov, or John Barth; to reify it into a collection of objects like Robbe-Grillet; or to *explode* it, like William Burroughs, to leave only twisted fragments of experience and the miasma of death. The latter seems, alas, the American way; and it is certainly the way which has haunted Burroughs, whose recent work has been impregnated with the image of the Nova, the flare-up of an exploding planet, which blends into, on the one hand, the glare and terror of the atom bomb, and, on the other, the spatter and release of orgasm. "A new mythology," Burroughs comments, explaining this very image like the good science-fictionist he is, "is possible in the space age."

But what form will emerge to embody that mythology? Surely nothing Burroughs himself has been able to contrive; for since he has been thrown back on his own largely mechanical and magical devices; since, that is to say, Ginsberg last put the semblance of a book together for him, he has seemed repetitious, dull, and long-winded. The nausea of the end has an intrinsic appeal as strong as that of pornography itself; but for a long time Burroughs has lived simply on the basis of that appeal. Only the belated discovery of his early work has given him now the reputation of a new and currently rewarding writer.

Perhaps, though, we do not have to believe Burroughs, who has a special stake in declaring the end of everything. Perhaps, after all, the novel still flourishes in the United States in forms too conventional to be noticed by those determined to pretend that we have still, or at last, an avant-garde. Are not many of our recent novels major efforts by major or immensely promising writers? Do we not have big books by James Baldwin and Philip Roth, Bernard Malamud, Robert Penn Warren and Mary McCarthy? Was there not a last book from Faulkner, as well as another by Nabokov, and even the twenty-years-promised-and-delayed magnum opus of Katherine Anne Porter? Indeed, in prospect, even those who know that fewer and fewer people buy novels these days, and who for a long time have had a prevision of the year in which every adult in the United States would write a novel which no one else would read— even such professional ironists have not been able to prevent a tremor of excitement from unsettling their tranquil sense of doom.

But how every one of these books (except the anti-novel of Nabokov) cheated our hopes: the Malamud slight and inconclusive; the Roth morally obtuse and ill-organized; the Baldwin shrill and unconvincing; the McCarthy intolerably "female" in the worst sense; the Porter appallingly obvious and dull. Surely there has never been so large a cluster of egregious flops in the span of a couple of years; and surely it is not merely that, for quite different reasons unconnected with each other or with the general cultural situation, so large a number of promising writers have betrayed not only their extravagant promises but even our quite modest expectations. Is there no relationship at all between so general a failure and the fact, reported by publishers and known to every writer, that at the moment, in our country of 180,000,000 people, a good first novel, prominently and favorable reviewed, may sell as few as 600 copies?

Yet any suggestion that the novel, after its brief two hundred years of existence, may be about to disappear, in the United States at least, lose its pre-eminence, its status as the reigning literary genre, is greeted by howls of dismay and hoots of contempt. Such predictions are received not with the pious lack of interest or mild concern common to literary statements, but with the sort of agitation more appropriate to a surmise that the United States may be approaching its final days as a significant power, or that the Church of Rome has outlived its last accommodation. To many earnest types I meet and read, forecasts of the death of the novel seem even *more* unnerving than comments on the death of the Republic or of God, the end of the family, or the overthrow of the male sex.

This must be, it occurs to me, because we cannot imagine anything after the novel that is still literature, cannot conceive of an alternative form which will provide all the satisfactions of the novel, including the exercise of those prestigeful skills we call "reading." Such a failure does not, I think, reflect the weakness of our imaginations, but rather our appreciation of the fact that the novel is the last narrative art-form invented, or capable of being invented, for *literates*. Beyond it, we sense, lie only those forms to which we who read cannot help condescending a little: comic books, movies, television, etc. Most of us find it personally upsetting to confess, even to ourselves, that the reigning narrative art of the not-so-distant future may well be one appropriate to a post-literate culture; and this despite our realization that it becomes more and more difficult to write what most people mean when they say a "book," a recognizable novel.

Still, we tell ourselves, there will always be the novels which have survived; even if no one ever writes another *Moby Dick*, someone will be around to read the first one.

And surely it will have been preserved to be read by an interested élite, however marginal literacy may become. That novels like *Moby Dick* will survive, I cannot doubt; and it pleases me to envision a tiny few gathering in that world, perhaps half-secretly, to discuss with each other the remaining great books, the reading of which has become an art as learned and abstruse, and suspect, as deciphering heiroglyphics. Meanwhile everyone else will be acquiring only the simple skills required to follow the pidgin used in the subtitles of foreign movies or to consult the schedule of the day's television programs.

If the novel disappears, then, it will have disappeared for two quite different reasons: First because the artistic faith that sustained its writers is dead, and second because the audience-need it was invented to satisfy is being better satisfied otherwise. From the consumer's point of view, the novel came into existence at the paradoxical insistence of a hitherto illiterate middle-class audience that everyone be given the skills necessary for deciphering words on a page, and yet that no one be required to practice those skills against his will. The demand for the extension of literacy and the reservation of the right to reject literacy were thus bound up together from the first, and no literary form extant at the moment of their formulation seemed capable of satisfying both at once. What history required (and what those who stood in its vanguard were willing to pay for) was a new genre which made possible symbolic, or perhaps better, demonstration literacy. This represents a typical demand and a typical solution of the modern world, of mass industrial society, which has gone on to demand and get, along similar lines, demonstration trials (the Reichstag trial, the Moscow trials) and demonstration voting—either in the form of the two-party-choice, much admired in the democracies, or of the single-party-plebiscite favored in totalitarian regimes.

From any traditional point of view, then, from the standpoint, say, of those still pledged in the eighteenth century to writing epics in verse, the novel seemed already anti-literature, even post-literature; that is, it appeared then precisely what we take television or comic books to be now. In the jargon of our own day, the novel represents the beginnings of popular culture, of that machine-made, mass-produced, mass-distributed *ersatz* which, unlike either traditional high art or folk art, *does not know its place*; since, while pretending to meet the formal standards of literature, it is actually engaged in smuggling into the republic of letters extra-literary satisfactions. It not merely instructs and delights and moves, but also embodies the myths of a society, serves as the scriptures of an underground religion; and these latter functions, unlike the former ones, depend not at all on any particular form, but can be indifferently discharged by stained-glass windows, comic strips, ballads, and movies.

Yet it is precisely this cultural *ambiguity* of the novel which made it for so long so popular on so many levels, at the same time creating those tensions and contradictions by virtue of which it is presently dying. From the first, there have been, certainly, two kinds of novel, not always clearly distinguished from each other (sometimes because of the blessed un-self-consciousness of their writers; sometimes because of their deviousness): the bestseller, ill-written and scriptural, and at home in the world of mass culture; and the art novel, a hybrid form into which men of talent and the highest ambitions have poured certain insights and perceptions no longer viable in traditional forms—including basic criticisms of mass culture itself. It is for this reason that the serious artist has had to *fight* for the attention of the audience which invented the genre he exploits and resents his attempt to use that genre against its own values and aspirations. But in modern times there has been no other audience.

The serious novelist has, then, tended simultaneously to woo and to war on the bourgeois world; which in turn has both wooed and warred on him by adapting to its own uses (i.e., by turning into stereotypes) the very devices he has used to mock it. Pornography, horror, the merciless docu-

[174]

mentation of the sordid which we call "naturalism," even the attack on mass culture itself, have been assimilated into mass culture; just as the favorite refuges of the artist, his bohemias and places of exile, have been transformed into tourist attractions; and his very vices, from tobacco to marijuana, have become country-club diversions.

The only unredeemable offense against middlebrow culture in the power of the novelist is to consider his work as absolute art: a form which aspires to the condition of poetry, and which refuses the weary reader any possibility of forgetting that he is reading *words*, dealing not with archetypes only, but with nuances of language, and the strategies of form. The perpetrators of that ultimate offense have already been immortalized in scandal; and the names of Proust, Mann, Joyce, and Kafka, for instance, stir still in some quarters the uneasy grimace and the embarrassed snicker. In the United States, however, there has never been an unequivocal avant-gardist among the novelists of first rank. What experimentalism there has been in our fiction has been imported and, at the moment of importation, accommodated to middlebrow demands. Think, for instance, of how the example of Joyce's *Portrait of the Artist as a Young Man* is modified in Thomas Wolfe's *Look Homeward, Angel*.

As early as the twenties, certain of our writers had learned from the example of the European avant-garde simply to do otherwise: Scott Fitzgerald, for instance, Glenway Wescott and, after a brief period of indecision, Kay Boyle. Others took longer to accommodate themselves, like Katherine Anne Porter, who only in the past few years has clearly exposed herself as having gone over to ladies'-magazine fiction; while Hemingway's and Faulkner's final apostasy to art is revealed only in their last works, and, especially, in the works of their followers. There is, in the American grain, an implicit anti-intellectualism, a contempt for mere art (of which Mark Twain is a chief source) which threatens always to turn our writers against their fellows and to deliver them into the hands of their enemies. However, so long as the counter-tendency to avant-gardism ran strong in the Western world in general, this native American know-nothingism cast a valuable counterbalance, protecting our novelists against becoming academicians of the new.

There is now, however, nothing to stem a world-wide drift toward middlebrow art except the sterile and academic nostalgia for yesterday's avant-garde on the part of such European writers as Alain Robbe-Grillet. Everywhere else there are signs of a great revolt against the aspirations of the novel to art, a turning on the part of novelists themselves— without outside pressure—toward the mass audience. Included in this great middlebrow revolt are writers as different from each other as Yael Dayan in Israel, Françoise Sagan in France, Kingsley Amis and John Wain in England; and in America, Jack Kerouac, J. D. Salinger, Truman Capote, Herbert Gold, Vance Bourjaily, perhaps even Philip Roth.

Some of these writers, in America, at least, are harder to recognize as Philistines than, say, Irwin Shaw or James Gould Cozzens because, to begin with, they are younger, and because there attaches to them, for one reason or another, a certain avant-garde cachet. They are likely to appear in magazines, with avant-garde pretensions or an avant-garde past (the *Evergreen Review*, for instance, or *Partisan Review*); and they may even lead lives more like those once led by avant-garde artists than by most of the readers to whom they actually appeal. Moreover, they have failed to develop a new or notable Philistine style, writing, whether ill or well, in manners associated not so long ago with experimental writers of the first rank. And finally, they may not even know they write for the great audience, since, in fact, they often don't get its attention. Certain writers of the school of Saul Bellow (not including Bellow himself), Herbert Gold, for instance, could in this regard cry out in all truth, "How can I be as bad as the critics say I am, when I'm not even popular?"

The disconcerting fact suggested by such cases is this: at the moment when a considerable wave of semi-serious writers find themselves, deliberately or not, wooing the mass audience for the novel, that audience has begun to detach itself from the novel completely. After all, what does the largest sub-literate public need fiction for? What documentary realism once promised to give them in novel form, non-fiction provides more efficiently, more painlessly. And the mythical reassurances they have long sought in books (boy gets girl, good man kills bad, etc.) the non-literary arts of television and film provide more vividly and at less intellectual cost. At the same moment, those non-literary arts satisfy more fully, less hypocritically than the hybrid novel form ever could, the revulsion of the great audience from the very act of reading, their half-secret, shamefaced hatred of the literacy which once they had found it politically expedient to demand.

In the end, what the neo-middlebrow movements succeed in doing is not (as some exponents of that movement may fondly hope) to raise the level of the mass audience, but to substitute, for the former élite, a pseudo-élite conditioned to *kitsch*, corn, and self-congratulation. The rejection of literacy by the mass audience and the betrayal of standards by the semi-artist combine with the onslaught against the novel form by the exponents of the alteration of consciousness to doom that genre, or at least to make the possibility of that doom a leading item on the agenda of contemporary criticism. I, myself, though I practice the art of the novel ironically and desperately in a world which provides me no assurances about the nature, or even existence, of such an audience as I dream, am inclined to believe that the history of the genre is approaching its end.

I do not mean, of course, that I have lost faith in the survival of the art of fiction, for I cannot conceive a human situation in which stories are not somehow told, and I do not myself foresee the end of man. Perhaps narrative will not continue much longer to be entrusted to print and bound between hard covers. But this does not especially dismay me, since I have no special affection for the novel as such: that fat, solid commodity invented by the bourgeoisie for the ends of commerce and culture-climbing. There is always the screen, if the page proves no longer viable: the

[177]

neighborhood movie, the drive-in, or the parlor television set. And I presume that if cinema eventually becomes a lost art, too, there will be some of us scratching pictographs on the walls of caves, or telling each other stories over bonfires made of the last historical romance hailed as the novel of the year in the last book review section of the last *New York Times*.

12

TRAITOR OR LAUREATE:
THE TWO TRIALS OF THE POET

In the United States, poetry has been for so long not so much bought and read as honored and studied that the poet has grown accustomed to his marginal status. Unlike the novelist, he takes his exclusion from the market place as *given*, not a subject for anguish and protest but a standing joke, partly on him, partly on those who exclude him. Edmund Wilson was able to ask, as early as the Thirties, "Is Verse a Dying Technique?" and the mournful answer is implicit in the mournful cadence of the question. But Mr. Wilson did not, of course, pose the question for the first time; behind his concern there is a tradition of discovering the end of verse which goes back as far as Thomas Love Peacock's "Four Ages of Poetry" and the earliest impact of advanced technology on the imagination of the West.

Long before the poets of the United States had found an authentic voice, the survival of poetry itself had come to seem problematical; and certainly today there is no American poet who does not suspect that his own verse is likely to live (once his small circle of admiring friends has died) in the classroom and library, rather than in the hearts of men. Meanwhile, he is inclined to feel, he must somehow sustain himself on the long, difficult way toward academic immortality, and to do so he must choose between being subsidized by foundation grants and university sine-cures, or earning his keep at some job completely unconnected with the making or reading of verse. Wallace Stevens was an actuary in, and then vice-president of, an insurance company; Robert Frost tried for a while to farm; William Carlos Williams was, all of his adult life, a family doctor; T. S. Eliot began his career as a bank clerk. Each choice is perhaps a metaphor for each poet's view of himself and his work: Stevens aspiring to the precision and objectivity of statistical analysis; Frost longing to root words in the soil; Williams thinking of himself as a healer and adviser to ordinary men in their daily suffering; Eliot viewing himself as the guardian of the treasury of culture. But all together, these choices surely reflect a common awareness of a common plight, the poet's inability to subsist on his poetry alone.

That plight, however, has sent more poets into the classroom than (with whatever metaphorical intent) into the great world of production for profit; even Robert Frost, for instance, ended up teaching, once he had discovered how little he could earn tilling the soil. It is not, I think, only the poet's aversion to a world of competition and economic risk which has led him more and more to seek refuge in the college, but a sense that there he is close to his own future, to the posterity for whom he writes. Certainly there he can, if he likes, tout himself and his friends, as well as abuse his rivals and detractors; and there he can set the captive youngsters before him the task of understanding and loving (or, at least, of seeming for a moment to understand and love) certain poems, including his own, more important to him than any of the goals—erotic, athletic, or technological—which those same youngsters pursue once out of sight. Sometimes he fears, in fact, that the *only* reading such poems will get in the world he inhabits is precisely this vicarious or symbolic one, between college walls and class bells.

All of the Southern agrarian poets from John Crowe Ransom to Randall Jarrell have ended up teaching at one university or another; and numerous other poets of quite different styles and persuasions from them and from each other (Delmore Schwartz and Robert Creely, John Berryman and Richard Wilbur, for instance) teach regularly if they can, irregularly if they must, or, best of all, enjoy the status and pay of teachers with a minimum of classroom duties. Even among the maddest of our poets, there are not a few to whom the academy seems the only real place preferable to the Nowhere that otherwise attracts their total allegiance. Sometimes, indeed, it seems as if the path which leads back and forth between the classroom and the madhouse is the one which the modern American muse loves especially to tread.

Yet the poet is finally aware that in the university he is expected not so much to write poetry, or even to teach it, as to be a poet: to act out a role which is somehow necessary to the psychic well-being of society as poems are not. And, similarly, it is the assumption of his poetic *persona* for which he is paid by grants and subsidies, and applauded at symposia and writers' conferences. After a while, it may even seem to the poet that he is being paid not to write; but this is not really so, and it is only a kind of desperate self-flattery which leads him to indulge in the conceit. In point of fact, our society does not really care whether he writes or not, so long as he does not do it on the time they ask him to spend in embodying publicly what they have rejected in themselves: a contempt for belonging and order and decorum and profit and right reason and mere fact; a love for exile and irrelevance and outrage and loss and nonsense and lies.

It is not merely himself that the poet is asked to play; if it were, there would be no temptation involved worth resisting. It is rather a *myth* of himself, or, more properly, perhaps, a myth of the poet in general which he is called on to enact. And he has, as a matter of fact, a choice of roles, for the morality play in which he is urged to assume a part demands, like all literature on the level of mass culture, heroes as well as villains, good guys as well as bad guys. But how can a poet be a hero? How can the projection of what the great audience rejects function for that audience as "good"? To be sure, we can imagine best-selling poets on the analogy of best-selling novelists, unequivocal spokesman for the mass audience and its values; but there is so steep a contrast between "best-selling" and "poet," between what the great audience demands and what verse, any verse, does, that the concept is soon abandoned.

At any rate, since the time of Longfellow at least, the largest public in the United States has decided it does not need such hybrids in the realm of verse. The fictionist, the journalist, and, more recently, the script-writer for movies or television, performs much more satisfactorily any tasks which could be imagined for them. The servile sub-poet does not cease to exist entirely, but he is barred from the place where poetry is chiefly read, judged, and preserved, the academy, and relegated to the world of commerce, where he produces greeting card mottoes, or to ladies' clubs, where he flatters vanity, or to the mass magazines, where he provides filler for the spaces between editorials and short stories. In return for such meager employment, he is asked to endure the indignity of being read, or listened to, without being noticed or remembered.

The "hero" of the popular socio-drama we have been discussing is not so simple and obscure a mouthpiece; he is, in fact, both problematical and ambiguous: a hero-villain, a good rebel, an admirable non-conformist. And what makes him good or admirable is his presumed attitude toward the great audience which notices him without ever reading him; for that audience, by certain mysterious processes of cultural transmission, comes, after a while, to know—or believe it knows—who in the realm of art is really on its side, who regards it without something less than contempt. The one thing it will never forgive a writer is despising its reading ability, which, to be sure, it does not usually get around to practicing. Such despite it regards as the ultimate treason, being willing, on the other hand, to forgive any challenge to its values or beliefs so long as that despite is not visibly present. As the critic at his best forgives a writer almost anything for writing well, the non-reader at his worst forgives him almost anything for writing ill—or simply for having the courtesy to *seem* to do so.

How can the great audience tell, after all, who is, in this

[182]

sense a friend and who a foe? The point is, of course, that they cannot really tell at all, that they are likely to be fooled by the most elementary sorts of duplicity, since all their judgments are rendered on the basis of a handful of lines quoted for the benefit of their immediate mentors (schoolmarms and leaders of P.T.A. discussion groups) in the columns of, say, the *Saturday Review*, the *New Yorker*, the front page of the *New York Times Book Review*, or the back pages of *Time*. As a matter of fact, the reviewers for such journals exist precisely in order to serve as prosecuting attorneys for the great public in its continuing case against the artist; and what they must establish in order to prove guilt is *that a given writer has produced passages which cannot be misconstrued or half understood without the reader's being painfully aware of his own failure.*

It is not, then, mere difficulty which constitutes the *prima facie* evidence of a writer's contempt for the mass audience, but *unaccustomed* difficulty, a difficulty different from the kinds long so familiar in the classroom that no one any longer expects himself to do more than recognize and label them: Shakespeare, Dante, Whitman, etc. Certain writers are, in fact, more flagrantly difficult than others, and sometimes they are deliberately so; but the public's consciousness of the writer's role in this regard does not always coincide with his own. As far as American serious poets are concerned, though all of them have known for generations that the onerous advantages of best-sellerdom are denied them, they have responded in two quite different ways: some of them writing *as if* for a very few, and some of them, nonetheless, writing *as if* for a popular audience.

What is, or at least, from any historical point of view, ought to be involved is rather a matter of stance than of genuine expectation; because in fact there is little correspondence between the poets' theoretical and actual audiences. Walt Whitman, for instance, theoretically popular poet that he was, had, at the time of publication and, I should guess, will have forever after, a much smaller readership than the theoretically anti-popular poet Edgar Allan Poe. Certainly school children, that largest audience of all, have never been urged to read Whitman as they have been urged to read Poe. Yet this has not kept certain later poets (irony breeding irony in the tangle of misunderstanding), dedicated to widening the audience of verse, from invoking Whitman as their model; while others, content to address an élite, have made their ideal Edgar Poe, at least as re-interpreted by the French *symbolistes*.

In the mid-nineteenth century, the great public needed neither Poe nor Whitman, having still at their disposal the respectable academic bard, Henry Wadsworth Longfellow, and not yet having acquired that fear of Harvard professors which now plays so large a role in political as well as literary matters on the level of mass culture. Both Poe and Whit-man were, therefore, found guilty in the treason trial for which only Poe had braced himself: Poe of drunkenness and drug-addiction and the celebration of death; Whitman of blasphemy and obscenity and the celebration of sex. Poe, at least, knew always that he was on trial, while Whit-man, more naïvely and more typical of the American writer, thought of himself as wooing an audience, which in fact saw itself not as his beloved but as his judge.

Essential to an understanding of the difficulties of the American writer (especially, but not exclusively, the poet) is an awareness of this conflict of imagined roles, the clash of metaphors on the border between art and life. The rela-tionship of the poet to the audience in the United States is—in *his* consciousness—erotic or sentimental; the relation-ship of the audience to the poet is—in *its* consciousness—juridical. While the writer may fancy himself pleading a tender suit, or carrying on a cynical seduction, the reader is likely to think of himself as hearing evidence, deciding whether to say, not "no" or "yes," but "guilty" or "inno-cent": guilty of treason, or innocent by reason of insanity—or even, as in the case of Ezra Pound, *both* at once.

It is, of course, Pound who comes into our minds when we reflect on the trial of the poet. A century ago, it might have been still Poe or Whitman, but neither of these long-dead (and therefore for us inevitably sanctified and forgot-ten) figures is capable now of stirring passion in the minds of sub-literates, who have no memory. Each age must have its own, brand-new defendants, and the mass audience sitting in judgment in the middle of the twentieth century has tried and sentenced the poet once more, yet as if for the first time, in the person of Ezra Pound. Indeed, they have condemned him with what, from their standpoint, is perfect justice. I do not mean merely that Pound was, indeed, guilty of the charges of abetting anti-Semitism (and more recently anti-Negro feelings), praising Fascism, and condemning the best along with the worst in his own country; the popular mind in America has often regarded with favor enemies of democracy, Jews, and Negroes. I mean that all of the ambitious long poems of our time have been written under Pound's guidance or inspired by his example: Eliot's *The Wasteland*, for instance, and Hart Crane's *The Bridge*, and William Carlos Williams' *Paterson*: all of those fragmented, allusion-laden, imagistic portraits of an atomized world which have so offended the Philistine mind. And I mean, too, that in his *Pisan Cantos* Pound, driven by his tribulations beyond the circle of his bad literary habits and his compulsive political idiocies, has caught the pathos and the comedy involved in the relationship between artist and society in the twentieth century with absolute precision. Both the self-pity of the artist and the complacent brutality of the community that needs and resents him have been dissolved in irony only to be re-created as improbable lyric beauty. These are offenses hard to forgive for those convinced that they should judge and not be judged— certainly not by a mad poet.

Precisely the qualities, however, which have made Pound the prototypical enemy of the people in our time have attracted to him not only certain impotent young cranks who might have been successful Hitlers had time and circumstances conspired, but also the sort of disaffected young poet who turns out in the end to have written the poetry by which an age is remembered. Both kinds of Poundians wrote on the walls of bars and taverns "Ez for Pres," both dreamed him as their ideal anti-President in the time of Eisenhower, while Pound in fact still sat in an insane

[185]

asylum in Washington—to which he had been remanded, just after World War II, by a jury of his peers, even more eager to find him nuts than to declare him a traitor. And what worthy living poet would such a jury not have found crazy enough to confine, whether or not he had made treasonable broadcasts for Mussolini?

The answer is easy: Robert Frost, through whose intervention Pound was finally released from the madhouse and allowed to return to the place from which he had once raged against his country. For Frost only could our whole nation have consented to parole Pound, just as for Frost only could it mourn officially and without reservations. Certainly it could not have mourned so for, say, T. S. Eliot, who, however sanctimonious in his old age, had once swapped citizenship; or for E. E. Cummings, who despised punctuation and the slogans of advertising; or for Wallace Stevens, who had obviously not even cared to be understood. Indeed, long before his death, the great audience had found Frost guiltless of the ultimate treason, the betrayal of what it defines as "sanity," and considers itself to possess in an eminent degree. Had certain poems of his not become so standard a feature of grade school and high school anthologies ("Mending Wall," for instance, or "Stopping by Woods") that one finally could respond to them no more than to yet another reproduction of the Mona Lisa? Were not other verses of his distributed every year as Christmas cards by his publishers, and were not still others quoted from station platforms and the backs of trains by candidates for political office?

Had he not even been invited by President Kennedy to read a poem of his own composing at the inaugural ceremonies, and had he not actually written one for the occasion, ending with the complacent boast that his appearance there itself inaugurated "A golden age of poetry and power/ Of which this noonday's the beginning hour"? Fortunately, fate fought for him against the adulation of politicians and the crowd, that kindly comic fate which protects great men from their own delusions; he could not read the text, the sun too bright in his aging eyes, and had to give up a tele-

[186]

vision première in favor of more conventional modes of publication. But the damage had already been done; Frost had become in effect the first Poet Laureate of the United States, an honor and indignity no other American had ever endured. And the nation, which is to say, the mass audience, smiled at his discomfiture and applauded his honors.

But why did they feel so at ease in his presence? Was it merely that he had lived so long? There was enough in his career to dismay them, had they known or cared. He had begun as alienated from them as any poet they had ever cast in the role of utter villain; had fled to England already middle-aged and convinced apparently that he could make his American reputation only second-hand; had withdrawn from the pressures of getting and spending, as well as the obligations of citizenship, to sit alone in a back-country which its own inhabitants were deserting as fast as they could; had boasted all his life long of preferring loneliness to gregariousness, night to day, cold to warmth, melancholy to joy; had mocked in more than one poem the penny-saved-penny-earned philosophy of the American Philistine's laureate, Benjamin Franklin; had celebrated himself as a genius "too lofty and original to rage," and hinted that his message was not for everyone but hidden away "under a spell so the wrong ones can't find it."

In a long and, I suspect, not much read poem called "New Hampshire," Frost has spoken, for once, without defensive pretense or disguise, as an artist—though he assumes the mask of a novelist rather than that of a maker of verses—and has identified without equivocation the bitterness that underlies his vocation as a poet.

> I make a virtue of my suffering
> From nearly everything that goes on round me.
> In other words, I know where I am,
> Being the creature of literature I am,
> I shall not lack for pain to keep me awake.
> Kit Marlowe taught me how to say my prayers:
> "Why, this is Hell, nor am I out of it!"

[187]

He has spoken elsewhere quite as frankly of his audience, remarking, with the quiet and devastating irony that characterizes his best verse:

> They cannot look out far.
> They cannot look in deep.
> But when was that ever a bar
> To any watch they keep?

Yet reading this epitaph upon the grave of their fondest pretensions, the great public, which does not recognize irony, could see only what short words Frost used and how he respected both the syntax and the iambic measure which they had learned in school to honor, if not use. If he was "lofty and original," he did indeed keep it a secret, as he slyly declared, from the "wrong ones," from the very ones who made up his mass following, who hated all other living poets, but loved him because he seemed to them a reproach to those others who made them feel inferior with their allusions to Provençal and Chinese poetry, their subverted syntax and fractured logic, their unreasonable war against the iambic, their preference for strange, Mediterranean lands and big cities. Even if they themselves inhabited such cities, the Frostians knew that it was not fitting to write poetry about them; one wrote, like Frost, *not* Eliot or Pound, about hills and trees, streams and animals. Was this not what the Romantic poets, whom certain wiseacre moderns liked to mock, had written about; and did they not now venerate the memory of those poets whom they had despised, perhaps, in school, but who at a distance benefited by the illusion of attractiveness which attaches itself to terrors far enough removed: home, mother, the bad weather of our childhood?

Pound and Frost: these become the ideal antagonists of contemporary culture for the popular mind, which knows such myths better than any poems. The award of the Bollingen Prize for Poetry to Pound in 1949, while he was still a patient in St. Elizabeth's Hospital, made it all a matter of public record. First the intellectual community itself was rent by disagreement about the wisdom of honoring the verse of one whose ideas they condemned (at the high point, an eminent poet challenged to a duel a well-known editor who, alas, never realized he was being challenged); and then the great audience, which has never noticed before or since any other winner of a poetry prize, found a voice in Robert Hillyer and through him joined the debate. In a series of articles for the *Saturday Review*, that second-rate poet vented his own frustration, as well as the public's rage, at the best poetry of the century, using Pound as his whipping-boy and Frost as his whip.

For this reason, then, we must come to terms with the legend of Pound and Frost, on our way toward a consideration of their verse. Indeed, not only the mass audience (to whom Pound is a curse-word in Hillyer's diatribe and a picture in *Life*, Frost an honorific in the same diatribe and a face on the television screen) but the poets themselves have been victimized by the myths mass culture has imposed on them. Under pressure, the poet tends to become his legend: Frost begins to believe he invented New England, and Pound to consider himself the discoverer of the Italian Riviera. And who is crude enough to remind the one that he was born in California, the other that he came from Hailey, Idaho? In the end, Frost almost succeeded in turning into the cracker-barrel philosopher from Vermont he played, spouting homely wisdom and affecting to despise the crackpot ideas of all intellectuals, while Pound came near to transforming himself into a caricature of the cosmopolitan esthete, a polyglot unsure before the fact whether the word trembling on his lips would emerge as Greek or Catalan or pure Mandarin.

Worst of all, Frost finally permitted himself to be cast—in complete contempt of his deepest commitments, which are to alienation and terror—as the beaming prophet of the New Frontier, court-jester to the Kennedy administration, even as Pound was content to mug his way through the role of traitor-in-chief to a nation, though he seemed more a clown in the entourage of Mussolini. And for accepting such public roles at the cost of scanting the private tasks imposed on them by their talents, these two chief poets of our time must stand trial in quite another court, the court of criticism. Before the tribunal of critics, they will not be permitted to plead that they voted right (or wrong), or even that they were in their writings comprehensible (or obscure)—only that, keeping faith with their gifts, they wrote certain lines which no literate American, perhaps no educated man anywhere, will willingly forget.

Similarly, the charges against them will not be that they voted wrong (or right), or that they were obscure (or comprehensible)—only that, pursuing their own legendary images, they wrote dull or trivial, arch or pedantic, smug or self-pitying verse; that, moreover, by their poses, they have made even their best work unavailable to certain readers: passionate liberals and sensitive Jews in the case of Pound, the disaffected urban young and a vast number of Europeans of all persuasions in the case of Frost; and that, finally, by a strange sort of retrospective falsification, they have seemed to alter the meaning, the very music of the lines in which they have, in fact, transcended the limitations of their roles and of the weaknesses in themselves out of which the mass mind created those roles to begin with.

How much time will have to go by before we are able to read either one of them without these prejudices? If there were, indeed, a justice in the world higher than that of the critics, as the critics' is higher than that of the mass audience, both Pound and Frost would be condemned to spend that time in purgatory—a single chamber in a shared purgatory, where Frost would say over and over to Pound:

> And lonely as it is that loneliness
> Will be more lonely ere it will be less—
> A blanker whiteness of benighted snow
> With no expression, nothing to express.
>
> They cannot scare me with their empty spaces
> Between stars—on stars where no human race is.
> I have it in me so much nearer home
> To scare myself with my own desert places.

while Pound would shout back ceaselessly:

> Thou art a beaten dog beneath the hail,
> A swollen magpie in a fitful sun,
> Half black half white
> Nor knowst' you wing from tail
> Pull down thy vanity
>   How mean thy hates
> Fostered in falsity,
>   Pull down thy vanity,
> Rathe to destroy, niggard in charity,
> Pull down thy vanity,
>   I say pull down.

13

THE UNBROKEN TRADITION

If the contemporary American poet must be understood in terms of his difficult and ambiguous relationship with the great audience, created by the dream of democracy and the fact of mass culture, he must also be understood in terms of his equally difficult and ambiguous relationship with the great tradition, impugned by the same dream of democracy and the same fact of mass culture. When Walt Whitman cries out, in his "Song of the Exposition":

> Come, Muse, migrate from Greece and Ionia,
> Cross out please those immensely overpaid accounts,
> That matter of Troy and Achilles' wrath, and Aneas',
>   Odysseus' wandering,
> Place 'Removed' and 'To let' on the rocks of your snowy
>   Parnassus,
> Repeat at Jerusalem . . .
> The same on the walls of your German, French and
>   Spanish castles . . .

he is echoing, as befits a poet who has chosen to play the impossible role of popular spokesman, the contempt for the remote classical past and the distrust of a more recent European one that move the American mass audience in its insecurity and pride. To be sure, he is also echoing certain European aspirations, accepting the Romantic image of America and reflecting a tradition of anti-tradition already invented in the shadow of "German, French and Spanish castles." But his *posture*, at least, signifies a resolution to reject the artistocratic past in favor of a democratic future.

Here once more posture answers posture, and Poe assumes the anti-Whitmanian role: setting his poems against backgrounds vaguely Italian or German or English, anything but native American, and affecting through allusion and quotation (often superficial or faked) the manner of one at home among old books and alien tongues, mouldering dungeons and mossgrown graveyards. In Poe and Whitman alike, however, in the unacknowledged borrowings of the one and the ostentatious references of the other, old-world models seem more parodied than emulated; as if in each, equal though opposite ambiguities undercut piety, turning *imitatio* to travesty. The absurdity of Whitman's attempt to dignify his diction with pseudo-borrowings from foreign tongues is well known, and there is scarcely an undergraduate in America who has not been taught to smile a little at his fondness for the non-existent word "camerados." But Poe is equally ridiculous when he affects the style of certain inferior English historical romances in "Lenore":

And, Guy de Vere, hast *thou* no tear?—weep now or
  nevermore!
See! on yon drear and rigid bier low lies thy love, Lenore!

It is not entirely fortuitous, after all, that the only poet writing in English who succeeded in imitating Poe's rhythm and diction with real faithfulness is that composer of nonsense verse for children, Edward Lear. From Poe's "dank tarn of Auber" and "misty mid-region of Weir" to Lear's "Hills of Chankley Bore" is a shorter distance than any of us find it convenient or comfortable to remember.

So, too, Longfellow, when he makes his very American attempt in *Hiawatha* to adapt the meter of Finnish epic to the matter of Indian life, produces the most easily and most often parodied poem in our language. Our main poetic tradition, in all of its various lines of development, can, then, be described as essentially, if sometimes unintention-

G

ally, comic or burlesque; and it is never funnier than when it seeks to emulate European models of greater or lesser antiquity. This fact, still largely unacknowledged in classrooms, the early Eliot (before respectability overtook him) and the early Pound (before madness undid him) brought to full consciousness in a series of anti-poems which have given our age its special American savor. Mock-epic is, of course, their chosen form, and satire their mode; but the device they make most their own is the travesty-allusion: the simultaneous evocation and parody of great verses out of the past. The reader remembering at the moment he reads in Eliot's *The Wasteland*:

> When lovely woman stoops to folly and
> Paces about her room again, alone,
> She smoothes her hair with automatic hand,
> And puts a record on the gramophone.

the lovely lines of Goldsmith to which they allude (or is guided to those lines by Eliot's mock-serious footnote, "V. Goldsmith, the song in *The Vicar of Wakefield*"), finally is unsure what is being mocked: Goldsmith, our relationship to him, us, or the poet himself? Perhaps it is really the poet, vainly attempting to hold onto a no-longer-viable tradition by means of pedantry and travesty and frustrated love. Certainly, in the great gallery of comic characters created by Eliot—Prufrock and Sweeney and Bleistein and Doris—it is the Old Possum himself who is least forgettable:

> How unpleasant to meet Mr. Eliot!
> With his features of clerical cut,
> And his brow so grim
> And his mouth so prim . . .

Yet no one has written more earnestly, and, after a while, more solemnly, about the "Tradition" and our need to attach ourselves to it than this same Mr. Eliot. Indeed, with the help of Ezra Pound, he has created a canon of works out of the past to which he has ceaselessly urged us to commit ourselves, presumably at the same moment that we embrace Anglo-Catholicism and even, perhaps, a more-or-less-synthetic British citizenship. What we are likely to overlook is the fact that his canon is home-made and—though studded with European writers—therefore peculiarly American, made in the U.S.A. at least. There is, that is to say, no desire on the part of Eliot and Pound to go back to the tradition so rousingly disavowed by Walt Whitman; for, whatever Eliot may say outside of his poetry, he knows that Americans must begin by recognizing their exclusion from the *organic* cultural community once the common heritage of all Europe. Our choice is always between living in a theoretical non-tradition made for us by Europe or in a synthetic European tradition of our own fabrication. In this sense, the effort of Pound and Eliot is a little like that of Longfellow in his raids on a score of literatures from Finland to Spain; nor is it very different from such attempts at synthesizing culture as last century's Harvard Twelve Foot Shelf of Books or this century's Hundred Great Books and Syntopicon as contrived at the University of Chicago. We may even be reminded of those contests, held annually in the provincial colleges of America, in which a prize is awarded for the best "new tradition" suggested by a student.

In any such contest, the "new tradition" of Eliot and Pound, with its demotion of Milton and Shelley, and its elevation of Donne, its snide devaluation of Goethe and its overt attack on Hugo, its apotheosis of Dante and its beatification of Guido Cavalcanti and Arnaut Daniel, would surely take the prize. In fact, it *has* been awarded the accolade of academic acceptance and is now embodied in a hundred textbooks and "taught" in ten thousand classes. Oddly enough, or perhaps not so oddly, at the moment when American literature enters the world scene, it has been accepted in some parts of Europe itself, and controls the assumptions of poets like, say, Eugenio Montale and Odysseus Elytis, and of the critics who admire them. Nonetheless, it is important to remember that the essential shape and direction of American poetry had been established by the middle of the nineteenth century, and that, far from radically altering this shape and direction, the "new canon" of Eliot and Pound is itself influenced by them.

No one writing poetry in the United States today, of course, can feel himself separate from an international movement whose boundaries cannot even be confined to what is at the moment called politically the West; nor can what has happened to American verse from, say, 1912 to the present moment, be understood unless one has taken into account the impact of French *symboliste* verse of the last century, Italian and Provençal verse of the late Middle Ages, the Japanese *Noh* play, and the short poems of Bassho, English religious poetry of the seventeenth century, and so on. Such influences have, however, been more than adequately treated in the most recent past, and offer now the rewards of scholarship rather than those of critical understanding. What needs to be emphasized is rather the sense in which American poetry has been *continuous* for the last one hundred years.

It is convenient, in attempting to make clear the nature of the continuity of American poetry, to speak of four lines of descent in our verse: the line of Longfellow, the line of Poe, the line of Whitman, and the line of Emerson. More commonly, critics speak of two only, that of Poe and that of Whitman, though sometimes they will cross generic or national boundaries and speak of Henry James or Baudelaire, rather than Poe, as the ideal anti-Whitmanian figure. Behind the twofold classification, there is always some myth of conflict, some legendary classification of the one as good, the other as evil. To V. L. Parrington, for instance, Whitman was the hero and Poe the villain; while, at a later date and under other pressures, critics like Yvor Winters or R. P. Blackmur reversed the labels, Blackmur insisting that "the influence of Whitman was an impediment to the *practice* of poetry, and that the influence of Baudelaire [he might equally as well have said Poe] is a re-animation itself." Whatever the original justification for such a twofold division, it has long worn out the' pedagogical uses it may once have had, and must yield to another analysis, more firmly based in literary history and critical discrimination.

For many decades now, we have simply not spoken of Longfellow in attempting to come to terms with contemporary verse, since his influence has seemed to us neither good nor bad, just non-existent. Yet, ceasing to function as high literature, his poems have assumed another kind of life, blending into the body of sub-literature which represents the nearest thing to a common culture we possess: the culture of grade-school children. Such poems as "The Children's Hour" and "The Village Blacksmith" have a status otherwise reserved for the lyrics of long-popular songs: "Home, Sweet Home," "The Old Oaken Bucket," "Way Down upon the Swanee River," or such occasional, semi-ritual poems as "The Night Before Christmas." The authors of such songs and verses are, however, almost inevitably forgotten, though their compositions survive in the popular mind, while Longfellow is, for precisely that mind, the typical poet. Indeed, he is for many semi-literate Americans the sole poet, besides Shakespeare (whom they are likely to think of as a playwright, anyhow), whom they know by name. Puns on his eminently punnable last name can be made in jokes for third-grade children, to whom parodies of his verses are also recognizable, needing no scholarly apparatus of the kind provided by Eliot for his more recondite rewritings of Goldsmith or Baudelaire.

By the same token, however, Longfellow provides a model to advanced poets of what they must define their poetry *against*, and they are haunted by his bearded presence, the patriarchal face which once hung over their desks in classrooms where their fellows learned to hate all verse. Whenever they turn from nostalgic and evocative parody to brutal satire and burlesque, mocking popular culture at the point where it becomes best-selling poetry, they are likely to be thinking of Henry Wadsworth Longfellow. When Auden, for instance, comments ironically on over-domesticated verse ("each homely lyric thing/ On sport or spousal love or spring/ Or dogs or dusters . . ."), or E. E. Cummings travesties the cultural aspirations of Americans abroad ("O to be a metope/ now that triglyph's here"), or Robert Frost parodies didacticism with an appallingly straight face

("Better to go down dignified/ With boughten friendship at your side/ Than none at all. Provide, provide!"), each may have quite other specific anti-poets in mind; yet the total effect is of an attack on Longfellow.

Other countries have had their own best-selling poets, dispensing culture and good advice. This we know (yet we cannot help feeling that we would have been better off with Victor Hugo or Tennyson). And we know, too, that none of the other founders of the main lines of American verse managed to die without leaving behind a contribution to popular sub-poetry. With uncanny accuracy of judgment, the mass audience has found them out, and does not forget Poe's "Raven," Whitman's "O Captain, My Captain," or Emerson's "Concord Hymn." A single slip is enough; the lonely error is canonized in the collections of anti-literature which serve as children's anthologies, and the great audience is revenged on the poet who has despised it. With Longfellow, however, it is not merely a matter of a poem or two on the level of debased taste, but of many scattered through a lifetime of providing the more educated, genteel, and securely Anglo-Saxon segments of the American middle class with lucid, simple, musical, sentimental, pious, often trite reassurances that the values of their class and race were not only universal, but would survive eternally.

> Life is real, life is earnest,
> And the grave is not its goal.
>
> Dust thou art, to dust returnest,
> Was not spoken of the soul.

It is his good poems which are irrelevant, as we must remember at the same moment we grant that he has written them. In recent years, he has found some learned and even sensitive defenders, and it is true, as they assert, that he has written subtle and moving verse, that especially in his Dantesque moments he possesses a genuine dignity and passion. But, alas, his artistic successes somehow do not count! The Longfellow who really survives is the one who has never died, but who is re-embodied year after year in volumes of poems published at their own expense by widowed grand-mothers or spinster aunts. It is not merely that he is banal or even Philistine, but that he is an "American" in a sense which had ceased, by the time he died, to move living writers: an Anglo-Saxon American comfortably at home, rather than an alienated American, a melting-pot American, a frontier American, or an expatriate American. Despite all his concern with European literature, he was for this very reason as unsympathetic to avant-garde Europeans as to the serious poets of his own land, and, unlike the other major lines of American verse, that which is derived from his example has been unable to influence or to be subsumed into the international modern style.

Certainly the line of Poe has fared much differently. He has, notoriously, influenced no adult twentieth-century American poet directly, yet his *presence* has haunted many, his ghost, for instance, inhabiting the very center of the American Hades imagined by Hart Crane in *The Bridge*. And scarcely anyone interested in verse has not, in his early adolescence, tried to write in the style of Poe; for adolescence is Poe's true homeland, the imaginary country out of space and in time of which he was, throughout his short life, a secret but loyal citizen. Grown-up Americans, however, have found it difficult to come to terms with Poe, except as re-interpreted by his great French admirers, Baudelaire and Mallarmé. He is at once too banal and too unique, too decadent and too revolutionary, too vulgar and too subtle, all of which is to say, too American, for us to bear except as reflected in the observing eye of Europe. And he is, further, the inventor of what was to become, by the twen-tieth century, a true international style—though it remained in his hands merely a synthetic non-national one, learned, allusive, at ease with no mythology but acquainted with many:

> Thy Naiad airs have brought me home
>   To the glory that was Greece
> And the grandeur that was Rome . . .

> Ah, Psyche, from the regions which
> Are Holy-Land!

The act which makes Poe a poet, which commits him to his muse is, then, an act of disengagement from the myth of America. Certainly, no poet who works in the tradition derived from him is aggressively patriotic, for the quarrel out of which he makes his poetry is inevitably the quarrel with his own country, and followers of Poe typically became expatriates—especially after World War I taught them the way to Europe. Before that time, their recourse was to total detachment from all the world they knew, and beyond which they could imagine no other, a flight to insanity based on the belief that there was no alternate way out of America. Indeed, the ultimate expatriation of madness seemed often to Poe identical with the most exquisite achievement of art, and he distinguishes scarcely at all between the poet, the aristocrat of the spirit, and the madman.

There is a politics of madness as well as an esthetics, and Poe subscribes to both. His ideal poet is an anti-democrat, too sensitive and refined to accept anything sponsored by the majority, including those norms of reality by which sanity is customarily judged. But syntax, logic, the act of predication itself, are concessions to sanity, and all these Poe, obsessively concerned with them elsewhere, would ban from the highest expression of art, from the poem.

Poe is in his verse not merely anti-rationalist, which he is willing enough to admit, he is also anti-literary, anti-communicative, which he finds it harder to confess even to himself. Yet it is for precisely this quality that the *symbolistes* hailed him, seeing in him that dissolution of statement into music which they so admired; and for this, too, Lear took him as a master, seeing in him that dissolution of sense into nonsense which so appealed to his imagination. Poe is the first modern poet, then, in the sense that he not merely registered his alienation from the larger audience, but wrote the kind of verse only the alienated poet is free to write—verse intended for fellow-poets or children, which is to say, "no one," as opposed to "everyone." Poe's awareness

[200]

of his revolutionary difference from other poets of his time is, however, rather dim.

He admired extravagantly, as everyone knows, the most conventional lady poets of his own day. And his famous quarrel with Longfellow, which began with an attack on didacticism, soon settled down into a quarrel about plagiarism. The truth is that Longfellow and Poe are *both* didactic poets, though the doctrine espoused by Poe is simply that art should not subserve morality. Children of the same romantic mode, Poe and Longfellow split the famous Keatsian chestnut between them, one asserting "Beauty is truth!" while the other retorted, "Truth is beauty!" How close they could come to each other in style and theme is attested by the fact that no critic now is sure whether Longfellow's "The Beleaguered City" is an imitation of Poe's "The Haunted Palace," or vice versa, or whether both borrowed from a poem by Tennyson called "The Deserted House." There is, at any rate, more of the Philistine and commonplace, more kinship with Longfellow, in Poe than is apparent at first glance; and this is a clue, perhaps, to why the school of Poe has, in the last decades, become as genteel and respectable a part of the American establishment as that of the New England Brahmins in the nineteenth century.

Even the poems which Poe wrote *about* his own loneliness scarcely rise above banality and self-pity of the most obvious kind. When he says in "Alone," for instance:

> From childhood's hour I have not been
> As others were—I have not seen
> As others saw—I could not bring
> My passions from a common spring—

he is contributing to a body of popular jingles on the subject, usually printed only in newspapers. If this represents the "school of Poe," that school reached its end with the convict leader of the last riot in the Montana State Prison, who was found dead after the shooting had died away, these verses by his own hand in one pocket:

[201]

> Nary a word said o'er my grave,
> Not a soul to rant and rave,
> No marker of errant past,
> An individualist to the last . . .

No, it is rather as in the final lines of "Ulalume," when the poet is no longer making meaning so much as sounds, when he is reproducing in pseudo-sentences the effect of hissing or singing *la-la-la-la*, that we are at last in the presence of *poésie pure*, which is to say, ultimate or last poetry, the sort of earnest parody of serious verse appropriate to a time when the average reader no longer understands such verse:

> . . . Have drawn up the spectre of a planet
> From the limbo of lunary souls—
> The sinfully scintillant planet
> From the Hell of the planetary souls?

Poe tried *deliberately* to write what other difficult poetry has *accidentally* become in the ear of the sub-literate; and this is the third kind of travesty appropriate to modern verse, the other two being the mockery of middlebrow poetizing, and the parody-allusion as practiced by Pound and Eliot.

But Poe's way, too, is a way to *épater la bourgeoisie*, as certain French poets not required to read Poe in school were quick to realize; and it is their *Edgairpo*, re-imported into the United States, who became the spiritual father of all our aristocratic anti-poets, from Eliot (who began by writing as often in French as in English), through Pound and Wallace Stevens to Marianne Moore, R. P. Blackmur, and beyond. Not only in his origins but also in his pose, Poe has appealed especially to poets of the American South, to the so-called Southern agrarians, cavalier dandies all, including John Crowe Ransom, Robert Penn Warren, and Allen Tate, the last of whom has begun a long, sympathetic study of the figure he calls "Our Cousin, Mr. Poe." It is tempting, as a matter of fact, to speak of the line of Poe as a "Southern line," appropriate to a part of our country

[202]

obsessed by myths of its aristocratic origins and high culture, and ridden by the fact of its impoverishment and defeat.

Utterly different in origin, tone, and appeal is the line of Whitman, whose pretensions are democratic rather than aristocratic, aggressively nationalistic rather than ostentatiously internationalist. To Whitmanians being American means despising the culture of Europe, indeed, all high culture, finally the very notion of culture itself; and, as we have already seen, their verse is dedicated not to the ironic evocation of the past in travestied quotation, nor to the creation of elegant nonsense in a simultaneous protest against and acceptance of the isolation of the poet, nor to an attack on popular vulgarization of language. The Whitmanian, indeed, has no quarrel with the esthetics of the masses, which he thinks of himself as trying to emulate; only with their politics and their morality, which he thinks of as somehow unworthy of them. His onslaught is directed against the artificial cultural heritage of the educated classes, which he regards as both pedantic and un-American, and he resists that culture in the name of the people, who for him represent the naïve, the natural, the *real*. It is raw experience for which he longs and for whose sake he disowns all literature except his own. He wants really to write the *first* poem of the world, even when he has come to his own second, or tenth, or one hundredth.

For the Whitmanian, consequently, the poet is conceived of not as the cosmopolitan dandy, but the provincial prophet, the man with a message from God, or from the people who are the voice of God. He does not, therefore, suggest or evoke, but asserts, yells, hollers, and screams, since for him poetry aspires not to the condition of music but to that of rhetoric, public speech. He has, perhaps, no assurance that he will be heard, only that he *must* be, and that is why his tone is rather the tone of one trying to shout down hecklers than of one preaching to the converted. Since he aims at convincing rather than delighting (like Poe) or instructing delightfully (like Longfellow), it is indifferent to him whether he writes in verse or prose; indeed, what he writes is likely to be deliberately ambiguous in this regard.

[203]

If there is a section of America with which poetry in the line of Whitman can be identified, it is the West, the part of our country mythically rather than historically defined. The "South" of Poe can be identified with Virginia, the "East" of Longfellow with Boston and Cambridge, but the "West" of Whitman (who, of course, did not really live in it or know it except out of books) is for one generation Kentucky, for another Ohio or Illinois, for the next Minnesota and the Dakotas, then California or Montana; and finally it ceases to exist at all except in poems like Whitman's, or in popular movies less unlike him than one thinks at first. The "West," that is to say, is not a fact of history defined once and for all and there to be accepted or rejected forever after; it is a fiction: the place to which we have not yet come or at which we have just arrived, a *theoretical* place. When Whitman talks of landscapes he knows, Brooklyn, Long Island, New York City, we believe what he writes; but when he cries, "I cross the Laramie plains, I note the rocks in grotesque shapes, the buttes. . . . I see the Monument mountain and the Eagle's nest, I pass the Promontory, I ascend the Nevadas . . ." we have the sense that he has worked it all up out of some gazetteer.

Yet actual Western poets in the generations which followed him have taken Whitman for a guide and model—Carl Sandburg, for instance, first poet of Chicago, and Edgar Lee Masters, who expressed, with political overtones, his appreciation of what is specifically new and, therefore, anti-Eastern about the author of *Leaves of Grass:* ". . . Whitman wrote for the American tribe and the American idea. . . . Whitman had the right idea, namely, that poetry, the real written word, must come out of the earth . . . It is no wonder that a man as sincere as Whitman . . . had to endure the sneers and chatter of New York critics . . . who often miss the important, the real and truly American art." To this classic populist statement, Amy Lowell gave the classic aristocratic answer, speaking from Boston and in defense of ideals more like Poe's: "Often and often I read in the press, that modern vers libre writers derive their form from Walt Whitman. As a matter of fact, most of them got it from French Symbolist poets . . ." And she adds, trying to take from Whitman his claims to Americanism as well as his prestige as a technical innovator, "It is perhaps sadly significant that the three modern poets who most loudly acknowledge his leadership are all of recent foreign extraction . . ."

Now it is, indeed, true that Whitman has appealed always to relatively *new* Americans, that is, marginal and therefore theoretical Americans, not to Anglo-Saxon Brahmins at home, like Miss Lowell, or such Brahmins exiled to the Midwest, like Eliot, nor to the offspring of upper-class Southern families, whose loyalties are sectional and whose origins tie them securely to Great Britain. It is to melting-pot Americans or to those on actual and recent frontiers, to those educated abroad, like William Carlos Williams, and whose America is therefore large and abstract, whose Americanism must be invented day by day, that he seems especially sympathetic. This is why he was at first the darling of the populist poets of the mid-West, like Sandburg and Masters, then the preferred muse of the Marxists in the United States, most of them children of recent immigrants and themselves just out of ghettos, or on the long hard way out. Americans, that is to say, who have yearned for, rather than endured, their Americanism have sought in Whitman a myth of their own lives and of their country.

Ben Maddow, a once-admired "proletarian poet" of the Thirties, will serve to represent the Marxist-Whitmanians as Edgar Lee Masters represents the populist-Whitmanians. In a poem called "Red Decision," he invokes the spirit of his master to help him prove in verse what the leaders of the American Communist Party were asserting in political manifestoes, that "Communism is the Americanism of the twentieth century":

> Broad-hearted Whitman of the healthy beard
> stiffen my infirm palate for this bread,
> whose gritty leaven shall embowel me
> to hold . . .
> in solemn hands, my tough majestic pen

This is rather Whitman parodied than Whitman emulated; for, indeed, the style of *Leaves of Grass* is, in its exaggeration, almost comic, almost caricature, a last desperate, delicate teetering on the edge of self-travesty—and pushed further it becomes a joke on those who use it. But worse was to come.

Transmitted, via the fake "native culture" (pseudo-Whitman, plus pseudo-folk-songs, plus pseudo-jazz) sponsored by the Popular Front movement, to the heart of the New Deal, this line of development from Whitman became a new official art and was exemplified, for instance, in the sound track of Pare Lorentz's *The River*, and other documentary films, as well as throwaways, campaign literature, etc. It was, at this point, that Whitmanian verse became to the living avant garde a butt and a laughing stock, not less scorned than ladylike effusions in the style of Longfellow; and W. H. Auden is able to include in a list of Philistine cultural horrors:

> . . . over-Whitmanated song
>   That does not scan,
> With adjectives laid end to end,
> Extol the doughnut and commend
>   The Common Man.

Yet just before World War I, poets in the line of Whitman and those in the line of Poe felt themselves allied in a common cause: a united front against the bourgeoisie and its dream of a poetry romantic and sentimental, Anglo-Saxon and genteel. At that point, the name of Whitman was the rallying cry of the whole literary avant garde; new sex, new society, and new poetry, these seemed the three persons of a single god (or better, devil), and Whitman was his prophet. *Poetry*, the magazine founded by Harriet Monroe, still carries a tag from Whitman, and in its pioneer days that magazine celebrated as a single syndrome, anti-conventional and anti-bourgeois, T. S. Eliot, Pound, Amy Lowell, imagism, free verse, Sandburg, Frost, and E. A. Robinson. To this blur of enthusiasm, the prophetic blur at the heart of the Whitman image corresponded exactly; he is the presiding genius of an alliance based on the single slogan: "Make it New!"

It was, however, an alliance that could not survive its first victories. Dismayed at the death of Longfellow as a living influence, the disappearance of an ideal against which to define themselves, and undone by the triumph and slow spread of the Russian revolution, its members divided against themselves. Quite soon, the socialist poets were regarding their converted Catholic confreres with hostility; the re-discoverers of metaphysical wit and classical form were watching warily the exponents of formless dithyrambics; the advocates of escape from emotion were wondering why they had ever enlisted beside the enthusiasts of phallic con-sciousness; the followers of *Edgairpo* separated themselves from the champions of *Leaves of Grass*. And though Ezra Pound tried to make peace ("I make a pact with you, Walt Whitman—/ I have detested you long enough), no one in Pound's own camp would believe him, Eliot insisting, for instance, "I am equally certain—it is indeed obvious—that Pound owes nothing to Whitman. This is an elementary observation . . ."

Yet one of the most admired American poets of the first half of the twentieth century attempted, in his most ambi-tious poem, to keep alive side by side not only the myths of Poe and Whitman but their actual influences. In *The Bridge*, Hart Crane confesses Poe as the ghost who haunts him and his country; but it is Whitman whom he honors as inspiration and guide:

> Our Meistersinger, thou set breath in steel;
> And it was thou who on the boldest heel
> Stood up and flung the span on even wing
> Of that great Bridge, our Myth, whereof I sing!

The Bridge, however, is a failure, incoherent throughout, despite occasional momentary successes; and it is never more incoherent than in the passages in which Crane attempts to evoke Whitman. Crane's whole relationship to Whitman was ambiguous in the extreme, and he had other troubles with his subject matter, each alone deep and dangerous enough to wreck a poem.

Nonetheless, the failure of *The Bridge* was interpreted not as Crane's failure but as Whitman's. The critical *locus classicus* is the review by Yvor Winters in *Poetry* for June 1930, which begins by admiring the "dignity and power" of Crane's attempt to make a Whitmanian epic, and ends by insisting that his lack of success proves "the impossibility of getting anywhere with the Whitmanian inspiration . . . it seems highly unlikely that any writer of comparable genius will struggle with it again." This contention became a basic dogma of those new critics who dominated the American scene for two decades; indeed, it is one of their few firm critical judgments about American literature, and one of the handful in any area upon which they unanimously agree. Allen Tate and R. P. Blackmur early expressed their concurrence, and by 1950 Winters' position had become orthodoxy in the academies. Here, for instance, is how the position is summed up in a handbook for college students: "But Whitman and his followers— like Robinson Jeffers, Vachel Lindsay, Edgar Lee Masters, Carl Sandburg, Stephen Vincent Benét . . . and later Paul Engle, August Derleth, Muriel Rukeyser, Ben Maddow, and Alfred Hayes . . . are not in the line of American writers who have deepened our knowledge of human motivation or action."

Not only is Whitman gone, according to this view, but two, three generations of followers with him, consigned to an outer darkness with all others who deviate "from the tradition which runs from Hawthorne and Melville through James and Eliot." Only in Europe did the wandering American, until very recently, encounter serious scholars and critics who wanted to discuss Sandburg or Edgar Lee Masters seriously, and who did not even know that Whitman's reputation had been challenged. At home only undergraduate versifiers, back-country bards, and provincial schoolmasters remained ignorant of the news that a god had died and that his prophets were unread. And these benighted few were advised, some years ago, on a black-bordered page in a little magazine called *Furioso:* WALT WHITMAN IS DEAD! As late as 1950, indeed, it would have been hard to persuade any reputable critic or respected younger poet that it would be possible ever again to write moving verse based on the example of *Leaves of Grass.*

Easiest of the lines of American verse to forget, or re-membering, to despise, is the line of Ralph Waldo Emerson. Europeans are likely to be quite unaware of its existence, and Americans to confuse it with the line of Longfellow (was not Emerson, after all, just another New England Brahmin?) or to dismiss it impatiently with a curt reference to the failure of Emerson's technique (was he not a lec-turer and essayist, a master of our prose, if of anything?). Edgar Lee Masters, who at least named Emerson in order to dismiss him in favor of Whitman, was apparently think-ing of *both* these objections: "It is not because Whitman is a better poet than Emerson that he may be called the father of American poetry. . . . It is because Whitman wrote for the American tribe." For a long time, indeed, it seemed as if Emerson were another once-admired poet doomed to live the sub-literary life of Longfellow: his "Rhodora" sung in occasional school concerts chiefly for the sake of its musical setting, and his "Concord Hymn" recited in school-rooms on patriotic occasions.

Without understanding Emerson, however, it is impos-sible to deal with two notable early modern American poets, Frost and E. A. Robinson, who seem otherwise unaccounta-ble eccentrics; nor can one understand the place of Emily Dickinson between Emerson's time and our own; nor, finally, can one appreciate the true meaning of Edward Taylor, that recently rediscovered American metaphysical poet who is Emerson's ancestor, as Emerson is Emily Dickinson's. We cannot now and never really could read with pleasure Anne Bradstreet and other pre-Republican American poets celebrated in the textbooks of a generation ago, but Taylor is a seventeenth-century poet as alive for us as his English forerunner John Donne. Lines from his poems have already made their way into our new anthologies and, more significantly, into our heads, from which they will not be dislodged: the first stanzas, for instance, of "Upon a Spider Catching a Fly":

Thou sorrow, venom Elf:
  Is this thy play,
To spin a web out of thyself
  To catch a Fly?
    For why?

I saw a pettish wasp
  Fall foul therein:
Whom yet thy whorl pins did
      not hasp
Lest he should fling
  His sting.

Thus gently him didst treat
  Lest he should pet,
And in a froppish, aspish
      heat
  Should greatly fret
    Thy net.

Whereas the silly Fly,
  Caught by its leg,
Thou by the throat took'st
      hastily,
And 'hind the head
    Bite Dead.

It is clear, as a matter of fact, that the sole line of American poetry which has an unbroken line of development as old as our country itself is the one that runs from Taylor to Emerson to Dickinson to Frost and beyond; and it is Emerson who brought it to full consciousness, at the very moment when the schools of Longfellow and Poe and Whitman were defining themselves for the first time. Yet Emerson does not exist for the imagination as do any of the other three, for he has not assumed mythic dimensions to Europeans, as have Poe and Whitman, or to the American middle classes, as has Longfellow. Emerson represents, that is to say, neither a European myth of America, nor an American myth of Europe—only a private myth of ourselves for ourselves, which somehow has appealed neither to Europeans nor to many of us. I do not mean to say that Emerson did not try to project his view of the poet in legendary guise; he was a deeply, if erratically, learned man, given to describing his ideal bard as Merlin or Uriel or Saadi; but somehow none of these tags caught on—perhaps because in his cool, almost antiseptic mind they were divested of the self-pity we seem to demand of our writers as our devil's due.

How, then, to define the Emersonian line? Perhaps the easiest way to begin is by locating it geographically in New England, in what seems at first glance the same Northeast out of which Longfellow speaks his bland and scholarly reassurance. In Longfellow, however, the emphasis is on the east of the compound sectional name; in Emerson the north. He speaks not for the self-satisfied urban center, not for the would-be cosy cosmopolitanism of Boston, but for a more provincial, a much colder Concord. He is the poet of winter, of an iciness which is not perhaps generous but is surely never sentimental. And, by the same token, he is the mouthpiece of essential Puritanism, that tough-minded view of man and God, immune alike to sentiment and gentility, which survived the collapse of the church that first nurtured it. That in our time the line of Emerson has been represented by a great poetic authority on snow and night actually called Robert *Frost* is one of those astonishingly happy accidents which almost persuade us that history is the subtlest allegorist of all. Trying to portray the typical American poet in his recent novel, *Pale Fire*, Vladimir Nabokov was unable to do better than model him on Frost

[211]

and name him analogously, though not quite as satisfactorily, "Shade."

The best brief description of the Emersonian countryside is in E. A. Robinson's "New England," which in scarcely more than four verses suggests to us not only the Emersonian setting but the special quality of feeling that setting begets:

> Here where the wind is always north-north-east
> And children learn to walk on frozen toes,
> Wonder begets an envy of all those
> Who boil elsewhere with such a lyric yeast
> Of love . . .

The language, the meter reflect more than some improbably imported ideal of neo-classicism. This is cool, if not downright cold, verse: a little tight and tending to the crabbed; sometimes—less in Robinson, perhaps, than in Emerson himself—as rocky and uncomfortable as the meager landscape against which it is written. At its best, however, it is quietly tough and masculine (even in the hands of Emily Dickinson, when her female instincts do not lead her into coyness or cuteness), neither sensually self-indulgent like Poe, nor ostentatiously loose like Whitman, in whom we sense the boast of masculinity rather than the fact. This is poetry of the middle-way, neither hypnotic nor hortatory, but it is saved from the smoothness of the golden mean by a kind of blessed clumsiness.

And behind it, of course, there is a different view of the poet than those which moved Poe and Whitman and Longfellow. For Emerson, the poet is neither dandy nor agitator nor domesticated paraclete; he is, rather, a lonely philosopher or magician; a rebel, perhaps, as much as Whitman's mythical poet, but one, in Frost's phrase, "too lofty and original to rage." The voice of such a poet is neither wholly musical nor wholly rhetorical, though it partakes of both elements. When it inclines to the rhetorical, it is the speech of a man urging himself on, rather than appealing to a crowd:

[212]

He shall not his brain encumber
With the coil of rhythm and number,
But leaving rule and pale forethought,
He shall aye climb
For his rhyme:
Pass in, pass in, the angels say,
In to the upper doors;
Nor count compartments of the floors,
But mount to Paradise
By the stairway of surprise.

When it inclines to the musical, it is like the overheard spell some amateur magician murmurs to himself:

Subtle rhymes with ruin rife
Murmur in the house of life,
Sung by the Sisters as they spin;
In perfect time and measure, they
Build and unbuild our echoing clay,
As the two twilights of the day
Fold us music-drunken in.

But at its best it is conversational, though not garrulous and effusive, rather like the cryptic interchange of two wise old friends, each of whom insists that between them the final words, the last things remain unspoken:

Askest, "How long shalt thou stay?"
Devastator of the day!
Know, each substance and relation
Through nature's operation,
Hath its unit, bound and metre . . .
But the unit of the visit,
The encounter of the wise,
Say what other metre is it
Than the meeting of the eyes?

Sometimes the Emersonian writer is content with pure musing or meditation, and stays within the confines of the

[213]

lyric; but often he is moved to try his hand at myth-making or narration, and produces poems like Emerson's "Uriel," which Frost thought to be one of the greatest poems in the language. Actually "Uriel" is a retelling of the first two books of *Paradise Lost* from the point of view of the Satanic party, very terse and very American. In it the fallen angel is Prometheus rather than the Devil; and Prometheus, biographically interpreted, turns out to be the transcendentalist Emerson or, prophetically understood, the scientific relativist, Albert Einstein:

> Line in nature is not found,
> Unit and universe are round;
> In vain produced, all rays return,
> Evil will bless, and ice will burn.

Emerson himself, however, was too short-breathed and gnomic to tackle seriously the really long poem, and it remained for Frost (less happily for E. A. Robinson, too) to produce in the twentieth century, after almost everyone else had abandoned conventional drama and story-telling in verse, large poetic narratives of considerable power. Such a poem as Frost's "Witch of Coos" stands nearly alone in a time when the chief American poets had decided its mode and methods were hopelessly outdated and were searching for hints in Whitman and Pound to help them construct pseudo- or mock-epics with imagistic rather than narrative techniques. Frost and Robinson alone resisted the drift toward studied incoherence, willed dissociation, and planned irrelevance that characterized the anti-poetry of the first half of the twentieth century, just as they alone clung still to the traditional metrical forms of English poetry despite Pound's battle-cry, "Break the iambic!" Indeed, in their resolve to write poetry that scanned and told a story, Frost and Robinson came to seem allies to the Philistine opponents of the new verse, and enemies to its practitioners.

Though Frost had made an appearance or two in *Poetry*, in the exciting days just before World War I, he did not seem part of the movement that was making room for the utterly new by destroying the old: old allegiances, old esthetics, old forms. Indeed, he had to go to England before he could make a poetic reputation; there he was able to profit by the cultural lag which has kept British poetry limping along behind ours through the whole of this century, and to be accepted along with certain of the English Georgian poets, with whom he only seemed to have something essential in common. That he wrote about the countryside rather than the city appealed to a backward English audience convinced that, in their land at least (unlike France or America), poetry was going to be kept where it belonged, that is, where Wordsworth had firmly placed it at the end of the eighteenth century. But what did the landscape evoked in the title of Frost's second published book, the bleak snow-bound world of "North of Boston," have to do with the Lake Country?

Robinson had the good grace, at least, to be born in the same decade in which the Civil War ended, and to die before World War II, so that he could be comfortably placed in the past and labeled a forerunner. But Frost disturbingly survived into the present, to be honored not by a remote Theodore Roosevelt (like E. A. Robinson) but by the living and reigning exponent of the New Frontier. What to do, then, in a time like ours, with poets still available to Philistines and even Presidents, with poets who neither pretend to write first poems, in the manner of Whitman—poems before which the reader could imagine no others—nor last poems, in the manner of Poe—poems after which the reader could imagine no others? Without a sense of the Emersonian tradition and its meaning, one is tempted to class them with the poets who wrote just poems, in the manner of Longfellow, poems whose whole function is to remind the reader of all the others he has read before and shall read after. But the relevance to our present situation of what Emerson and his followers were after, and the sense in which they stand beside the Whitmanians as dissenters and disturbers of the peace (after all, it was Emerson alone, of all the poets of his day, who hailed the publication of *Leaves of Grass*), we are just now beginning to understand.

14

TOWARD THE SUBURBS:
THE FEAR OF MADNESS
AND THE DEATH OF THE "I"

What, then, of poetry today, of the so-called "beat move-ment" in verse and the unforeseen triumphs of certain poets as cabaret entertainers—with or without benefit of jazz backgrounds to their recitations? How did poetry get out of the classroom and into the nightclub, out of libraries and back into bohemia? To understand any of this, one must understand first, I think, how complete was the triumph of the poetic line which, beginning with Poe, passed via the French *symbolistes* to T. S. Eliot, and from him to certain quasi-official bards of the academy and the suburbs. What had begun as a revolutionary movement in the arts, in the years just before World War I, had in the three decades stretch-ing roughly from 1925 to 1955 become an almost unchal-lenged orthodoxy. Anyone who picks up, for instance, the anthology of American verse compiled by Oscar Williams and published in 1955, will be struck by the sameness of certain poems he includes, particularly by writers born from 1915 on. They are characterized by a uniform style, a uni-form subject matter, a uniform broad range of erudition, and a uniform high level of technical excellence—impres-sive, but somehow more than a little depressing.

A whole school of younger poets was, at mid-century, writing in a style derived from Eliot, though not, to be sure, from the irreverent author of the Sweeney poems, skeptical, gross, and moving always on the edge of nausea and madness:

Yes I'd eat you!
In a nice little, white little, soft little, tender little,
Juicy little, right little, missionary stew.
You see this egg
You see this egg
Well that's life on a crocodile isle . . .
You'd be bored.
Birth, and copulation, and death,
That's all the facts when you come to brass tacks:
Birth, and copulation, and death.
I've been born, and once is enough.
You don't remember, but I remember,
Once is enough.

These lines are from the unemulated Eliot, from *Sweeney Agonistes*, a poem he could not finish after he had decided to exorcise once and for all the alter ego of his youth, Sweeney: for once Sweeney was dead, only the proper, Anglo-Saxon Eliot was left, with his "features of clerical cut" and his commitment to a higher and higher seriousness. Sweeney, vulgar Boston-Irish comic, represented Eliot's tribute to all he was not: his awareness that no American, no matter how proper his own Bostonian forebears, could afford to be, as a poet, all Anglo-Saxon; since no one so pure in origin could make, in the twentieth century, moving and authentic poetry for Americans. It is, however, precisely the later, the successful and Sweeney-less Eliot whom Oscar Williams' younger poets seek to emulate. In their work, his wit (a little attenuated), his posture of anti-Romanticism, and especially his fondness for symbol and allusion remain. But his aspirations to vulgarity and nuttiness are gone. Sweeney is gone! And the finished form, which a certain blessed uncertainty had prevented Eliot himself from attaining, though he talked about it at great length, has replaced, in their poems, the tentative, awkward rhythms of his.

At the moment, then, that the Eliotic new poetry triumphed in the United States, it was already well on the way to becoming academic and genteel, well-behaved and passionless, a convention made out of a revolt; but all revolutionaries really aspire to make their manifestoes conventions. It was with Eliot's implicit consent, as well as the best intentions, that certain critic-professor-poets of the Eliotic persuasion (Allen Tate, R. P. Blackmur, and Robert Penn Warren, for instance) revised the college curriculum and rewrote the college textbooks of literature, in order to prepare their students first to read Eliot and the earlier poets he admired, then to write poems like his. Meanwhile, a new genteel audience was being formed to replace the old one destroyed by the First World War, the first great prosperity, and the great depression: a liberal, culture-hungry, new bourgeoisie, with a taste for irony, who had admired Franklin Roosevelt but whose true culture hero was Adlai Stevenson; and who, with the coming of the second great prosperity, moved from the cities to the suburbs, from which they sent their sons to Harvard, Yale, Princeton, and the smaller quality colleges, where the professor-poets were waiting for them with the new orthodoxy.

The new audience no longer hated literature *per se*, as had many of their parents and grandparents; they only feared madness and unrestraint (though they had read Freud), like their spiritual ancestors, the audience which had sustained Longfellow and Lowell and Oliver Wendell Holmes. And they found bards appropriate to their fears and allegiances in their actual or spiritual offspring, whose names one can read at hazard out of the index of Oscar Williams' *New Pocket Anthology of American Verse*: Joseph Bennett, William Burford, Donald Hall, W. S. Merwin, Howard Nemerov, etc. etc. Best of the group by far, however, is Richard Wilbur, who was born in the suburbs of New York in 1921 and was educated first at Amherst, then at Harvard, where, appropriately enough, he worked on a long study of the concept of the dandy. It was a book he never completed, but parts of it appear as the introduction to an edition he has recently prepared of the poems of Edgar Allan Poe. The choice seems almost disconcertingly apt; though, to be sure, Wilbur makes the low estimate of Poe's poetic achievement customary among followers of

[218]

Eliot, who settle usually for preferring not Poe but other poets who preferred him, e.g., Mallarmé or Baudelaire.

Wilbur is a versatile craftsman, capable of assimilating to his own uses the techniques of poets as peculiar and difficult as Marianne Moore; and he controls, always with deceptive ease, whatever he sees (the cultivated countryside just out of cities), feels (the loveliness of the created world), imagines (Noah, dead heroes) or muses upon (the meaning of art). His language is never banal and never outrageous; his music never dull and never atrocious; he knows what he can do and is never tempted to exceed it. Most of his adult life he has spent teaching in a university, but he has a sense of his obligation to those outside it, and has tried to extend the range of his voice in the theater: translating, for instance, with astonishing fidelity and grace, Molière's *Le Misanthrope*, and writing the lyrics for a musical comedy based on Voltaire's *Candide*. Just past forty, Wilbur has already had an effect on the work of younger poets, particularly in the universities, and has come to be spoken of widely as an influence on current poetic practice.

Indeed, not only his example but his taste is helping to determine the shape of poetry at the present moment; for he is one of the editors of a series of volumes of new poetry being published by the Wesleyan University Press, as well as the chief editor of a series of paperback anthologies of great poets of the past, English and American, and he has recently been called on to help update the Untermeyer anthology of English and American verse, widely used as a basic school text. A sense of the special quality of his work, though by no means of its scope, is perhaps sufficiently suggested by the following short poem. Like the work of many other poets now at or around their fortieth year, his belongs neither with the hopeful efforts of those who hope to invent first poems nor the desperate achievements of those who suspect they are writing last poems. "Museum Piece" assumes the existence of a living tradition, an accepted and up-to-date set of standards, in light of which it must be read simply as a good poem. Not only in its range

[219]

of reference, but in its tone, diction and metrical form, it postulates an enlightened good taste, which may grow, perhaps, more enlightened, more tolerant, more broadly inclusive, but which can never be completely overthrown, being, as it were, the product of what everyone knows is the final great revolution in taste:

> The good grey guardians of art
> Patrol the halls on spongy shoes,
> Impartially protective, though
> Perhaps suspicious of Toulouse.
>
> Here dozes one against the wall,
> Disposed upon a funeral chair.
> A Degas dancer pirouettes
> Upon the parting of his hair.
>
> See how she spins! The grace is there,
> But strain as well is plain to see.
> Degas loved the two together:
> Beauty joined to energy.
>
> Edgar Degas purchased once
> A fine El Greco, which he kept
> Against the wall beside his bed
> To hang his pants on while he slept.

There are wit and grace in these lines, as there are in all of Wilbur's poems; and there is an impulse—far from ignoble—to write at every moment as well as one can; but there is no personal voice anywhere, as there is no passion and no insanity; the insistent "I," the assertion of sex, and the flaunting of madness being considered apparently in equally bad taste. But this is the influence of Eliot, though of his criticism rather than his poetry, with its insistence upon objectivity, control and form—all flagrantly disregarded in the verse itself. In Eliot, the injunctions against an excess of feeling were balanced by the pressure of emotion one senses in him everywhere; in Wilbur, they seem to accord only too well with a temperamental distaste for excess.

Wilbur is not an epicene poet, much less a homosexual one, but the face which his poetry presents and the voice in which it speaks seem de-sexed, or, rather, smack of that intersex which aged men and women alike approach somewhat faster than they do death. Aptly enough, the model for many of his early poems was found in the work of Marianne Moore, already old when he began. There is more sense of the aroused and living flesh, of bodies savored and seed sown, and, therefore, of a creating "I," in the work of certain women poets, especially Ruth Stone, whose debut was simultaneous with Wilbur's (they were both, improbably, members of the Harvard Poetry Society just after World War II), but who still remains undeservedly little known.

Mrs. Stone's single small published volume is unfortunately titled *In an Iridescent Time*, suggesting poems more feminine and less female than hers actually are; but even a few stanzas of a single poem are enough to indicate the presence in her work of whatever is the female equivalent of *cojones*; and of the acuteness of her nose, that ordinarily attenuated sense without which we cannot fully know our existence in the flesh:

> When I was young I knew that I would die.
> The fear of an old death went out with me.
> The rank green wasted; fiddle, so did I,
> But I was long-lived as the hemlock tree.
>
> Yes, I was strong as juniper. The pitch,
> The amber resin, all of those strong tars,
> The pungent aromatics of the bitch,
> I kept in fascinating rows of jars.
>
> All those other odors. Love's a smell.
> I'll dance the diddy on a wrinkled knee;
> The empty udders dangle on the shell.
> Now the fat's gone, some gnaw the bone with me . . .

Not all the neo-genteel poets in the line of Eliot, however, represent so disheartening a diminution of passion as we have noticed in Wilbur. Particularly in the work of the first generation of "New Poets," there remains, to the end of their careers, evidence of how revolutionary their impact was on an audience still conditioned to nineteenth-century verse long after the nineteenth century had died. Wallace Stevens, for instance, utterly baleful as an influence on the young—and unfortunately addicted, through the latter part of his writing life, to poetry about poetry about poetry— produced, after all, "Sunday Morning." And "Sunday Morning," harmless anthology piece that it has come to seem, remains the only moving death-of-god poem in the American canon: the musing of a Nietzschean dandy who has chosen to take on the mask of a woman, though everyone knows that the woman is the opposite of the dandy, and represented to Nietzsche the ultimate enemy. Moreover, tags of Stevens continue to ring in our heads, not as remembered glories out of an irrelevant past, but as living language:

Let the lamp affix its beam.
The only emperor is the emperor of ice-cream.

. . . Is not the porch of spirits lingering.
It is the grave of Jesus, where He lay.

And you, and you, be thou me as you blow,
When in my coppice you behold me be.

His firm stanzas hang like hives in hell
Or what hell was . . .

                            . . . the softest
Woman with a vague moustache and not the mauve
Maman. His anima liked its animal . . .

Only, here and there, an old sailor,
Drunk and asleep in his boots,
Catches tigers
In red weather.

Of that generation, too, John Crowe Ransom refuses to be entombed in the definitions he himself helped formulate. Founder of the *Kenyon Review* and of the School of Letters, dean of the Southern agrarians and veteran of close textual analysis, he is associated in our minds with the rigid pieties of the new criticism and the nostalgic politics it so often implies. But his generosity of spirit and questing intelligence kept him from ever closing off the literary precincts he controlled from sensibilities alien to his, and even from kinds of madness and passion (my own, for instance) he would have considered it poor form to flaunt, as, in the generations since his, it has become fashionable to do. There is a pathos of lastness about him and his accomplishment, the sense of a world already lost to his audience even as he continued to exploit it; but there is never a hint of smugness. And always at work beneath his surfaces, there are, thank God, his own kind of madness and passion—plus a sense of humor both mad and passionate—thrusting against the tight control, the polished form; making the ordered lines buckle, the controlled metaphors blur, the well-bred voice break. Few twentieth-century poems, at any rate, remain as uncomfortably vivid in my memory as his "Captain Carpenter," which I rediscover with surprise on the printed page, having come, I suppose, to believe it a remembered nightmare, or a frightening story heard in childhood from some amiable, terrible old man:

> God's mercy rest on Captain Carpenter now
> I thought him Sirs an honest gentleman
> Citizen husband soldier and scholar enow
> Let jangling kites eat him if they can.
>
> But God's deep curses follow after those
> That shore him of his goodly nose and ears
> His legs and strong arms at the two elbows
> And eyes that had not watered seventy years.
>
> The curse of hell upon the sleek upstart
> Who got the Captain finally on his back
> And took the red red vitals of his heart
> And made the kites to whet their beaks clack clack.

[223]

It is possible that Ransom will be remembered as the poet of childhood, for most of his best work rings as if in the ear of a child, or is about childhood itself: that last area of wilderness left to the genteel imagination. A later generation of poets will view themselves as children, their own savages, noble or ignoble, and exploit the wilderness of their own lives. Ransom's excursions into disorder, passion and natural terror are likely to be disguised as the adventures of a child he no longer is, as in "First Travels of Max":

> In the middle of the wood was the Red Witch.
> Max half expected her. He never imagined
> To find a witch's house so dirty and foolish,
> A witch with a wide bosom yellow as butter,
> Or one that combed so many obscene things
> From her black hair into her scarlet lap . . .

Even in generations more recent than that of such founding fathers, however, there are *symboliste* poets who seem finally neither academic nor suburban. Two, at least, have maintained, into the Sixties, some sense of the madness that moved the author of *The Wasteland*, and have managed to keep some measure of faith with the attack on sense inherited by Eliot, through whatever intermediaries, from Poe. These are W. H. Auden, who was born in 1907, and Theodore Roethke, who was born a year later. Despite their considerable seniority over Wilbur and the other members of the new-genteel school, they seem still poets of the moment; and the recent death of Roethke makes all the clearer that, along with Auden, he had come to seem, over the past decade, one of the two most eminent poets producing verse in America.

In England, to be sure, Auden is still thought of as a poet of the Thirties; and, as an *English* poet, so he is, though the thesis that he died forever as a poet at the moment of his emigration to America just before World War II will not hold up under examination. Such a point of view is necessary, perhaps, in England, where writers, at a time of small accomplishment, find satisfaction in the myths of cultural anti-Americanism; but Auden's difficulties with his art after 1940 should not be compared solely with those of his fellow-emigré Christopher Isherwood to make the pat anti-American case. No, the circle should be extended to include certain English stay-at-homes like Louis MacNeice, C. Day Lewis, and Stephen Spender, to make clear that what is involved is a failure of certain Oxford undergraduate communists to come to terms with a world in which their growing up coincided precisely with the destruction (for all intelligent men in the West) of hopes for society and art too closely associated with the political fate of the Soviet Union.

Not only for Englishmen, but for Americans as well, who had learned to write in the shrill accents of the Thirties and in praise of that decade's ideals, the Forties proposed an unforeseen choice: *die forever or be totally reborn.* Only Auden, of the group of young poets who moved and astonished the English in the era of the great depression, has been successfully born again; and in his second birth he is an American, an American poet of the Fifties. The work he produced in the early Forties seems to us now, in large part, tentative and uncertain, though, alas, not frankly so; for he had invented a rhetoric to conceal from himself and his readers alike his failure to find, at that point, satisfactory themes and an adequate new voice. But beginning with *Nones* and *The Shield of Achilles*, the second Auden, the American Auden, had entered into full and secure possession of his craft again, rendering, in poems like "In Praise of Limestone," reflections of the Mediterranean landscape in an American eye; in others, like "The Shield of Achilles," a view of the Eastern European scene out of the deepest American political imagination; and making, in his Phi Beta Kappa poem, delivered at Harvard just after World War II, a new American Decalogue:

> Thou shalt not answer questionnaires
> Or quizzes upon World-Affairs,
>   Nor with compliance

H

> Take any test. Thou shalt not sit
> With statisticians nor commit
> A social science . . .

We hear, to be sure, echoes of Byron, to Auden always the model for the artist in conflict with his world; but there are present, too, traces of Eliot's satirical style, and, finally, a sense of the American poet in his endless comic war against the American comic cliché.

Unlike Auden, Theodore Roethke seemed not so much twice-born as late-born. He had been writing, indeed, for a long time; but only recently, deep into the Fifties, when he himself was approaching his fiftieth year, did he begin to receive at last the general notice and the critical acclaim he has all along deserved. In terms, then, of felt presence and living influence, he belongs to poetry now. Roethke who had lived earlier in Michigan and Pennsylvania, made his home, in the years before his death, far from the centers of American publishing and book-buying, in the remote Northwest of the United States; and this choice, if it was choice rather than mere accident, had perhaps something to do with the slowness with which he moved from the periphery to the center of our concern. Moreover, though Roethke, like Wilbur, taught at a university, taught, indeed, the history and craft of poetry, he has remained the least academic and, therefore, the least teachable, of poets.

To categorize him is, under the circumstances, perhaps irrelevant, even insolent; yet it is hard to resist saying (and, surely, it is useful to say) that he represents a return to all that is truly subversive in the line which comes down to us from Poe by way of *symbolisme*. Particularly strong in his work are evidences of surrealism, which elsewhere our tradition so strongly resists. Indeed, in our verse as in our prose, we have seen writer after writer flirt with the ultimate abandonment of sense only to retreat before the final embrace; though perhaps in this regard our poets have been somewhat bolder than our novelists. Only Nathanael West —and Hemingway once in *The Torrents of Spring*—accepted the surrealist mode; but Hart Crane, and Eliot, and Pound, even E. E. Cummings on occasion (usually he only fakes), have moved to the edge of incoherence—from which their followers have then withdrawn. Eliot and Pound themselves, however, as well as Crane and Cummings (and Poe before them all), have been finally too involved with *culture* to make the final plunge into the abyss of the unconscious; their madhouses are inhabited by the ghosts of books rather than those of unconfessed or unfulfilled desires. Roethke, on the other hand, has been willing, in his flight from the platitude of meaning, not only to work on the very edge of psychic disaster, but also to seek in the absolute privacy of his own dreams, rather than in decaying culture, his ultimate images and myths. Like all the other American poets who descend from Poe, he is a Gothic writer; but at the center of his universe of horror there stands not the ruined castle of Europe, only the greenhouse of his dead father, back in Michigan or wherever:

> The way to the boiler was dark,
> Dark all the way,
> Over slippery cinders
> Through the long greenhouse.
>
> The roses kept breathing in the dark.
> They had many mouths to breathe with.
> My knees made little winds underneath
> Where the weeds slept.
>
> There was always a single light
> Swinging by the fire-pit,
> Where the fireman pulled out roses,
> The big roses, the big bloody clinkers . . .
>
> Pipe-knock.
>
> Scurry of warm over small plants.
> Ordnung! Ordnung!
> Papa is coming!

[227]

And there ring in his haunted inner ear not scraps from the great tradition of Italy and Provence, Greece and Rome ("these fragments I have shored against my ruins"), only nursery rhymes read in the voice perhaps of his dead mother:

> Is it soft like a mouse?
> Can it wrinkle its nose?
> Could it come in the house
> On the tips of its toes?
>
> Take the skin of a cat
> And the back of an eel,
> Then roll them in grease,—
> That's the way it would feel.

In Roethke's verse, at any rate, father and mother are dead before the poetry begins; and it is against the looming threat of annihilation, the prescience of the death that cut him off just as he was attaining full recognition, that he asserts the frail "I" which the cult of objectivity would have had him disavow. He can never cease to travel the road to Woodlawn, for him the archetypal cemetery, but thinking of it he asserts his ego with special passion: "I miss the polished brass, the powerful black horses . . . I miss the pallbearers momentously taking their places . . ." Nowhere else does he remind us so strongly of Whitman, of the "Song of Myself." Present madness, moreover, as well as future annihilation, threatens always to dissolve the integrity of Roethke's "I"—by blending with his public voice the secret voice of another, buried self, an anti-self he hears often from the dark innards of the earth to which he lays his ear:

> I sang to whatever had been
> Down in that watery hole:
> I wooed with a low tune;
> You could say I was mad . . .
>
> Mouth upon mouth, we sang,
> My lips pressed upon stone.

Indeed, during a large part of his life, Roethke would end up in the madhouse at regular intervals; though between times he lived in the university, moving and loving his students; even writing for one of them, a girl called Jane ("My Student, Thrown by a Horse"), perhaps the first classroom elegy in recorded history, though—as he explains in the poem—he had "no rights in the matter,/ Neither father nor lover." He responded to more on the campus, however, than the pathos of the death of the young, commenting ironically on his colleagues (the "critic, pitched like the *castrati*") and on the prospects for himself, remarking, in a poem called "Academic":

> The stethoscope tells what everyone fears:
> You're likely to go on loving for years,
> With a nurse-maid waddle and a shop-girl simper,
> And the style of your prose growing limper and limper.

But the satirical tone seems less essentially Roethke's than the melancholic or elegiac, and the bitter jokes at the expense of those who worked beside (and against) him less moving than his vision of the sadness implicit in the appurtenances of offices, the small furniture of the world of clerks:

> I have known the inexorable sadness of pencils,
> Neat in their boxes, dolor of pad and paper-weight,
> All the misery of manila folders and mucilage . . .
> And I have seen dust from the walls of institutions,
> Finer than flour, alive, more dangerous than silica . . .

A third poet of real merit who stands in age between Wilbur and Roethke is Robert Lowell; and Lowell, too, has seemed—or at least did seem for a while—to be affiliated with the school of Eliot. Certainly he wrote, up to his latest volume, elegant stanzas respectful of the iambic beat, and exploited a kind of metaphor related to the "metaphysical conceit": that extended, enigmatic comparison based on steep contrast which Eliot had celebrated in the poetry of

John Donne. To be sure, Lowell had always seemed more "baroque" than the other followers of Eliot, his verse more tautly drawn by the tension between his strict over-all form and his passionately centrifugal detail; but this seemed for a while irrelevant. Only in the past several years have we come to appreciate how little there is in him of *symbolisme*, and how much of a more native metaphysical strain, capable of providing those dissatisfied with suburban Eliotics deeper, if more disquieting pleasures.

It is, of course, to the Emersonian tradition that Lowell belongs, as is proper in a poet whose name declares him native to New England, kin of James Russell Lowell and of Amy Lowell, but whose work reveals him as constantly at odds with that region and those relatives. To be of New England *uncomfortably* is precisely to be an Emersonian; and Lowell is uncomfortable enough with all he has inherited: at times embracing pacifism and Roman Catholicism, always committed to anti-Puritanism and the struggle against the complacencies of genteel Boston. Yet to Boston he has been drawn again and again, in search of themes and subjects as well as of a place to live. No ancestor worshiper, he has still had to endure being haunted by his forebears whose ghosts possess his verses as they must his life. From their allegiances and creeds he has struggled to be free, and out of that struggle has made his best poems.

In no other poet of the line of Emerson, except to some degree in Frost, does there exist so extreme a contrast between the controlled tone and tight form on the one hand, and the hysterical fervor and explosive passion on the other. In this sense, the earlier verse of Lowell can be thought of as a continuation and fulfillment of what Frost —in the interests of his mask and his public—censored in himself: banned Frost. To understand the affiliation of the older and the younger New England poet the reader must know Frost's "The Subverted Flower," originally published in *A Witness Tree*, omitted in the Modern Library *Poems*, and reinstituted only in the very late *Selected Poems* published by Rinehart.

She heard him bark outright.
And oh, for one so young
The bitter words she spit
Like some tenacious bit
That will not leave the tongue.
She plucked her lips for it,
And still the horror clung.
Her mother wiped the foam
From her chin, picked up her comb
And drew her backward home.

In Lowell, however, there is at once more complication
of stanzaic form and a deeper implication with the mythology of New England history and literature—though no less
terror; as in these lines from "Mr. Edwards and the Spider,"
in which not only the spider in the flame out of the great
Puritan divine's sermon on damnation but also the spider
we have seen in the poetry of Edward Taylor live again
as genuine terrors:

I saw the spiders marching through the air,
Swimming from tree to tree that mildewed day
  In latter August when the hay
   Came creaking to the barn. But where
     The wind is westerly,
Where gnarled November makes the spiders fly
Into apparitions of the sky,
They purpose nothing but their ease and die
Urgently beating east to sunrise and the sea;

On Windsor Marsh, I saw the spider die
When thrown into the bowels of fierce fire:
  There's no longer struggle, no desire
  To get up on its feet and fly—
    It stretches out its feet
And dies . . .

Yet Lowell deals not only with the historical roots of his
own horrors, which are America's, but also with the double

horror of our present attempts to achieve, if not release from them, at least the semblance of surcease granted by tranquilizers. So in "Man and Wife," he has moved from the real hells threatened by Puritan preachers to the artificial paradises promised the children of Puritans by the corner druggist:

> Tamed by *Miltown*, we lie on Mother's bed;
> the rising sun in war-paint dyes us red;
> in broad daylight her gilded bed-posts shine,
> abandoned, almost Dionysian . . .

15

INTO THE CAFES:
A KIND OF SOLUTION

Robert Lowell is included, of course, along with Richard Wilbur and W. H. Auden, in the 1955 anthology of Oscar Williams; but absent from those pages is a whole group of poets—some senior to Mr. Wilbur himself, and almost all older than such favorite versifiers of Mr. Williams as W. S. Merwin, for instance, and Donald Hall. These poets, called generally, largely by their own choice, "the beats," had begun to be known to a small group before the middle of the Fifties, though the publications which made their fame national were still to appear. Allen Ginsberg's *Howl*, for instance, around which an "obscenity" trial of truly comic proportions unfolded, was not published until 1957, and Lawrence Ferlinghetti's *A Coney Island of the Mind* reached print in 1958. Yet Ginsberg was born in 1926, Ferlinghetti in 1919, and the relative lateness of their entry onto the national scene must surely be explained by something more general and symptomatic than their own slow maturing. True, they both published in San Francisco, a cultural backwater from which, ten years ago, no one was expecting anything of interest in the arts; but more apropos, they both needed for their full development a new kind of audience with quite other expectations than those satisfied by Williams' anthology. Writers in the mode can blossom and be praised early; those who work against the mode move more slowly toward recognition and acclaim.

The triumphs of Ginsberg and Ferlinghetti, as of Gil Orlovitz and Gregory Corso and others who share their methods and their mystique, have been linked with the re-emergence of the "I" at the center of the poem, and the reappearance of Walt Whitman as a considerable force in our poetry, as well as the rejection of the objectivity and the metaphysical-*symboliste* tradition sponsored by T. S. Eliot. The battle was fought first in the cafés and cabarets, where no one was looking, and where poetry was performed rather than assigned for classroom discussion; but the inhabitants of those cafés and cabarets were none other than students enjoying a recess from the classroom, and they have carried their new enthusiasms back with them to school (leaving behind the marijuana and the strumming of guitars). Willy-nilly the "beats" have triumphed in the academy, too, and Whitman with them.

As a matter of fact, the author of *Leaves of Grass* has become to those who turn to him, presumably to be delivered from a bondage to mythology and allusion, the center of a new mythological cult and a new source of allusion:

> Out of the table endlessly rocking,
> sea-shells, and firm,
> I saw a face appear
> which called me dear . . .

writes Robert Creeley, who is surely the best of the skinny-poem wing of the "beats." And Norman Mailer tops him with an even skinnier poem (thinner than the thinnest of William Carlos Williams, who is the beginning of it all):

> . . . what do you think
>   of the Chinese Communists?
>   asked
>   the poet
>   (who
>   thought
>   of himself
>   as a
>   blade of g
>   r
>   a
>   s
>   s

But Mailer may not even have been aware of what he was doing, since Hemingway seems to be his only acknowledged source.

Other poets of the hyper-urban new dispensation have many sources. Indeed, some of them possess (and deploy in the name of freedom from pedantry) a terrifying erudition, beside which the efforts of Eliot in *The Wasteland* seem the feeble attempts of a man who—we remember—never made it through Harvard, while Pound's *Cantos* are revealed as the poor best of a would-be professor who could only hold his teaching job at Wabash College for three months. Charles Olson, a kind of secular dean to the new school of anti-academics (Creeley pays him the proper respect in a dedication or two), begins with what seems merely negative allusion, aimed, we presume, at ending all allusion, and certainly at cutting down the great alluders of the last generation:

> Style, est verbum
>
> The word
> is image, and the reverend reverse is
> Eliot
>
> Pound is verse

But he continues on into recondite scholarly worlds of his own, reminding us that he was educated at Wesleyan and Yale *and* Harvard and that, though he has given up formal teaching, he still practices as an expert in Melville, as well as in Sumerian and Malayan archeology. That these do not define the limits of his learning, however, his poems demonstrate:

> Observing
> that there are five solid figures, the Master
> (or so Aetius reports, in the *Placita*)
> concluded that
> the sphere of the Universe arose from
> the dodecahedron . . .

Never mind, we tell ourselves; this is the learned wing of the "beats," their hostages to the educational system they have defined themselves against. Nor does it dismay us to discover in Jack Gilbert, self-declared mediator between the suburban and hyper-urban poets and a recent favorite of all camps, a poem different from Wilbur's more in its absence of rhyme than in its second-hand relationship to "real" experience, its declared connection with the "tradition":

> Poetry is a kind of lying,
> Necessarily. To profit the poet
> Or beauty. But also in
> That truth may be told only so.
>
> Those who, admirably, refuse
> To falsify (as those who will not
> Risk pretensions) are excluded
> From saying even so much.
>
> Degas said he didn't paint
> What he saw, but what
> Would enable them to see
> The thing he had.

It is when Allen Ginsberg joins in the allusion game that we are surprised, though, after all, his father was a high school teacher of English, and his mentor Lionel Trilling; and most of all we are taken aback when Ferlinghetti, the nearest thing to a best-selling poet we have had since Frost (though his audience consists of bad boys rather than good ones), plays hide and seek with quotation and paraphrase. Ferlinghetti, as a matter of fact, is given to quoting not once but twice, perhaps out of some anachronistic notion of fair play:

> just off the Avenue
>   where no birds sang
> and the sun was coming up on time
>   in its usual fashion
> and just beginning to shine
>   on the statue of Saint Francis
> where no birds sang

Surely the repetition of the tagline from Keats ought to be enough to alert the unwary; but a similar strategy misfired recently in learned circles, among hardened explicators of poems conditioned by years of allusion-hunting. At the national meeting of the Modern Language Association in 1962, a poet-professor (taken in, perhaps, by the manifestoes of the "new wave"—or maybe only condescendingly certain that bookstore-owner-poets do not remember what Shakespeare they may improbably have read) failed to recognize the obvious and deliberate echoing of Prospero's farewell speech in the following lines:

> and he is an old man perpetually writing a poem
> about an old man
> whose every third thought is Death
> and who is writing a poem
> about an old man
> whose every third thought is Death . . .

The poem is called "He" and is clearly about William Carlos Williams thinking of Shakespeare thinking of Prospero (the whole farrago, I cannot help believing with some embarrassment, suggested by a critical essay of mine printed years ago in an eminently scholarly volume). The academic-poetic commentator, however, found the Shakespearean phrase, "every third thought is Death" not only "colloquial" but "jazzy," and took its use to indicate Ferlinghetti's resolve to seek a "particular elevation" which was not of "the traditional poetic kind." So much for believing poets rather than their poems!

Even that favorite rediscovered *naïf* of the newest generation, Eli Siegel, who had been known in the Village during the Twenties as the "*Narr*," which is to say, the fool, is in fact a failed pedant. His archetypal bad poem, "Hot Afternoons Have Been in Montana," awarded the *Nation* poetry prize in 1925 and laughed at for the next twenty-five years, is a potpourri of absurdly assorted misinformation, mostly historical and geographical. William Carlos Williams, who first nominated Siegel's tribute to Montana the "single poem, out of a thousand others written in the past

[237]

quarter century" which "secures our place in the cultural world," spoke of him as one "undamaged by the past"; but it is, of course, the past which obsesses Siegel, as it must all extra-academic superacademics:

> (Indians ambushed Braddock in the Allegheny Mountains; the woods, once quiet, once dark,
> Sounded sharply and deeply with cries, moans, and shots; Washington was there:
> Washington Irving wrote of Washington, so did Frenchmen who knew Voltaire;
> In 1755, Braddock was ambushed and died, and then, in Paris men and
> women wrote of philosophy who were elegant, witty and thought spirit
> was of matter; say, Diderot, Helvetius, and Madame du Deffand; Samuel
> Johnson was in London then; Pitt was in England; men lived in Montana,
> Honolulu, Argentina and near the Cape of Good Hope . . .)

But the rediscovery of this is a piece of scholarship in itself, as well as a joke on the pretensions to scholarship of what Williams calls slightingly "the authorities."

Similarly—however hard this may be for certain neo-Whitmanians to grant—the re-emergence of Whitman as a living force is an academic event, already prepared for in the university itself by such teacher-critics as Randall Jarrell and Richard Chase and I, who had, for more than a decade before the appearance of *Howl*, been attempting to rescue Whitman from the pious clichés of his liberal-Philistine admirers, and to reveal him again as a poet profoundly comic and tragic, as well as truly what his earliest detractors had called him, "the dirtiest beast of the age." Karl Shapiro, himself a professor at the University of Nebraska and a poet of considerable talent, has pressed hardest the new case for Whitman, hailing him as "the First White Aboriginal" and crying out that, "Because Whitman is beyond the law of literature, he is condemned to extinction from generation to generation."

[238]

It is Shapiro, too, who has led the attack on T. S. Eliot, even to the point of denying that Eliot has, in the recent past, functioned as an influence on poetry at all; and to help prove this point, Shapiro has excluded from his own collected poems certain verses obviously written under that very influence! But it is the sense of "lastness," i.e., the inheritance of Poe, that really dismays Shapiro when he confronts Eliot, just as it is the sense of "firstness" which exhilarates him when he reads Whitman. "We should remember Eliot's lifelong interest in the final this and the final that, and at least entertain the possibility that the *Four Quartets* were intended to stand as the last poem in the Great Tradition," Shapiro observes; and concludes, horrified, "Eliot and Pound have both shown themselves capable of such arrogance."

It is, in part, Shapiro's sense of his own Jewishness and his rage at the anti-Semitism of Eliot and Pound (both its existence, and its acceptance in genteel academic circles) which has led him to re-examine and reject their world-view and their esthetics as well as their verse; and if he finds Whitman preferable in these regards, this is perhaps because he reads Whitman (as Allen Ginsberg does, too) back *through* William Carlos Williams, who was himself partly Jewish. Yet, ironically enough from Shapiro's point of view, Williams himself apparently came to Whitman with the help of Ezra Pound, most inglorious anti-Semite of them all; and if his *Paterson* seems the most Whitmanian of all recent long poems, it is by the same token the most Poundian. For Williams, in fact, there is only a single enemy: T. S. Eliot, to whom he opposes both Whitman ("Whitman as a symbol of indiscriminate freedom was completely antipathetic to Mr. Eliot who now won the country away from him again.") and Pound ("A new era . . . was gratefully acknowledged by the universities, and Mr. Eliot, not Mr. Pound, was ultimately given the Nobel Prize."). It is clear from Williams' critical writings that he considers neither Whitman nor Pound to have succeeded finally in inventing a new kind of verse which, abandoning all homage to the "classics," would have fought its way through *vers libre* to a hitherto unimagined order of form.

[239]

In the quest for a truly free verse, however, he finds Eliot to have failed cravenly, Whitman to have foundered heroically.

But for Williams the American has a duty beyond and above that of inventing an anti-classical form—that of honoring his country and its language. In this regard, he has no difficulty in finding Whitman successful, for as Ezra Pound all along understood, Williams is as theoretical an American, perhaps an even more theoretical American, than Whitman himself. "The foreign observer," Pound aptly calls Williams, and points out how he spent his life not so much seeing, as sight-seeing, America. Born of mixed ancestry, in part Jewish-Creole, Williams spent the early part of his life abroad, looking back at America, and he continued to see not only his land but himself—and this is the hallmark of the true Whitmanian—as a visitor from abroad might have seen them; for only from abroad is it possible to believe that there are not only Negroes and whites, Westerners and Easterners, big city people and provincials, New Englanders and Southerners—but "Americans" on our continent. And only one who feels himself such a mythical "American" can speak on funerals, for instance, as Williams does in a poem to his townspeople called "Tract":

> For heaven's sake though see to the driver!
> Take off the silk hat! In fact
> that's no place at all for him
> up there unceremoniously
> dragging our friend out to his own dignity!
> Bring him down—bring him down!
> Low and inconspicuous! I'd not have him ride
> on the wagon at all—damn him—
> the undertaker's understrapper!

It is all there: the hortatory voice, the mild profanity, the schoolgirl punctuation compounded of dashes and exclamation points, the true Whitmanian style; but the injunction, "Bring him down!" is out of Pound; and, in-

[240]

deed, Williams' Whitman—the Whitman of us all today —is Pound's. Pound, unhonored still by the Nobel Committee and once more in exile, is, then, not once only, but twice over the father of our verse. One line, which reaches him from the Provençal poets and the Medieval Italians, runs via Eliot to Richard Wilbur; but another strain passes through him from Whitman and descends via Williams to Allen Ginsberg. No wonder Ginsberg began by honoring Pound: inscribing on walls "Ez for Pres" and even anti-Jewish slogans out of the *Cantos*, though in the end his affiliation is indirect only; and he is less at home with the boy from Hailey, Idaho, who ended in Rapallo than with his more immediate neighbors: Whitman who moved from Long Island to Brooklyn to Camden, and William Carlos Williams who settled in Paterson, New Jersey. Ginsberg himself was born in nearby Newark and brought up in Paterson, taking the road west that Whitman had only dreamed and ending in California. But they are bounded by a small circle, Whitman and Williams and Ginsberg, their imaginations made in the world defined by the shadow which New York City casts one way toward New Jersey, the other toward Long Island.

It is a little misleading, I think, to speak of Ginsberg in terms of a movement, and to attempt to define his achievement in light of what he and the other "beats" have thought or said they stood for. He stands alone, or almost alone, surely, in his preference for the long, swinging line that breaks the verse pattern expected by the eye; and his thick columns of prose-verse surmounted by single-word titles like "Howl" make quite the opposite design on the page from the tau cross shape of the poems we have already seen (such as the one by Creeley, for instance) whose diet-slim bodies are sometimes surmounted by titles longer than their lines (say, "All that Is Lovely in Men"). Besides, in terms of merit, he stands out above those who cluster about him and with whom he is sometimes driven to identify himself out of personal loyalty or programmatic solidarity: a closing of ranks against the "squares."

Finally, it is he alone who has single-handedly, in less

than a decade, moved to the center of the national scene, capturing the newest anthologies and pre-empting the imaginations of the young; so that at a moment when his own talent already seems (quickly, quickly) to be flickering out, a resistance to his influence is beginning among even younger poets, annoyed at how difficult it has become to be printed in certain little magazines without accepting his poetic credo, or at least affecting his style. Some older critics, on the other hand, have never accepted him at all, quoting against him his own worst efforts, which are very bad indeed; and yet no one, entrenched critic or competitive new poet, can deny that since the appearance of *Howl* it has been made clear at least that Walt Whitman is *not* dead, the Whitmanian tradition not exhausted. The question once smugly closed by Blackmur, Tate, and company has been reopened and placed high on the poetic agenda of the moment. Perhaps this, after all, is the cause of the often irrational rejection of Ginsberg by those who would find it easy enough to accept a young poet, but cannot abide honoring in him the influence of an old one they had long since written off.

Everything about Ginsberg is, however, blatantly Whitmanian: his meter resolutely anti-iambic, his line-groupings stubbornly anti-stanzaic, his diction aggressively colloquial and American, his voice public. The title of his first book was, we remember, *Howl*; and though the Whitmanian roar has become in him a little shrill and tearful, it is no less obnoxiously loud. Yet he is a follower of Whitman along utterly unforeseen lines, owing no debt to such professional Westerners as Sandburg or Masters, much less to the Popular Front or liberal-Philistine bards, who long claimed exclusively to represent the Master. The Whitman he emulates is the "dirty beast" out of the East who once shocked even Emerson; and he manages to be dirtier and more bestial, a deliberately shocking, bourgeois-baiting celebrator of a kind of sexuality which the most enlightened post-Freudian man-of-the-world finds it difficult to condone.

Ginsberg is, moreover, an urban Whitman, frankly a city-dweller and a singer of cities, as his prototype was but did not always admit; and he is, like that prototype, a homosexual, though, unlike Whitman, he has abandoned all subterfuge and disguise. It is, indeed, characteristic of Ginsberg's generation to have turned, in a way almost un-American and certainly unforeseen, all the best-kept secrets of our tradition into public boasts. No longer does he feel obliged to pretend that his espousal of madness is the advocacy of some higher form of mental health, or his programmatic homosexuality a kind of pure and disembodied love. His declared heroes are those, on the one hand,

> . . . who were given instead the concrete void of insulin
>   metrasol electricity hydrotherapy psychotherapy
>   occupational therapy ping-pong & amnesia,
> who in humorless protest overturned only one symbolic
>   ping-pong table, resting briefly in catatonia . . .

and, on the other, those

> who blew and were blown by those human seraphim, the
>   sailors, caresses of Atlantic and Caribbean love,
> who balled in the morning in the evenings in rosegardens
>   and the grass of public parks and cemeteries scattering
>   their semen freely to whomever come who may . . .

And had not Brother Antoninus already called upon his Lord, with somewhat more delicacy than Ginsberg could muster, and considerably greater piety:

> Annul in me my manhood, Lord, and make
> Me woman-sexed and weak . . .
> What is the worth of my own sex
> That the bold possessive instinct
> Should but shoulder Thee aside?

It is, in any case, the dark side of *Leaves of Grass* that Ginsberg reflects or, more properly exposes, presenting himself as the apostle not of self-adulation but of self-pity, not of joy but of terror, not of sanity but of insanity. Whitman liked to boast that he drank nothing but pure water; Ginsberg tells us he smokes marijuana. Whitman saw himself as a kind of mystical healer; Ginsberg celebrates himself as an angel of death and derangement. He is a prophet not of the beginnings of man, but of his end; and if, like Whitman, he tries to write first poems, they are the first poems of the next evolutionary stage beyond us, anticipations of the verse of meta-humans.

Yet is must be confessed that though there is no joy in Ginsberg, there is a good deal of humor; for he never quite forgets how funny it is to be a Jewish, homosexual Walt Whitman, a parody of a white Indian, the bearded secular saint, into which Whitman's first followers had transformed him. It is not in the egregious self-pity and uncertain tone of the title poem of *Howl* that one finds the authentic Ginsberg, the Whitman no one had expected; but in "America," his *Leaves of Grass* one hundred years later, a poem comic enough to be appropriate to our time:

> America I used to be a communist when I was a kid I'm not sorry.
> I smoke marijuana every chance I get.
> I sit in my house for days on end and stare at the roses in the closet.
> When I go to Chinatown I get drunk and never get laid.
> My mind is made up there's going to be trouble.
> You should have seen me reading Marx.
> My psychoanalyst thinks I'm perfectly right.
> I won't say the Lord's prayer.
> I have mystical visions and cosmic vibrations.
> America I still haven't told you what you did to Uncle Max after he came over from Russia.
>
> America is this correct?
> I'd better get right down to the job.
> It's true I don't want to join the Army or turn lathes in precision parts factories, I'm nearsighted and psychopathic anyway.
> America I'm putting my queer shoulder to the wheel.

There are jokes on Ginsberg, however, as well as in him; and the greatest of all, of course is his success. Who could not have foreseen the pictures in *Life*, the fellowships to Chile or the Pelopponesus or whatever, the journey to Israel (with required verses on Martin Buber and Gershom Sholem), the pilgrimage to the banks of the Ganges (reported fully in *Esquire*). Nobody is to blame, nobody has betrayed anybody, it is simply the way it goes in America. "America," says Ginsberg, "I still haven't told you what you did to Uncle Max after he came over from Russia." Nor what it did to Uncle Max's nephew after he returned east from San Francisco—not yet, not quite, not ever. So far, Ginsberg has resisted a regular teaching job, but not the occasional lectures at New York's City College and Columbia, not the appearances at writers' conferences, nor the speeches at benefits for sympathetic little magazines.

And what can he do about his imitators, his adulators? He wanted to reform poetry, to redeem it from what he takes to be the idiocy of the iambic; but to succeed even partially in so large an ambition is to become an institution, an academy. Old-line poets, with a sense that the tradition in which they began has failed them, latch on: Karl Shapiro producing, in "The Bourgeois Poet," a tribute and an imitation only slightly embarrassing.

> Where did you study the physics of the epic? What is
>   this eternal conspiracy of distraction? Why are the sick
>   the most articulate? Poetry weaving at the bar, go home.
>   Somebody call a cab.
> Who are these that compound the mystery? Tell me about
>   the Dewey Decimal System.
> Do something about the sour smell of schools. Call the
>   Americans!

Meanwhile, a quite young poet like Jack Hirschman, a disaffected academic still in the academy, pays his kind of tribute in a tighter form than would please Ginsberg, with frank Jewish commitments that would dismay Ginsberg, yet in a language influenced by his:

[245]

His howl grabbed me by my high intangibles;
His humor, of the ghetto-American, riddled
Me silly as Fosdick of the cops
My gassy dialectic escaping to be filled
By dancing in between despairs, and flops.

And Shapiro writes the introduction.

Robert Creeley, too, hails the master, and with him others of the gang, in a poem dedicated to James Broughton and beginning like this:

Oh god, let's go.
This is a poem for Kenneth Patchen.
Everywhere they are shooting people.
People people people people.
This is a poem for Allen Ginsberg.
I want to be elsewhere, elsewhere . . .

It is a gang finally that is invoked, a small circle of friends dedicating books to each other, mythicizing each other from poem to poem,* giggling in the background of the execrable recordings of "Howl," and around them a gaggle of name-dropping sub-acquaintances—who once might have been proud to know "Wystan" or "Stephen," the old gang, but now refer with studied casualness to "Gregory" or "Allen." Some, indeed, manage to maintain a friendly relation with both like Alan Ansen, who dedicates his book of verse to Auden *and* Corso.

Once begun, the process does not stop; generation begets generation with the terrifying speed of drosophilae. Creeley, who hails Ginsberg, has already a group of undergraduate emulators who publish, out of British Columbia, a mimeo-graphed magazine called *Tish* (it was Dylan Thomas, I suppose, who invented the practice of spelling one's contempt for the world backwards). And there are other in-

* Even languages and national boundaries do not limit such chumminess. There is, for instance, a poem of Olson's entitled "To Gerhardt, there among Europe's things of which he has written us in his *'Brife an Creely und Olson.'* "

group magazines (*Evergreen Review, Big Table, Journal for the Protection of All Living Beings,* etc.), in-group anthologies (by Charles Olson and Donald Allen), even an in-group freshman textbook: the *Casebook on the Beat,* out of which young instructors with underground anti-academic leanings can teach standard disaffection to the young.

Whatever the merits of Ginsberg's poems—and they possess merit in considerable measure—he has not destroyed a world, but only displaced a tired style; has not created a new heaven and new earth, but only made a school; has not reached everybody, but only pleased a tight circle of friends. In the imagination of those friends, and in that of the popular press, he has seemed sometimes an Attila at the gates; but it was wish and fear, more wish than fear, that fed such fantasies. Our world still stands, alas; and our waiting for the end—with the dream of an unimaginable beginning beyond it—seems already, or again, an affectation, a classroom topic, a literary theme. The last word was spoken long ago and far away, by Constantine Cavafy, one of the founders of modern Greek poetry, discovered first for the West By E. M. Forster and emulated most lately by Lawrence Durrell. But Cavafy died in Alexandria in 1933, at the pit of the Depression and before the Second Great War and the long prosperity had set us to dreaming of a *Götterdämmerung* once more, so that his voice comes to us like a prophecy from the grave:

What does this sudden uneasiness mean,
and this confusion? (How grave the faces have become!)
Why are the streets and squares rapidly emptying,
and why is everyone going back home so lost in thought?

Because it is night and the barbarians have not come,
And some men have arrived from the frontiers
and they say that there are no barbarians any longer.

And now, what will become of us without barbarians?
Those people were a kind of solution.

[247]

Finally the "beats" have made no difference. The old order is basically unchanged; the colleges brim full and overflow; the curriculum is expanded to include Burroughs and Kerouac; what was shuddered at only yesterday is today anthologized and assigned. Certain quite old poets imitate the anti-iambics of Ginsberg, while certain very new ones rediscover iambic pentameter with a thrill; and our basic consciousness remains unaltered, though new kicks have been added to old, marijuana to martinis, mescalin to bourbon on the rocks. In a few decades, the "pot" party will have replaced the cocktail party as a social obligation and a bore, beards will have become required or passé, and homosexuality will no longer seem an intolerable offense to even the most backward provincial. Only cleanliness will not have been replaced by dirtiness as next in rank to godliness; there is too much money invested in soap.

In any case, we have begun to realize that it is not Armageddon which confronts us (not as imagined by the "beats" or the Marxists or the ban-the-bombers), only a long slow decadence in which the arts will continue to thrive, to the confusion of everyone. John F. Kennedy as Louis XV, rather than Allen Ginsberg as Attila, seemed up to the moment of his assassination the true symbol of our cultural plight; not only our first sexually viable president in a century, after a depressing series of uncle, grandfather and grandmother figures, but the very embodiment of middlebrow culture climbing. And even his death has no more signified an apocalypse in the realm of the arts than it has a revolution in the realm of politics. To be sure, the sporting on the White House lawn has become, since the advent of Lyndon Johnson, more bucolic than pastoral; but already the literary columnists have begun to assure us that Mrs. Johnson, at least, reads books—and that authors will still be asked to Washington to dine, dance, perhaps even talk.

Certainly the library chosen for Kennedy by the Chief Librarian of Yale University will remain on the presidential shelves, come Republicans or Democrats, Jeffersonians or Jacksonians; the plans for a great cultural center in the

[248]

national capital continue to be executed. And from the pages of a recent book called *Creative America*, the late President (along with Eisenhower and James Baldwin among others) lectures us all on the errors of our anti-cultural past. "Too often . . ." he tells us, "we have thought of the artist as an idler and a dilettante and of the lover of arts as somehow sissy or effete. We have done both an injustice." But, of course, like most presidential calls to action, whether posthumous or "live," this, too, comes a little too late. For a long time the index of literacy has crept inexorably upward, the paperbacks in supermarkets have proliferated until there is scarcely room for bread and milk; and the boards of directors of large corporations have invited intellectuals to lecture their junior executives on Dostoevski and Kierkegaard and Freud. Most appalling of all, in the past couple of years, for the first time in our history, more Americans have attended cultural events than have paid to watch sports.

But even this is not the end. Our writers will learn to bear the indignities of success, as they have born those of failure; and out of these, too, with luck and skill, they will make the stuff of art. What new apocalypse they will dream as they work, we cannot even imagine; and if we know that, whatever its nature, it will fail them, like all the others, that is a truth we had best keep to ourselves. In any event, no one younger than we will listen; but it does not matter, for there is no end.

INDEX

[251]

[253]

[255]

WESTFIELD UNIV. LONDON COLLEGE